THE IMPERATIVE OF HEALTH

THE IMPERATIVE OF HEALTH

Public Health and the Regulated Body

Deborah Lupton

SAGE Publications
London • Thousand Oaks • New Delhi

SAGE Publications Ltd
6 Bonhill Street
London EC2A 4PU

SAGE Publications Inc
2455 Teller Road
Thousand Oaks, California 91320

SAGE Publications India Pvt Ltd
32, M-Block Market
Greater Kailash – I
New Delhi 110 048

British Library Cataloguing in Publication data

A catalogue record for this book is
available from the British Library

ISBN 0 8039 7935 5
ISBN 0 8039 7936 3 (pbk)

Typeset by Photoprint, Torquay, Devon
Printed in Great Britain by The Cromwell Press Ltd,
Broughton Gifford, Melksham, Wiltshire

Contents

Acknowledgements

I am grateful to the University of Western Sydney, Nepean, for providing me with a grant allowing release from some of my usual teaching duties in second semester 1994 to assist in the completion of this book. I thank the two anonymous reviewers of the penultimate draft of the book for their helpful critical comments. Thanks are due too to Gamini Colless for his continuing support of my work.

Parts of my article 'Risk as moral danger: the social and political functions of risk discourse in public health' published in the *International Journal of Health Services*, 1993, 23(3), 425–35, are reproduced in Chapter 3. Chapters 4 and 5 include reworked excerpts from another of my articles, 'Consumerism, commodity culture and health promotion' which was published in *Health Promotion International*, 1994, 9(2), 111–18.

Introduction

> The imperative of health: at once the duty of each and the objective of all.
>
> (Foucault, 1984a: 277)

When undertaking a Master of Public Health degree several years ago, I found the limited approach of the subjects I was studying and the literature I was reading a source of consternation. Unlike the vast majority of the other students in my year, who were qualified in such areas as medicine, nursing and health services management, I held two degrees in the humanities and social sciences, majoring in sociology and anthropology. Having emerged from a tradition of socio-cultural and political critique, I found the extent to which the rationale, models of human behaviour, methods of research and major strategies of public health were accepted uncritically by many academics, researchers and students in the field surprising and unsettling. Over the past decade, new directions in socio-cultural and political theory have incited an upheaval in the ways that concepts such as knowledge, power relations, society and the human subject have come to be understood in the humanities and social sciences. Despite the importance of this literature, its insights and concerns have yet to be taken up by scholars and researchers in public health and health promotion to any significant degree. While public health research is often described as 'multi-disciplinary', quantitative sociology, biostatistics, epidemiology, social psychology, demography and the stimulus–response model of communication have traditionally dominated. Due to its close links with biomedicine, which favours positivistic forms of inquiry based on the gathering of empirical quantifiable data, public health research has tended to undervalue the more humanistic, critical, theoretical and interpretive approaches. Disciplines such as anthropology, philosophy and history have been marginalized; at best treated with suspicion, at worst denigrated for being 'soft' and non-practical. The tendency has been to accept the prevailing orthodoxies of public health and health promotion, focusing upon statistical measures, cost effectiveness and the evaluation of measurable effects, but devoting comparatively little attention to the critical analysis of the political implications of such endeavours. While health promoters and researchers have for some time critiqued the ideologies underlying medical practice, they have not fully directed this critique at their own epistemology and practices.

In my previous book, *Medicine as Culture: Illness, Disease and the Body in Western Societies* (1994a), which, as its title implies, focused specifically on the doctor–patient relationship and the illness experience, I was able only briefly to touch upon some of the issues around public health and health promotion. In many ways this present book develops and complements *Medicine as Culture* by exploring these latter areas of medicine and health using contemporary socio-cultural and political theory, particularly that building on Foucault's writings on subjectivity, embodiment and power relations. Public health is a form of medicine, social medicine, which directs its professional attention towards the health of populations, aggregated bodies, instead of individual bodies. As in my previous book, *The Imperative of Health* combines sociological, anthropological, historical and cultural studies approaches to analyse the symbolic nature of public health practices, going beyond their surface rationales to explore their underlying meanings and assumptions and incorporating an historical understanding of the dynamic nature of such meanings and assumptions. The book emphasizes that the practices and discourses of public health are not value-free or neutral, but rather are highly political and socially contextual, changing in time and space.

The ideological underpinning of the institutions of public health and health promotion rests upon their utilitarian objective to accomplish a continuing good health status for all. This in itself is difficult to question: what could be more individually and socially beneficial than promoting good health and reducing the misery created by illness and disease at the population level? In adopting and carrying out the strategies of public health and health promotion, the state is seen as acting in its citizens' best interests, seeking to improve their health and lengthen their average lifespans. These institutions are manifestly progressive, employing the ideology of post-Enlightenment humanism in their quest to measure, order and contain illness and disease at the population level. However, a growing critique of public health and health promotion has challenged the notion that the state has a right to 'interfere' into the everyday activities of its citizens. Ironically, the conservative critique of health promotion overlaps in some ways with that of the radical critique. The right-wing position considers health education and promotion activities as apparatuses of an overly-authoritarian and preaching 'Nanny State' (see, for example, Davies, 1991). It is argued that the state should let its citizens conduct their lives as they choose fit, without intervening. In Britain, right-wing individuals supportive of the *laissez-faire* model of government have historically expressed dismay at state intervention into public health matters. In the late nineteenth century, for example, the Conservatives claimed that legislation directed at the regulation of sanitation and water supply was interference into private property and local government and disruptive of individual rights (Porter and Porter, 1988: 100–1). It was argued that '[a]gainst the body of a healthy man Parliament has no right of assault whatever under the pretence of the Public Health; nor any the more against the body of a healthy infant' (quoted in Porter and Porter, 1988: 106–7).

Scholars from the political economy of health perspective have also questioned the authoritarian and patronizing tenor of much health promotion rhetoric. Their concern lies, however, not so much with the restriction of personal autonomy but with the focus of public health on individual behaviour to the exclusion of challenging the structural causes of ill-health. Rather than championing the freedom of the market, they have called for greater state intervention to be directed towards industry in the interests of the population's health. Critics from the left are concerned about the elements of 'victim-blaming' discourse which attracts attention away from the structural, political and economic causes of ill health such as unsafe working conditions and environmental health hazards (Crawford, 1977; Brown and Margo, 1978; Wikler, 1978; Rodmell and Watt, 1986; Minkler, 1989). Radical critics have called for a return of an 'ecological' perspective, including paying attention to improving living conditions for the under-privileged, alleviating poverty and malnutrition and focusing on the physical environment. They have pointed to the continuing disparities between the morbidity and mortality rates of the poor and working classes and the privileged classes in developed societies. They have called on health educators and promoters to become more questioning and radical, to facilitate social change, to enable people to act to challenge and remove health-damaging conditions. This approach centres on the strategies of community development and advocacy politics. The solution to ill-health, argue proponents of this perspective, is to 'empower' citizens, make them aware of the hidden socio-economic reasons for ill-health, and assist and encourage them to act collectively to overcome social inequality, to 'free' themselves from the bonds of power. A dichotomy is thus set up between the state and the people, in which it is argued that the former possesses power and acts as an instrument of oppression, actively serving to constrain the freedom and undermine the health of the latter, who lack power. Critics from the political economy perspective generally accept the knowledge claims of medicine and public health, questioning the uses to which they are put rather than seeking to explore the assumptions that underlie them.

This book adopts neither of these critiques of public health and health promotion. While the focus of the book is upon power relations in the context of public health, it is argued that power relations are not structured by traditional oppositions between the state and civil society and coercion and consent. Rather than acting simply to constrain citizens, power works to produce or 'make up' citizens who are capable of autonomy and 'a kind of regulated freedom' (Rose and Miller, 1992: 174). Therefore, the book seeks not simplistically to condemn public health and health promotion as oppressive of citizens' rights in the state's quest for power, nor to argue that individuals need to be 'empowered' to challenge the power of the state. Nor is it contended that public health and health promotion should be wholeheartedly supported for their potential to liberate the public's health and happiness. Such dualisms are too reductive of the complexity of the nexus between public health, the state and other social institutions and apparatuses such as the family, the education system, mass media and commodity culture, and the individual or social group. Rather, this book seeks to explore the ways in which some of the knowledges and practices of public health and health promotion in western societies have been developed and articulated, how they are justified, what ends they seek, their alliances and dependencies, and how they are embedded into broader historical, socio-cultural and political settings.

For quite some time, the western system of medical knowledge and practice, often referred to as 'biomedicine', was rarely examined by sociologists, anthropologists or historians for its socio-cultural nature, but was accepted as neutral and 'scientific' (unlike the medical belief systems of non-western cultures). It is only relatively recently that scholars have approached biomedicine as a symbolic system of beliefs and a site for the reproduction of power relations, the construction of subjectivity and of human embodiment (see, for example, Foucault, 1975, 1979; Wright and Treacher, 1982; Turner, 1984, 1992). While this area of inquiry has produced fertile debate, particularly in the wake of Foucault's writings on medicine and the body, one dimension of medicine, that of public health, has tended thus far to be neglected. Yet just as biomedicine is socially and culturally constructed, public health and health promotion are socio-cultural products, their practices, justifications and logic subject to change based on political, economic and other social imperatives. Just as bio-medical knowledges, discourses and practices create their objects and fields of interest – disease, illnesses, patients, surgical techniques – the knowledges, discourses and practices of public health serve both to constitute and regulate such phenomena as 'normality', 'risk' and 'health'. Just as moral systems draw distinctions between 'good' and 'bad' patients in biomedicine, so too are such moral judgements central in the logic of public health. As in any field which relies for its authority on knowledge, the relationship between power and knowledge in medicine and public health is often obscure. Public health practitioners make claims to truth and use these claims for strategic purposes just as do members of the medical profession.

In this secular age, focusing upon one's diet and other lifestyle choices has become an alternative to prayer and righteous living in providing a means of making sense of life and death. 'Healthiness' has replaced 'Godliness' as a yardstick of accomplishment and proper living. Public health and health promotion, then, may be viewed as contributing to the moral regulation of society, focusing as they do upon ethical and moral practices of the self. Public health and health promotion have adopted insights from a range of human sciences – psychology, demography, sociology, sexology, economics – to categorize and construct the human actor. This book argues that while the rise of public health and health promotion in western countries has been associated with improvements in health status at the population level, the discourses and practices of these institutions have also worked to produce certain limited kinds of subjects and bodies, drawing upon binary oppositions associated with discriminatory moral judgements. What needs to be brought to light and critically interrogated are the covert political and symbolic dimensions of these institutions; the ways in which the practices and policies of public health and health promotion valorize some groups and individuals and marginalize others, the concepts of subjectivity and rationality they privilege and exclude, the imperatives emerging from other socio-cultural sites that intertwine and compete with those of public health and health promotion, and the discursive processes by which these institutions are constituted and supported. It is also important to consider the ways that individuals are interpellated, or hailed, by the discourses of public health and health promotion. How do individuals recognize themselves as subjects of the discourse, or else reject the discourse as pertaining to them? That is, how are subjects and subject positions voluntarily produced, and under what conditions? The complex socio-political context in which individuals make choices regarding their everyday activities must be also acknowledged.

Public health and the civilized body

In the past decade there has been an increasing interest in the socio-cultural dimensions of the human body on the part of social theorists and researchers. A continuing debate has ensued over the extent to which the body is a physiological product or a social construction. Some scholars argue for a view of the body that has no existence outside social relations, and thus is purely constructed and amenable to transformation. Others insist that there is a grounded biological dimension to the body: for example, all bodies die and decay. I favour a dialectical approach to body, which recognizes the location of bodies in nature, but also the ways in which discourses act to shape bodies, and experiences of bodies, in certain ways over which individuals have only a degree of control. That is, 'people make their bodies through labour, sport and play, but they do not make them in circumstances of their own choosing' (Shilling, 1991: 665; see also Turner, 1994: 24–6). Hence, throughout the lifespan the body is taken up and transformed by social relations, but within certain limits imposed by biology. There is, therefore, a symbiotic relationship between the body and society which defies determinism of either a biological or social constructionist nature.

Post-Foucault, it has become recognized that the body is the site at which power struggles are enacted and become 'real'. For Foucault, power does not exist independently of the body, is not external to the self, but acts to construct the body in certain ways. As he argues, 'nothing is more material, physical, corporal than the exercise of power' (1980a: 57–8).

Foucault's notion of the 'inscribed' body, 'written on' by discourse, has become an important conception for understanding the nexus between anatomy and society: 'The body is the inscribed surface of events (traced by language and dissolved by ideas), the locus of a dissociated self (adopting the illusion of a substantial unity), and a volume in perpetual disintegration' (Foucault, 1984b: 83). From this perspective, it may be argued that the discourses and practices around the promotion of health have been central to constituting the contemporary human body. More so perhaps than any other apparatus or institution, discourses on health and illness serve as routes through which we understand, think and talk about, and live our bodies.

Foucault identified two dimensions of what he termed 'biopower', or the ways in which power relations work in and through the human body. The first discursively constitutes the individual body, and is exercised in interpersonal relations in the medical encounter, while the second exercises disciplinary power over the body politic, intent on the documenting and regulating of the health status of populations. The focus of this book, centring as it does on the institution of public health, is on the latter dimension of biopower. Turner (1984: 2, 90ff.) has built upon Foucault's concept of biopower to construct a conceptual framework which categorizes the ways in which the state must deal with bodies: the reproduction of populations in time; the regulation of bodies in space; the restraint of the 'interior' body through disciplines; and the representation of the 'exterior' body in social space. Turner goes on to outline the institutional subsystems which are responsible for these categories: for reproduction, patriarchy; for regulation, panopticism; for restraint, asceticism; and for representation, commodification. The discourses and practices of public health and health promotion attempt to serve all these functions. For example, arguments of health are used to encourage people to have more or less children, to seek health care deemed appropriate by the state when undergoing pregnancy and labour, to desist from or engage in abortion, sterilization or contraception. As I will outline in Chapter 1, the concern with the reproduction of the labour force at the turn of the twentieth century was a major impetus for the public health movement's focus upon infant mortality and fertility rates. Systems of regulation are constantly used to survey populations' health status (the questionnaire is the most obvious example). The latter two ways outlined by Turner in which the state deals with bodies are also highly relevant to the activities of health promotion, in its concern with self-surveillance, discipline and control; for example the discourses valorizing dietary and body weight control in the name of good health first, and good looks, second.

It is not only the shape and deportment of the human body that is constructed through the discourses and practices of public health, but also subjectivity, or the 'inner self'. The concept of subjectivity is central to an understanding of the ways in which people negotiate the imperatives of public health and health promotion. Subjectivity may be defined as a sense of self or self-identity. It is socially constructed through interactions with others; thus we are not born with subjectivity, we acquire it from infancy. Language and discourse are central in the constitution of subjectivities, in a complex relationship with other sources such as sensual embodied experience and the unconscious. Subjectivity is fragmented, highly changeable and dependent on the context. There are numerous, often contradictory ways in which individuals fashion subjectivities. That is not to argue, however, that individuals have a totally 'free' and unrestrained choice of subjectivities. Subjectivity is constructed through and by the articulation of power, for 'it is already one of the prime effects of power that certain bodies, certain gestures, certain discourses, certain desires, come to be identified and constituted as individuals' (Foucault, 1980b: 98). There are strong structural constraints placed on the range of subjectivities available; for example, individuals born with female genitals are directed from birth in ways both subtle and overt to behave, dress, think, feel and express themselves in ways consonant with current broad understandings and assumptions of femininity. While there may be a number of choices within the range of accepted versions of femininity, these will always be limited.

Each era privileges certain kinds of subjectivity. The modern subject is characterized by an interest in the deportment of oneself and others in the social realm, a belief that one's appearance and behaviour are reflective of one's disposition and a new self-consciousness about one's individualism, one's separateness from others. Hence the interest in finding one's unique character and defending it evident today: 'Each person's self has become his [sic] principal burden; to know oneself has become an end, instead of a means through which one knows the world' (Sennett, 1976: 4). Consonant with this version of subjectivity is the Enlightenment or Cartesian notion of mind/body dualism. In this conception, the mind is considered to be separate from and transcendent over the body, ideally having the power to control the urges and emotions of the potentially recalcitrant flesh. The mind/body dualism is linked to others that distinguish reason from passion, outside from inside, depth from surface, reality from appearance, culture from nature, humanity from animality, male from female and Self from Other (Grosz, 1994: 3–4; Turner, 1994). This understanding of the body views it as a possession or an instrument of consciousness, subject to the control of external forces and needful of careful training and discipline. Co-existing with this conception is that of viewing the body as a vehicle of expression, communicating the thoughts and feelings of its 'owner' (Grosz, 1994: 8–9). The creation and presentation of the self is thus intimately linked to the body as project; the body is viewed as mirroring the authentic inner self (Turner, 1994: 14). If the body appears uncontrolled, then the self is revealed as undisciplined.

Related to the mind/body dualism is the distinction drawn between the 'civilized' or 'classical' body and the 'grotesque' body. The civilized body is constructed through dominant aesthetic standards and is considered much closer to culture, while the grotesque body is close to nature in its uncontrolled state. Historically the civilized body has been considered sacred and aristocratic, while the grotesque body is profane, associated with the peasantry and the carnivalesque (Elias, 1978; Morgan, 1993: 81–2). Elias (1978) argues that the concept of the civilized body emerged through court society after the Middle Ages. He examined books on manners published in Europe between the thirteenth and nineteenth centuries which dealt with matters of bodily propriety. He noted that during the Middle Ages, behaviours now deemed embarrassing and unmentionable (such as burping and urinating) were discussed openly in such texts, as were behaviours which have disappeared altogether (such as sharing beds with strangers in an inn). By the Renaissance, such matters had become more shameful, and there was a greater emphasis on the management of emotion (Mennell, 1992: 36–7). Hence it was concepts of respect towards others of higher ranking in one's presence and a desire to identify and maintain one's social standing that encouraged the differentiation of behaviours. The higher people aspired to a place in court society, the more control they needed to have over their bodies: thus, 'body management norms became internalized. Instead of being imposed from outside, through the threat of sanctions, codes of behaviour became adopted partly at a subconscious level to the point where they were followed irrespective of the presence of others' (Shilling, 1993: 159). In the eighteenth and nineteenth centuries, systems of knowledge such as medicine and psychiatry began to act as normative systems of power. With the advent of industrialism, the ability to control one's private thoughts and feelings, to be the author of one's character, to remake the self, became essential to material and social success (Sennett, 1976).

The civilized body is controlled, rationalized and individualized, subject to conscious restraint of impulses, bodily processes, urges and desires. This mastery, it is believed, is what sets humans apart from animals: the more an individual can display self-control, an unwillingness to 'give in' to the desires of the flesh, the more civilized and refined that individual is considered. Under this model, the individual who chooses to engage in intemperate behaviour is less than civilized, indeed is bordering on the animalistic. Hence the common justification for the categorization of non-white peoples, women and members of the working class as more 'primitive' and 'closer to nature' than the ideal of the European middle-class male. Since the nineteenth century, for example, women have been deemed inferior to men – as 'incomplete adults' – because of their supposed animality and lack of control caused by the ruling of their bodies, emotions and behaviours by their hormonal systems, their uteruses and ovaries (Laqueur, 1987; Moscucci, 1990). This ideology is still evident in discourses around the pregnant or premenstrual woman today, whose behaviour is popularly believed to be dominated by her hormones, causing her to lose control over her emotions and power of rational thought.

Health promotion relies upon the model of the rational, unified self, consciously making decisions about one's conduct in everyday life in the quest for self-improvement and social success and integration: 'The mastery of the self is thus a prerequisite for health; the lack of self-mastery, accordingly, is a "disease" prior to the actual physical complaint, whose symptoms are detectable as behavioural, psychological and cognitive patterns' (Greco, 1993: 361). Sickness has become a marker of the body 'taking over' reason, revealing the essential nature of the body as fragile and mortal (Kirmayer, 1988: 76). The response to illness or its threat is to champion greater rationality and bodily control, pushing the materiality of mortal bodies away in a vain attempt to defy corporeal disorder and death.

Public health and governmentality

The notion of governmentality, which Foucault believes has dominated political power since the eighteenth century, is highly relevant to the exercise of biopower at the level of the population. As the concept of governmentality incorporates an analysis of both the coercive and the non-coercive strategies which the state and other institutions urge on individuals for the sake of their own interests, it provides a means of understanding the social and political role of public health and health promotional discourses and practices. Governmentality incorporates both techniques or practices of the self – self-government – and the more apparent forms of external government – policing, surveillance and regulatory activities carried out by agencies of the state or other institutions for strategic purposes. Foucault (1991) traces the gradual emergence of governmentality from the sixteenth century and its links with 'normalization', or the establishment of disciplines, knowledges and technologies that serve to proffer advice on how individuals should conduct themselves (Gane and Johnson, 1993: 9).

The concept of governmentality avoids the notion of the state as an overarching, coherent, repressive authority intent on maximizing power and seeking to constrain the liberty of its citizens (Gane and Johnson, 1993: 7). Rather, it sees power relations as diffuse, as emerging not necessarily from the state but from all areas of social life. Unlike sovereignty, which is always directed towards the end of maintaining that sovereignty, governmentality is directed towards a plurality of specific aims (Foucault, 1991: 95). Indeed, as noted above, the techniques and strategies of governmentality emerge not simply from the state. While the state is important as part of the structure of power relations, so too are the myriad of institutions, sites, social groups and interconnections at the local level, whose concerns and activities may support, but often conflict with, the imperatives of the state. Governmentality locates regulatory activities at all levels of social institutions, from the family, the mass media and the school to national bureaucratic agencies such as parliament, the legislature and the police force. While the state is involved in providing the conditions for the maintenance of professional exclusivity and prestige, it does not overtly act in a directive or dominating fashion. Indeed, the apparatus and logic of governmentality is strongly linked in its development to that of the liberal state, which historically has emphasized individual freedom and rights against encroachment or excessive intervention on the part of the state: 'the characteristic outcome of power is not a relationship of domination but the probability that the normalized subject will habitually obey' (Johnson, 1993: 142).

Governmentality depends on systems of knowledge and truths, both to constitute and define the object of its activities, and continually to monitor its progress, to 'make it thinkable, calculable, and practicable' (N. Rose, 1990: 6). It therefore includes not only 'ways of theorizing, knowing, and classifying' but also 'forms of treatment, relief, discipline, deterrence, and administration' (Dean, 1991: 9). Experts and their expertise, particularly those related to the modern professions, are central to governmentality (Johnson, 1993: 150). By the process of normalization, attempts are made to construct a privileged type of subject through the web of expert judgements surrounding the body. This expertise is employed in the measuring of populations, documenting and establishing trends against which to compare individuals and to make decrees on their relative 'normality' in comparison to others. Experts play an important role in mediating between authorities and individuals, 'shaping conduct not through compulsion but through the power of truth, the potency of rationality and the alluring promises of effectivity' (Miller and Rose, 1993: 93). It is the role of experts to argue that the personal capabilities of individuals can be managed to achieve socially desirable goals, build upon political concerns and generate new fields of problems which they then show they can overcome using their expert knowledge (1993: 97).

It is clear that public health and health promotion may be conceptualized as governmental apparatuses. The institution of public health has served as a network of expert advice, embodied in professionals such as doctors and health promoters, who have dispensed wisdom directed at improving individuals' health through self-regulation. As Turner (1994: 27) points out, medicine and public health have strongly coercive elements in that they set out to shape and normalize human behaviours in certain ways. Indeed in contemporary western societies they have replaced religion as the central institutions governing the conduct of human bodies. However these institutions, like the educational system and religion, are often not recognized as coercive because they appeal to widely accepted norms and practices. While the institutions of public health and health promotion often display very overt signs of the state's attempts to shape the behaviour of its citizens, where this attempt at control becomes invisible is in the justification used. In the interests of health, one is largely self-policed and no force is necessary. Individuals are rarely incarcerated or fined for their failure to conform; however they are punished through the mechanisms of self-surveillance, evoking feelings of guilt, anxiety and repulsion towards the self, as well as the admonitions of their nearest and dearest for 'letting themselves go' or inviting illness. Therefore it is not the ways in which such discourses and practices seek overtly to constrain individuals' freedom of action that are the most interesting and important to examine, but the ways in which they invite individuals voluntarily to conform to their objectives, to discipline themselves, to turn the gaze upon themselves in the interests of their health.

The imperatives explicit in health promotional activities initiated and carried out by state bodies are supported by a proliferation of agencies and institutions, including commodity culture, the commercial mass media, the family, the educational system, advocacy groups and community organizations. Those individuals who are part of the framework of public health making judgements about relative states of health and normality include – in addition to medical practitioners – teachers, social workers, public and private bureaucrats, parents, community action groups, economic advisers and epidemiologists (Kendall and Wickham, 1992: 11). Some of these agencies and individuals deliberately and consciously set out to uphold state activities; others are vigorously opposed. While they have different and often competing objectives and tactics, all these agencies and institutions often articulate common discourses and encourage certain practices concerning the primacy of health and the importance of rational action. All are directed at constructing and normalizing a certain kind of subject; a subject who is autonomous, directed at self-improvement, self-regulated, desirous of self-knowledge, a subject who is seeking happiness and healthiness. All depend upon a limited collection of valorized knowledges and experts to support their claims.

The major concerns of institutions, groups and individuals in contemporary western societies revolve around the regulation of bodies in space, the monitoring of the surfaces of bodies and the relationships between bodies (Turner, 1994: 28). But governmentality is not just directed at bodily practices, but at the very constitution of the self. In late modernity, our personalities, our subjectivities, our relationships with others, while considered 'private' by most people, are intensely governed, such that even aspects of the self deemed intimate and individual such as thoughts and feelings are socially organized (N. Rose, 1990: 1). In the first volume of his *History of Sexuality* (1979), Foucault uses the example of sexuality, which he argues has been subject to a web of surveillance emerging from the state and elsewhere. Rather than issues of sexual behaviour being repressed, Foucault argues, they have been increasingly brought into the spotlight, constituted as problems, subject to incessant public discussion and discourses of regulation. Sexuality, and the sexual body, have therefore been produced by the discourses of medicine, psychiatry and public health, among others.

In his later writings, particularly *The History of Sexuality* Volumes 2 and 3 (1985, 1986), Foucault moved away from examining the external features of governmentality (those formulated and disseminated by institutions and agencies) to the autonomous modes of self-government engaged in by the individual as part of everyday life. He became interested in the 'care' or the 'practices' of the self, or the ways in which individuals act on their bodies, souls, thoughts and conduct 'so as to transform themselves in order to attain a certain state of happiness, purity, wisdom, perfection, or immortality' (Foucault, 1988a: 18). Through the notion of the practices of the self, Foucault reflected on the processes by which disciplinary power is internalized, seeking to explore the manner in which dominant discourses may be taken up, negotiated or resisted in the individual's fashioning of his or her existence as an ethical project of the self. The care of the self involves largely subliminal socialization rather than active, conscious decisions. It is about how people constrain themselves rather than being forcibly constrained by external agents, involving not generally explicit moral codes but a shared understanding of what a 'good person' is in a particular community (Hoy, 1986: 15–17). The practices of the self are not directed by the oppression of subjectivity, but by the enhancement of pleasures and desires, the happiness and fulfilment of the self, the health of the body, in ways consonant with political, social and institutional goals; they are, as Rose puts it 'therapies of freedom' (N. Rose, 1990: 257). In achieving and maintaining subjectivity, the contemporary individual has become a 'producer-consumer . . . the entrepreneur of himself or herself', ceaselessly engaged in the activities directed at reproducing and improving oneself as 'one's own human capital' (Gordon, 1991: 44).

The contemporary linking of morality with the rational, self-regulated subject intent on discovering the authentic self is historically and culturally contingent. The practices of the self are inevitably chosen from the range accessible to an individual in a given culture; they are not invented by the individual but are over-determined by the socio-cultural context (McNay, 1992: 61). Foucault argues that for men, the ethic of the care of the self at the time of the ancient Greeks and Romans was not individualistic but rather was highly related to political life (women were not considered citizens and thus did not have ethical obligations): 'The individual's attitudes toward himself, the way in which he ensured his own freedom with regard to himself, and the form of supremacy he maintained over himself were a contributing element to the well-being and good order of the city' (1985: 79). While self-knowledge was considered important, it was not directed at the discovery of the 'true self', but at refining the self in the context of one's public service to others (Cotton, 1993: 101). However, by the first and second centuries AD, self-knowledge had become an end in itself. This ethic became independent of political life and became invested in the body and its health status: 'One must become a doctor of oneself' (Foucault, 1988a: 31). By the Christian period, it was expected that each person had the duty to 'know' him or herself, to be true to the self, to acknowledge faults and resist temptations and to disclose these via the confession to God and to others. Purity of the soul was deemed impossible without self-knowledge (Foucault, 1979). To use Foucault's terminology, individuals become self-governed: individuals engaged in socially acceptable behaviour of their own free will, constrained by a sense of embarrassment and propriety that operated even when they were alone. The 'civilized' body became the ideal body. By the secularized era of the late twentieth century, the Christian confessional had been rephrased into other sites: notedly the 'psy' disciplines of psychiatry, psychoanalytic therapy and psychology, the educational system and media and popular culture, in which the imperative of 'knowing one's true self' is constantly articulated as a strategy of self-management.

Discourse and reflexivity

Like public health and health promotion, the social sciences and humanities are systems of knowledge that seek to describe and define the nature of social life, contributing to the vast network of governmental activities surrounding the human subject. The disciplines of sociology and psychology, in particular, have been important in contributing knowledges of human behaviour and reasoning to contemporary public health and health promotion, particularly in the form of data collected in the social survey (Figlio, 1987: 78–9). Until recently, these approaches have rarely challenged the assumptions and knowledge claims of medicine and public health. Hence, this book itself and its social analysis of public health may be viewed as constructing a certain field of knowledge around public health, health promotion and the human body. As no discourse or knowledge is value-free, there is no way of escaping this position, but it is important to be aware of one's position as producer and reproducer of certain discourses and practices, and the personal commitments and values inherent in the use of such discourses and practices (Fox, 1991: 711). Such awareness is often referred to as reflexivity.

The feminist writer Dorothy Smith (1990: 4) defines reflexive inquiry as being directed towards explicating the conditions of one's own existence and ideological practice so as to expose one's participation in power relations. For public health workers and researchers, reflexive practice involves the ability critically to interrogate their use of knowledge and to become aware of the interests they serve and reproduce as part of their working lives. Reflexivity requires a sensitivity to the manner in which ways of knowing are generally accepted as common-sense and taken-for-granted. Attention to language and discourse is central to any activity seeking to facilitate reflexivity. In producing their world individuals' practices are shaped in ways of which they are usually unaware by social structures, relations of power, and the nature of the social practice in which they are engaged. So too, individuals' practices themselves influence social structures, relations and struggles around them (Fairclough, 1992: 72–3). The linkages between discourses, social processes and power are generally 'opaque', and the critical awareness of language and discourse is directed at rendering this opacity more transparent (Fairclough, 1993: 135).

Fox (1993: 19) has developed the perspective he has dubbed 'the politics of health-talk', which centres its focus around the following methods of reflexivity at the site of health care and public health: a concern to explore and deconstruct the minutiae of discourses and discursive formations at the site of action or power; a concern with the constitution of subjectivities through discourse, knowledge and power, with the understanding of the subject as fragmented and constituted in difference and of power as productive and contested; a scepticism around commonsense understandings of the social world; a concern with desire and its role in the suppressed and the unconscious; a concern with intertextuality, or the way texts and discourses interact with each other; and finally a keen awareness of one's own production of texts. The term 'text' as it is used here includes such phenomena as written documents, verbal interaction and visual imagery. In the context of public health, reflexive practice includes the critiquing of such taken-for-granted notions as 'health', 'fitness', 'responsibility', 'empowerment', 'self-efficacy', 'taking control', 'risk' and 'participation' and the dominant discourses of healthism, self-control, surveillance, discipline and rationality that pervade the health promotion and health education literature.

This book is such an attempt to explore the processes of the production of subjectivities and bodies in public health and health promotion. The point of the book is to undermine and contest accepted understandings and assumptions about public health and health promotional practices, to incite critique and ask questions about dominant belief systems; in short, to disrupt the complacency of these knowledge/discourse systems and to open up the space for alternative 'truths' and realities. The areas of endeavour, models of human behaviour and theoretical perspectives which are embraced under the rubric of public health and health promotion are numerous and extensive. I have not attempted a broad examination of all of these but instead focus the concerns of this book on examining several key themes. One is public health's role, as a powerful social institution, in the processes of rationalization, normalization and social ordering, or the ways in which the discourses and practices of public health serve the post-Enlightenment ideal of control over the destiny of humanity. The book adopts an historical approach to look at the questions of how the health of populations first emerged as a problem, how certain 'rational' strategies, apparatuses and discourses were constructed to deal with this problem and how, in turn, the subject of public health has been constituted and reproduced. The ways in which notions of civility, or the 'proper' deportment of oneself – including one's state of personal cleanliness, one's diet and one's bodily shape and size – were integral to the discourses and practices of the emergent public health movement, and remain central in contemporary public health and health promotion, are examined. The book also features a discussion of the practices of the self, or the ways in which individuals conduct their bodies in response to imperatives about health. Attention is paid to the role of emotion, desire, pleasure and the unconscious in negotiating the imperatives of public health and health promotion, as well as the influence of such social structural factors as gender and social class.

Chapter 1 sketches a history of the present of public health, examining the development of dominant discourses and ideologies inherent in public health knowledges and practice. It reviews the ways in which the problems of disease, dirt, miasma, odour, contagion, cleanliness, spatiality, epidemics, microbes, sexuality, reproduction, childhood and the family have been constructed by public health, and outlines the major strategies of surveillance and regulation developed to govern these problems, including quarantine, isolation, the medical police, inspection, hygiene, disinfection, deodorizing, vaccination, screening, contraception, photography, statistics and education. The next three chapters go on to examine closely the prevailing discourses and practices of contemporary public health and health promotion. Chapter 2 describes current issues and themes in the 'new' public health and health promotion, looking at the uses of the discourses of 'rationality', 'health', 'community', 'theory' and 'lifestyle' and the strategies of prevention, empowerment, community development, demography, epidemiology and health economics. Chapter 3 examines more specifically the central discourse of risk and the strategy of diagnostic testing as they are employed in public health. Chapter 4 critiques the use of mass media and marketing strategies in public health, including discussion of the naive understanding of communication that is demonstrated in health promotional attempts to 'advertise' behaviours deemed health-enhancing, the constitution of the subject in health promotion campaigns and the political function served by such campaigns.

Chapter 5, the penultimate chapter, takes a somewhat different tack in moving from the analysis of the external imperatives of public health and health promotion to examining the ways in which individuals respond to these imperatives in the context of everyday life. The chapter examines the desires, emotions and anxieties invested in practices of the self at the conscious and the unconscious levels, and explores the ways in which health promotional imperatives paradoxically incite 'sinful' pleasures at the same time as they seek to contain and control them. The Conclusion returns to the issue of reflexivity and discusses ways in which it may be fostered in the training of public health and health promotion workers and adopted in alternative health promotional practices.

1

Governing the Masses: the Emergence of the Public Health Movement

It is difficult fully to understand the rationale and logic of contemporary institutions such as public health without some awareness of their historical underpinnings. Armstrong (1993: 405) has identified four major regimes of public health over the past two centuries: quarantine, followed by sanitary science, the regime of interpersonal hygiene and lastly the 'new' public health. As he observes, all of these regimes deal with drawing boundaries and circumscribing spaces: between geographical places, between the body and the external environment, between one body and another body. The quarantine regime was dominant up to the mid-nineteenth century, when the public health movement began to focus on environmental conditions. During the nineteenth century, new forms of surveillance of populations were developed in the fields of public hygiene and mental health, along with state policies and programmes. A concern with personal hygiene arose from developments in bacteriology in the late nineteenth century, leading to an emphasis on education around the proper deportment of the body. The 'new' public health movement emerged in the 1970s, refocusing attention on the social and environmental conditions of health patterns, with an interest in radical change. In this chapter the first three 'regimes' of public health are discussed, while Chapter 2 goes on to examine public health and health promotion in the late twentieth century.

Traditional historians of public health have tended to describe a narrative of progression. For these historians, the advent of the public health or sanitarian movement in the nineteenth century, particularly as it emerged in Britain and continental Europe under the dynamic interventions of the great reformers (almost invariably all white, bourgeois men), was the beginning of a 'modern', rationalized approach to protecting and preserving the public's health. The standard narrative of such histories begins by discussing the filth, squalor, ignorance and superstitious beliefs that prevailed before the nineteenth century and recounts the progressive introduction of the sanitarians' ideas into hygienic conduct as a continuing fight against general apathy, ignorance and dirt. The discovery of the microbe in the late nineteenth century is hailed as the watershed for a 'scientific' public health, enabling public health reformers to strengthen their arguments for a web of governmental regulations around public and private hygiene (for an example of such a history, see Duffy, 1990). Other histories of public health have taken a social history perspective, adopting a somewhat more critical stance in highlighting the inequities inherent in the nineteenth- and early twentieth-century public health movements' treatment of groups such as women, immigrants, non-whites, the working class and the poor (for example, Rogers, 1992). Those adopting a social constructionist approach have located their histories in the broader socio-cultural context, seeking to explore the symbolic and ideological dimension of public health practices (Brandt, 1985; Corbin, 1986; Herzlich and Pierret, 1987; Davenport-Hines, 1990). The advent of HIV/AIDS in the early 1980s, with its evocation of ages-old meanings around disease and epidemics, has had a particularly stimulating effect on the writing of histories of public health from the social history and social constructionist perspectives (see, for example, several of the essays collected in Fee and Fox, 1988, 1992).

A further, more radical historical approach has built upon the work of Michel Foucault in his genealogical analyses of medicine and public health. Genealogy is a term used by Foucault to describe his method of tracing the emergence of discourses, bodies of knowledge and power relations over time, to write a 'history of the present'. In genealogy, lateral connections are as important as causal or development connections (Grosz, 1989: xviii). Genealogy seeks to show that previous discourses and practices have their own logic and are internally coherent, even if they are radically different from present day practices and logic. As such, it demonstrates the contingent nature of the present. According to Foucault (1984b: 80) the genealogist 'needs history to dispel the chimeras of the origin', to demonstrate the fragmentary and heterogeneous nature of knowledges. Genealogy is also a means by which to trace the inscription upon the human body of events, to describe 'the articulation of the body and history' (1984b: 83). In doing so, Foucault was concerned to emphasize the discontinuity and non-linear nature of social change, to focus on local knowledges, or 'discreet and apparently insignificant truths' (1984b: 77). These include human emotions and abstract concepts such as morals, ideals, liberty, sentiments, love, conscience, instincts and how they emerge and re-emerge in different roles or are absent at certain moments.

The histories written by social constructionists and Foucault and his followers have demonstrated that a close analysis of the emergence and development of the public health movement reveals not a steady progression from primitive, 'unenlightened' thought to 'modern' ideas and practices, but a series of eras characterized by regressions and political struggles. Their histories have shown that while it is standard to describe the 'old' public health and the 'new' public health as related but very different traditions, much of the discourses and practices of the 'old' public health movement can be currently seen in the 'new' public health. They have also revealed that for centuries the institutions of medicine and public health have been central in constituting the 'normalizing gaze' as part of mass observation and social regulation. This chapter primarily draws upon the insights of such histories to discuss the key problems identified and constructed by public health and the strategies of surveillance and regulation developed to govern these problems. The history and philosophy of the public health and social hygiene movements as they emerged in the eighteenth century in western societies are reviewed, with a particular focus on Britain and continental Europe as the 'birthplaces' of the public health/sanitary movement. The discussion begins with medieval attempts to respond to epidemics, moving onto the Enlightenment and the emergence of the social hygiene movement, then to the implications of the discovery of the microbe for public health practice. The chapter focuses in particular on the ways in which the bodies of individuals have been constructed and regulated via the discourses and practices of public health in its various forms, centring on the constitution of such problems as dirt, miasma, odour, sexuality, reproduction, childhood and the family as matters requiring the attention and expertise of public health reformers.

Public health before the Enlightenment

Two kinds of public health measures dominated western societies until the late eighteenth century: emergency measures dealing with outbreaks of epidemic disease, and everyday regulations dealing with municipal nuisances such as waste disposal. Illness during this era was characterized by three primary dimensions: 'numbers, impotence and death, and exclusion' (Herzlich and Pierret, 1987: 3). Epidemic disease such as the plague created intense activity and extreme measures, which subsided after the threat had passed, while endemic diseases were taken-for-granted. When epidemics broke out, they were dealt with by invoking such measures as quarantines, sequestration and *cordons sanitaires*, and temporary institutions such as boards of health were set up to manage the crisis (La Berge, 1992: 10). From the Middle Ages onwards, more permanent public health measures were instituted, governing street cleaning, sewage disposal, the free-flowing of water courses, the zoning of industries, and hygiene in meat, fish and fruit markets (Palmer, 1993: 66).

The recurrence of plague in Europe throughout the fourteenth and fifteenth centuries engendered a concern with its control, with the high death rates inspiring the introduction of new measures to counter its spread. Of the European countries, Italy was in the forefront of establishing a system of epidemic control, having set up in the fourteenth and fifteenth centuries permanent magistracies charged with overseeing moral and physical hygiene in the major cities (Cipolla, 1992: 1). The Italians introduced new techniques of isolating the sick and those who had come into contact with them, establishing special isolation hospitals, requiring that the dead's clothing and effects be burnt and imposing restrictions on travel and trade with infected areas. Travellers were required to present a bill of health stating that they did not carry infection before they were allowed to enter a city or a port (Herzlich and Pierret, 1987: 14). Some

Italian cities set up 'books of the dead' to record mortalities and follow the course of epidemics (Park, 1992: 87). In the northern and central cities of Italy the health magistracies also concerned themselves with wider regulatory measures such as the quality of food sold, sanitary conditions in houses of the poor, prostitution, sewage, the activities of medical workers and the issuing of health passes (Cipolla, 1992: 2).

The word 'quarantine', still in common use today, originates from the Italian for 'forty days', as that was the length of time deemed necessary to isolate the ill. Quarantine was the first public health strategy used to police boundaries. This strategy was developed from the contagionist understanding of disease; that is, the belief that illness could be spread from body to body, and that the ill and the infectious should therefore be isolated from others to control the spread of epidemics. Under this notion, 'illness somehow resided in places, as it was places that had to be kept separate', while human bodies were seen as the vectors between places of infection and places of purity (Armstrong, 1993: 395). The contagionist model relied upon the identification of stigmatized groups as the dangerous Other, the site of contagion. For example, in medieval times lepers were separated from others, and were publicly denounced and expelled from cities or confined to hospitals outside the city walls. They were deprived of all property and forced to live on public charity (Herzlich and Pierret, 1987: 5; Park, 1992: 87). During the fourteenth century, Jews in particular were singled out as spreading plague, and were subsequently persecuted and killed in large numbers (Frankenberg, 1992: 74–5).

Two other central theories of disease causation underlay public health measures for several centuries; the miasmic and the humoral theories. From the time of the ancient Greeks and Romans, it was believed that the environment, in combination with individuals' constitutions, were influential in affecting people's state of health. The humoral theory of disease incorporated an understanding of the healthy body as maintaining a balance of the four humours, blood, phlegm, black bile and yellow bile, four elements, earth, air, fire and water, and four qualities, hot, cold, wet and dry. Both one's diet and the climate one lived in were deemed important to one's state of health (Nutton, 1992: 23). The longevity of the humoral theory of disease is demonstrated by its recurrence in lay and medical explanations of ways to maintain good health in the sixteenth and seventeenth centuries. During this time it was believed that 'the different qualities vital for life had to be kept in a good balance. The body must not be allowed to become too hot or cold, too wet or dry (fevers and colds would result)' (Porter, 1992: 95). It was further believed that the six 'non-naturals' – diet, evacuations, exercise, air, sleep and the passions – should be regulated by individuals to ensure good health (Porter, 1992: 99; Risse, 1992: 171). In the seventeenth and eighteenth centuries a series of books, manuals and pamphlets building on the humoral model were published, encouraging individuals to adopt a regimen directed at strengthening the body's constitution and giving advice on the types of food it was best to consume, the frequency of exercise that should be taken and so on. Such publications urged their readers to adopt a sober, rational approach to their lifestyle, privileging asceticism as the route to good health. They were directed at literate, wealthy, 'well-disposed' people who were expected to spread this knowledge among the less well-privileged (Turner, 1992; Risse, 1992: 187).

The miasma theory of disease was prevalent in Europe from ancient times right up until the discovery of microbes. This was the notion that 'bad air' – air that was damp, odorous or polluted – in itself caused disease. It was believed that the sticky miasmal atoms lodged in bodies, wood, fabrics, clothing and merchandise and could be absorbed through the skin or by inhalation and could therefore pass from person to person or animal to person through contact (Corbin, 1986: 63; Cipolla, 1992: 4). The theory was thus similar to the contagionist model, but was more specifically related to substances of contagion that could be identified by the senses: dirt and odour. The miasmas issuing from diseased, dead and decomposing bodies were considered especially dangerous, capable of causing such conditions as gangrene, syphilis, scurvy and pestilential fevers by breaking down the equilibrium of the living body (Corbin, 1986: 17). The miasma theory, in conjunction with the contagionist and humoral models, was able to account for a wide variety of disease. The chain of infection was believed to be the sequence of dirt leading to smells leading to miasma leading to pestilence. For example, it was noted that plague epidemics often broke out in the hot summer months, and this was explained by the fact that the heat intensified the bad odours associated with miasmas. Little attention was given to another phenomenon of this season: the increase in the number of rats and the fleas they carried (Cipolla, 1992: 5).

Because of the belief that smell was an indicator of the contagious nature of air, odour has been a particularly important dimension of beliefs about the causes of diseases and ways of preventing against epidemics. It was believed that confinement in spaces that smelt malodorous, such as ships, jails, hospitals and latrines, was especially dangerous (Palmer, 1993: 66). During an outbreak of the 'Black Death' (as the plague was called at that time) in 1348, the Italian town of Pistoia regulated the depth of burials ' "to avoid a foul stink" . . . and banned the tanning of hides within the city walls "so that stink and putrefaction should not harm the people" '. In 1522, the city of Venice ordered the compulsory hospitalization of people with syphilis found begging in the town because of the concern that their 'great stench' could bring the plague (Palmer, 1993: 65). In sixteenth-century England it was strongly believed that the countryside was far healthier an environment to live in than urban areas, partly because of the abundance of fresh air and lack of overcrowding. Tobias Venner, an English physician, wrote in 1628 in his treatise on healthy living that marshy or damp air produced nearly all 'the diseases of the braine and sinews, as Crampes, Palsies etc. with paines in the joynts; and to speake all in a word, a general torpidity both of minde and body' (quoted in Wear,

1992: 133–4). Methods of disinfection used aromatic substances to 'purify' the air and rid bodies or materials of the miasmic atoms (Corbin, 1986: 62–3). The sense of smell was employed to determine whether an environment was healthy or unhealthy, and people used sweet odours to combat the ill effects of bad air, carrying fragrant flowers or herbs around with them or using fumigation in dwellings, ships and hospitals (Corbin, 1986: 64–5; Wear, 1992: 137). As late as the eighteenth century in France, individuals would douse themselves liberally with perfume in the belief that doing so would protect themselves by purifying the surrounding air (Corbin, 1986: 63).

While factors such as the climate, diet and odours were believed to play an important part in causing disease, the ultimate cause was deemed to be God's will: disease was God's punishment for the sins of humankind (Herzlich and Pierret, 1987: 103; Porter, 1992: 96). A supernatural understanding of how disease was engendered thus overlay the other models, and provided an explanation when other rationales failed. It also allowed the expression of overtly moralistic statements concerning the relative sinfulness of individuals and certain social groups such as the poor (Tesh, 1988: 18–19); a tendency that has pervaded public health discourses for centuries.

Public health during the Enlightenment

The age of the Enlightenment, emerging around the end of the seventeenth century and lasting until the late eighteenth century, was a transitional era characterized by a reaction against unquestioning religious and superstitious belief, and a strong optimism in the ability of humans to control their destiny to their own convenience. It was believed that nature was patterned and predictable, and that its laws could be discovered using human insight. The uncovering of truth using rational thought, scientific method, experiment and calculation was believed to be the key to human progress. The public health movement (more often referred to at that time as the social medicine or social hygiene movement) as it developed in eighteenth-century Europe adopted many of the concerns and approaches of Enlightenment thought, including an emphasis on progress, rational reform, education, social order, humanitarianism and scientific method (La Berge, 1992: 11). It was believed that there were underlying laws of nature governing disease and epidemics that could be revealed through scientific inquiry and the gathering of empirical data (1992: 12). Once such laws were established, then disease could be controlled, removed and prevented by deliberate and rational action (Risse, 1992: 172).

This was also the time in which the concerns and strategies of governmentality became a central feature of the state's relationship with its citizens. The concept and apparatus of governmentality sprang from the Enlightenment ideal of the rationalization and ordering of society. Foucault (1991: 87–8) argues that governmentality first emerged as a general issue in the sixteenth century, associated with a number of social and economic phenomena: the breakdown of the feudal system and the development of administrative states in its place which were based upon rationality and legitimate rule, and the questions of spirituality and self posed by the Reformation. According to Foucault, by the eighteenth century, due to the emergence of the problem of the growth of the population, the notion of governmentality expanded beyond the aegis of the state (1991: 98–9).

The concept of 'social medicine' originated in the eighteenth century in association with a trend towards paternalism involving greater state intervention and regulation of citizens at the level of the population (Turner, 1990: 5). The ideology of statism, or the notion that it was the responsibility of the state to provide for public health through administrative, legislative, and institutional means, dominated the social medicine movement. It was believed that good health was a natural right of all citizens and as a result, if states' duty was to protect their citizens' rights, then public health was the duty of the state and a proper area for intervention and control (La Berge, 1992: 16). The movement was also influenced by scientism, or the notion that science was the key to progress, and hygienism, an ideology combining medicalization and moralization directed at preventing and containing the feared social disorder looming as a result of industrialization and urbanization. To achieve the goals of social medicine, its practitioners realized that they needed to increase their authority to gain legitimization, and to work towards professionalization and the development of the movement as a science (1992: 2). The proponents of the social medicine movement saw health reform as interlinked and broad, ranging from poverty, prostitution, venereal disease, infant abandonment and mortality and housing (Jones, 1986: 11–12; La Berge, 1992: 4). It was considered important to avoid the emergency approach to containing disease that characterized the Middle Ages by moving to a preventive model, using administrative procedures.

The goals of public health were predicated upon the rise of the modern European states during the seventeenth and eighteenth centuries, allowing the institution of effective political and bureaucratic organizations with national scope (Risse, 1992: 171–2). Enlightenment medicine began to regard health as 'a positive tenet which could be attained, preserved, and even recovered with the aid of a proper life style, public and personal hygiene, and the aid of medicine' (Risse, 1992: 195). By the early eighteenth century, the attention of public health reformers moved to endemic disease, devoting particular attention to occupational hygiene (La Berge, 1992: 18). This change in emphasis can be linked to the public health movement's concern with ensuring the health of the labour force in the context of rapid industrialization and urbanization. The goal of the public's health became an essential objective of political power. In concert with the economic imperatives of the emergent capitalist system, the health of the population became of central importance, especially that of the poor (Dean, 1991; Risse, 1992). It was in the interests of the modern European state to ensure that its citizens were healthy so as to promote productivity: to move beyond a concern with individuals and small groups to regulate health at the level of the population as a whole. Where Italy led the way for the management of public health in the Middle Ages, France dominated the social hygiene movement in the late eighteenth century, by virtue of its role as the intellectual leader of Europe, its framework of centralized bureaucracy and the broader major reform movement in the 1770s and 1780s accompanying the decline of the Ancien Régime and the changes wrought by the Revolution (La Berge, 1992: 17–18).

In two works, *The Birth of the Clinic* (1975) and the essay 'The politics of public health in the eighteenth century' (1984a), Foucault discussed in detail the changes taking place in the eighteenth century around the control and documentation of epidemics, leading to the expansion of medical jurisdiction. Epidemic medicine involves attributing causality and searching for an essential coherence in the patterns of disease and death (Foucault, 1975: 26). Foucault (1975: 25) notes that 'whether contagious or not, an epidemic has a sort of historical individuality'. It thus requires a complex method of observation, a multiple gaze which recognizes the uniqueness of each epidemic. It was this multiple gaze which was being institutionalized at the end of the eighteenth century in concert with an apparatus of intervention. The medical gaze thus became extended beyond the body of the individual to that of all aspects of society, involving 'a clinical recording of the infinite, variable series of events' including study of geographies, climate and weather (1975: 29). Medical knowledge became two intersecting bodies of information, between the individual's disease and the separate events that could be linked to it; thus 'medical space can coincide with social space, or, rather, traverse it and wholly penetrate it' (1975: 31). The 'pathogenic' city became a site for medicaliza-tion, in its open spaces, its sewerage and drainage, abattoirs and cemeter-ies, prisons, ships, hospitals, housing. As a consequence, a 'medico-administrative' knowledge developed, rendering medicine as a 'general technique of health' and not simply a means of ministering to or curing the ill. Medicine was enfolded within a system of administration, rendered part of the machinery of power, serving as the core of the 'social economy' (Foucault, 1984a).

As part of these changes, the 'population' became constituted as a problem, a target for surveillance, regulation, analysis and intervention (Foucault, 1984a: 278). There was constructed 'a politico-medical hold on a population hedged in by a whole series of prescriptions relating not only to disease but to general forms of existence and behaviour (food and drink, sexuality and fecundity, clothing and the layout of living space)' (1984a: 283). Bodies – those of individuals and those of populations – became bearers of new values relating to their productivity, use and general state of health (1984a: 279). Doctors became the 'specialists of space', posing problems of the co-existence of individuals, their density, their proximity with each other and with environmental aspects such as water, sewage, animals, the dead and housing (Foucault, 1980c: 150–1).

The medical police was a central element of bio-politics (Hewitt, 1991: 238); indeed, Foucault (1984a) contends that a 'medicine of epidemics' could exist only if supported by a medical police. The use of the word 'police' here denotes not simply the word as we use it today, to describe a body of officers employed to repress outlaw elements. As the term 'police' was used in continental Europe it more broadly denoted a condition of order in a community and those regulations employed to establish and maintain this order, as well as self-control and good manners on the part of an individual: 'The targets of policing included, inter alia, religion, customs, highways, public order, commerce, health, subsistence and the poor' (Hewitt, 1991: 238). Policing was a primary technology of rationality, directed at the problems of the administration and normalization of the body and the population: 'when people spoke about police at this moment, they spoke about the specific techniques by which a government in the framework of the state was able to govern people as individuals significantly useful for the world' (Foucault, 1988b: 154). Policing by the eighteenth century became a technique for achieving certain goals, directed at the prevention of threats to the social order (Dean, 1991: 55–7). The concept of the 'medical police' first arose in this century in Germany, and eventually spread to other European countries and the United States (Rosen, 1974). In Germany, which at that time had not adopted the emphasis on individual freedom that had developed in Britain, the concept had an authoritarian and paternalistic character, concerned with the passing of laws (Rosen, 1974: 143; Turner, 1990: 5). The ideal as it was developed in that country was to establish a coherent policy which was especially directed at the poorer classes.

Along with the political objectives of maintaining public order and economic regulation, the policing functions of societies were directed towards enforcing general rules of hygiene, such as the water supply and the cleanliness of the streets. The notion of the state as protector of the people, in exchange for the relinquishing of certain rights on the part of its citizens – the 'social contract' – lay behind the concept of the medical police (Risse, 1992: 172–3). For example, one treatise at the time identified medical police as 'the science which teaches how to apply dietetic and medical principles to the promotion, maintenance and restoration of the public health' (Professor E.B.G. Hebenstreit, 1791, quoted in Rosen, 1974: 145). To this end, German states enacted ordinances directed towards such activities as the control of epidemics, the regulation of prostitution, the qualifications and duties of medical personnel, the supervision of the food supply and of hospitals (Rosen, 1974: 147). The term 'medical police' was not generally taken up in France because of the overthrow of the Ancien Régime and the institution of parliamentary constitutionalism (Rosen, 1974: 155). However, the term continued to be used in Britain, Germany and Italy throughout the nineteenth century (1974: 151–2). It was not until the final decades of the nineteenth century that the terms 'public health' or 'social hygiene' began to supersede 'medical police' (1974: 153).

Along with the physician, traditionally considered a public health expert, other specialists were needed to collaborate in the goals of the social hygiene movement, including pharmacist-chemists, veterinarians, engineers, architects, scientists and administrators (La Berge, 1992: 15). Indeed, the movement was initially led by social reformers rather than medical specialists. It was not until public health became professionalized that medical practitioners began to play a more dominant role, especially with the introduction of 'preventive medicine' as a medical specialty in England. To meet the goals of public health, it was also essential to have measures of the number and 'value' of the people, especially those deemed to be most productive. When this need was recognized in the seventeenth century, the science of statistics was applied to measure the public health (Rosen, 1974: 177–8). The emergence of statistics as a form of organizing knowledge was vital to governmental practices, to render an 'unruly population' manageable and amenable to rational forms of administration (N. Rose, 1990: 7). It was also vital to support the concept of public health as a 'scientific' and 'professional' discipline (La Berge, 1992: 29). Documenting, recording and statistically manipulating information about individual bodies were thus central activities for the public health movement as it developed in the eighteenth century.

This new approach to medicine, that of the epidemiological surveillance of populations rather than the clinical examination of the individual body, had to address itself to time, to the persistence as well as the variability of disease in the community, 'to the movement of pathology rather than its localization' (Armstrong, 1983: 18). To maintain a 'technology of population', such techniques as demographic estimates, life expectations, mortality rates and the documenting of marriage and procreation rates were developed and exercised (Foucault, 1984a: 278–9). This ceaseless collection of figures became self-perpetuating, with one set of statistics serving to provide legitimization for further surveillance. As more and more statistics were gathered, expectations around 'normality' were constructed, based on the range of variation in large groups, against which individuals and groups could be measured. The technology of the population survey was an important strategy in providing data on populations. As Armstrong argues:

> The sample survey also embodied the panoptic principle of inverted visibility: all seeing yet unseen . . . The survey therefore constituted an apparatus for distributing the effects of a disciplinary gaze throughout society; a device for individualizing through measuring the differences between people; a means of constructing healthy bodies through its analysis of the normal. (1983: 53)

While the eighteenth-century European states were developing apparatuses to measure, document and regulate patterns of disease and death in populations, a new focus on the domestic sphere began to emerge in relation to the health status of the child. From the middle of the eighteenth century, the family unit was incorporated as a secondary element of the broader population, albeit fundamental to its government and privileged as a means of gaining information concerning the population (Foucault, 1991: 100). The problem of the 'child' developed, including a concern with the number of children and their growth and survival rates, and a proliferation of texts on the care of the child's moral and physical well-being emerged. By these processes, an 'infrastructure of prevention' was erected around the child and a series of educative measures set in motion to save him or her (Donzelot, 1979: 97). These new problems involved a new set of obligations for parents and children, including the control of bodily hygiene, diet, housing, clothing, physical exercise and familial relation-ships. The family unit was charged with the responsibility for developing and maintaining the child's body: 'health, and principally the health of children, becomes one of the family's most demanding objectives. The rectangle of parents and children must become a sort of homeostasis of health . . . from this period the family becomes the most constant agent of medicalization' (Foucault, 1984a: 280). The practices of vaccination and inoculation are examples of the regulation of the child which developed during this episteme (1984a: 280–1). The site of the family thus provided a link for the 'private' ethic of good health, as espoused and championed for individual families, and general political objectives regarding the health of the social body (1984a: 281).

The 'modern' public health movement

The 'modern' public health movement, emerging in the early nineteenth century, was led by British reformers in response to the problems of the towns in the wake of rapid industrialization and urbanization, including those of dirt, sewage disposal, poor water supplies, overcrowding and dangerous housing. By this time, it was not epidemics that brought about substantial public health reform, but concern about endemic diseases such as smallpox, typhoid and chronic illness caused by malnutrition and poor living conditions (Fee and Porter, 1992: 250). The movement was based largely on the tenets of miasma and contagionism. Its central problem was therefore constituted as that of the nexus between dirt, odour and disease. From medieval times well into the closing years of the Victorian era, European towns and cities were characterized by filthy streets littered with human and animal excrement and rotting garbage. Sewage either was thrown into the street or flowed from privies into streets and rivers, animals were kept and slaughtered and their hides tanned side-by-side with human housing. As recently as a century ago, in large cities such as London thousands of the poor lived in damp, overcrowded cellars prone to flooding, and even the olfactory senses of the most privileged regularly endured the pong of discarded human waste. Living conditions in the country were little better, with housing for the underprivileged characterized by dampness, overcrowding, lack of sanitation and running water and people commonly sharing their rooms with their animals (Wohl, 1983; Corbin, 1986; Cipolla, 1992). Even royalty was not spared the indignities of olfactory assault. At Versailles in the nineteenth century the cesspool was located next to the palace, and courtyards and buildings were littered with human and animal excrement (Corbin, 1986: 27). As late as the end of the nineteenth century the household of Queen Victoria experienced malodorous emanations from the Thames and problems with its sanitary system (Wohl, 1983: ch. 1).

Writers of the time were unsparing in their vivid description of the environmental fouling created by industrialization and urbanization. Friedrich Engels, in his *The Condition of the Working Class in England* (1845) described the slums of Manchester in condemning detail as a prelude to his collaboration with Karl Marx on *The Communist Manifesto* (1848). Charles Dickens' many novels included several damning details of life in urban industrial England and another well-known author of the time, Charles Kingsley, described the streets of a Victorian London slum thus in his novel *Alton Locke*:

> Fish stalls and fruit stalls lined the edge of the greasy pavement, sending up odours as foul as the language of sellers and buyers. Blood and sewer water crawled from under doors and out of spouts, and reeked down the gutters among offal, animal and vegetable, in every stage of putrefaction. Foul vapours rose from cow sheds and slaughterhouses, and the doorways of undrained alleys, where the inhabitants carried the filth out on their shoes from the backyard into the court, and from the court up into the main street; while above, hanging like cliffs over the streets – those narrow, brawling torrents of filth, and poverty, and sin – the houses with their teeming load of life were piled up into the dingy, choking night. A ghastly, deafening, sickening sight it was. (reproduced in Abrams, 1979: 1646–7)

By the mid-nineteenth century, attention was beginning to be paid to the condition of the working classes in France and Britain. In France, the migration of rural inhabitants to the cities and the changes wrought by industrialization created public health problems seen to demand attention (La Berge, 1992: 2–3). The concern was not related to humanitarian philosophies around the quality of life of the masses of industrial workers, but rather to fears around the threat of the deteriorating work capacity of people weakened by ill-health and the looming threat of insurrection and revolution on the part of the working classes (1992: 40–1). The early 'modern' public health movement which emerged in Britain in the 1840s under the renowned reformer Edwin Chadwick was also directly linked to the ideologies of capitalism. Public health reformers asserted that ill-health and premature death led to loss of worker productivity and thence to reduced profits. Using government money to improve public health would ultimately save the state money in providing poor relief for widows and orphans (Tesh, 1988: 30).

Chadwick produced his famous *Report on the Sanitary Condition of the Labouring Population of Great Britain* in 1842, demonstrating that current patterns of disease were closely related to environmental conditions, especially the water supply and housing conditions and the odours emanating from poor drainage, garbage disposal and sewage provisions (Rosen, 1974: 195; Tesh, 1988: 28–30). He therefore saw the problem as that of engineering, not medicine, writing in his report that:

> The great preventives, drainage, street and house cleaning by means of supplies of water and improved sewerage, and especially the introduction of cheaper and more efficient modes of removing all noxious refuse from the towns, are operations for which aid must be sought from the science of the Civil Engineer, not from the physician, who has done his work when he has pointed out the disease that results from the neglect of proper administrative measures, and has alleviated the sufferings of the victims. (quoted in Rosen, 1974: 196)

The aim of Chadwick and his like-minded reformers was 'to rationalize the principles of government, to remove waste, inefficiency and corruption' in order to make the free market more effective and to maintain and improve national prosperity (Jones, 1986: 6). Jones describes this approach as 'health care as a form of wise housekeeping'; it was argued that 'a little expenditure to prevent ill-health would lead, eventually, to a greater saving of money' (1986: 10). This argument promoted widespread public support for public health measures, particularly among the newly prosperous industrialists. There was no suggestion that industrialization should be halted or scaled down; on the contrary it was argued by the reformers that industrialization was beneficial in the long run in raising the standard of living for all (La Berge, 1992: 4).

The nineteenth-century public health movement became interested in the spread of illness and death within geographical space. When mapping distributions, public health reformers noted the link between geography, social class and patterns of mortality and morbidity (Prior, 1989: 123). Public health reformists like Chadwick used comparative statistics to demonstrate the new-found link between ill health and mortality and degree of wealth. French public health reformers were particularly influenced by the early nineteenth-century statistics movement, and contributed to it, seeking to make every area of investigation related to public hygiene quantifiable in a 'scientific' manner. Life tables were important in persuading them that the main causes of premature mortality were socio-economic, yet most of them stopped short of advocating large-scale social reform 'adopting instead a meliorist stance, according to which their responsibility was merely investigative . . . They assumed that a problem, once pointed out and understood, would either be addressed by the authorities or solved by long-term socioeconomic change' (La Berge, 1992: 3–4).

Well into the nineteenth century, odour continued as a prime marker of disease. The miasmic theory was adopted by Chadwick and became the official orthodoxy of the British General Board of Health (Fee and Porter,

1992: 253). 'Chadwick and his collaborators acted and behaved not only as if all "smell" was disease but also as if all disease was "smell" ' (Cipolla, 1992: 7). The hygienists believed that most diseases were spread by filth, poverty or climatic conditions, not living organisms, and therefore strategies were directed towards cleaning up the environment or sanitary conditions and alleviating poverty (La Berge, 1992: 20–1). They consequently 'embarked on a vast inventory of smells that – along with the other administrative inventories of the period – sprang from the desire to ensure the efficient functioning of the city; thus health administration was built upon a catalogue of noxious odours' (Corbin, 1986: 57). As a result, despite the discourse of reform articulated by members of the public health movement, the measures they introduced differed little from those adopted by the Italian states between the fourteenth and seventeenth centuries, centring as they did on the removal and control of dirt, excrement and rubbish and their associated bad smells (Cipolla, 1992: 6–7).

However, instead of the emergency measures of epidemic control typical of medieval Europe, the emphasis in the mid-nineteenth century shifted to the application of a permanent set of regulations and measures to prevent the spread of disease (La Berge, 1992: 21). Legislation was set in place to enshrine the concerns of the public health movement under the aegis of state authorities. In Britain, the result of Chadwick's report was the enactment in 1846 of a series of Nuisance Removal Acts, which gave justices the power to prosecute those responsible for 'nuisances' such as poor housing, garbage accumulation and foul cesspools or drains. The Public Health Act of 1848 built on these acts by establishing a General Board of Health and empowering local authorities to set up local boards of health, responsible for the regulation of sewage, 'nuisances', drainage, water supplies, gas works, housing, parks, burial grounds and public baths (Wohl, 1983: 148–9). The General Board of Health, however, operated under conditions of constraint set by the general *laissez-faire* ideologies of early capitalism. It did not have the right to enforce local authorities to act unless a certain death rate was reached in the area, and was the subject of much criticism for its interference. Only a minority of regions took the opportunity to establish local boards of health, and the General Board was forced to dismantle in 1858 as a result of sustained opposition, its function absorbed by the Privy Council (1983: 149–53).

It was not until the 1866 Sanitary Act that compulsory clauses were introduced for the direction of local authorities (Wohl, 1983: 155), but officials still encountered difficulties in implementing reform. Local boards in charge of sanitary conditions tended to be comprised of men involved in mercantile, building and manufacturing activities, with medical practitioners in short supply (1983: 168). As a result, '[u]nless an epidemic or some other emergency created an atmosphere favourable to reform, most public health measures were generally viewed with suspicion, or open hostility, by the ratepayers and the officials who were returned to power on the cry of low rates and economy' (1983: 170). Despite a united concern in achieving maximum prosperity by maintaining the health of the workers, there was thus a continuing tension between the long-term goals of the public health movement and the short-term concerns of those in power. However, Wohl (1983: 203) argues that by the end of the nineteenth century the notion of the 'sanitary idea' had slowly become an accepted part of local government.

The new technology of photography that developed from the mid-nineteenth century became a valuable strategy in the documentation of patterns of disease and illness, and the construction of sites of dirtiness and contagion. Just as photographs were used to depict the physical characteristics of disease and sexual 'deviancy' in the context of the hospital and clinic, thereby constructing the visual difference between the 'normal' and the 'abnormal' (Marshall, 1990), photography was an important tool in the documenting of the urban spaces that required surveillance. It was also used extensively to show public health officials at work in their unceasing quest to cleanse cities of contagion. In their historical study of British and American photographs of medicine since 1840, Fox and Lawrence (1988: 51) noted that representations of public health efforts in the late nineteenth century and early twentieth century tended to link dirt, lack of hygiene, poverty and slum housing with illness and disease. These images of the 'unclean' were juxtaposed with images of the medical profession actively working to disperse filth and bring hygiene to the great unwashed masses. Together with maps, photographs of city areas were used to chart the location and movement of disease outbreaks, highlighting 'trouble spots' and 'suspects', or buildings considered to be incubating disease, thereby rendering contamination visible (Grace, 1993: 159–61).

Public health in the 'New World'

Due to Australia's isolation from the Old World sources of infection and its small and dispersed population, major outbreaks of infectious disease did not occur until the mid-nineteenth century, when an influx of immigration dramatically swelled the population, causing urbanization and associated overcrowding, polluted water supplies and poor sanitation (Curson, 1985: 9–15). The scarlet fever epidemic of 1875–6 in Sydney was the first real outbreak of infectious disease to excite official and public concern and to occasion the development of official policy on public health (1985: 87). Although Sydney had previously experienced outbreaks of illness, including a mysterious virulent infectious disease that severely affected the Aboriginal population of the Sydney area in 1789 (a year after Europeans settled in Australia) and a measles epidemic in 1867, the scarlet fever outbreak occasioned large-scale fear because it affected European adults. It was not until the influenza epidemic of 1891 that Sydney experienced a major pandemic of infectious disease with widespread effects. Public health legislation in New South Wales was drawn up from the 1880s. A

Central Board of Health was established in 1881 and a new Public Health Act was passed in 1893 giving local municipalities the authority to survey housing conditions and to cleanse and disinfect premises considered contagious or unhygienic, and making compulsory the notification of a range of infectious diseases (1985: 17–19).

In Australia, as elsewhere, the old techniques of quarantine and isolation were reinterpreted through the hygienist ideal. The epidemics that caused the highest mortality (measles and scarlet fever) engendered less public reaction of hysteria, panic and fear than did outbreaks of the dread diseases (smallpox and bubonic plague) that resulted in fewer overall cases and deaths (Curson, 1985: 170). Minority groups were blamed for introducing and spreading contagion. For example, when an epidemic of smallpox broke out in Sydney in 1881, the New South Wales press and parliament first blamed the epidemic on Chinese immigrants living in the city. Their attention then turned to the poor residents of Sydney, who were castigated for their 'inordinate, unseemly, and perverse fondness for dirt . . . [and] daily defiance of sanitary laws' (*Daily Telegraph* [Sydney], 11 August 1882, quoted in Mayne, 1988: 227). In response, the Sydney City Council embarked upon a programme to 'clean' slum areas which was met with hostility by their inhabitants; understandably so, for it involved compulsory eviction, barricading, the burning of clothing and furniture, the closing of schools and the disinfecting of all public conveyances and evacuation of all suspected cases and their contacts to the local quarantine station (Curson, 1985: ch. 6; Mayne, 1988: 234).

The police force was employed to guard infectious houses, and many of those boarded up inside were left without medical care, food or other supplies. Teams of 'Ambulance and Disinfecting Corps' under the charge of a police constable moved from house to house, burning clothing, bedding, carpets and mattresses, stripping the paper off walls and applying carbolic acid and lime-wash to walls and ceilings. Some houses were demolished. Chinese immigrants, in particular, were subjected to forcible quarantine and vaccination and extreme levels of racism and violence (Curson, 1985: ch. 6). During this epidemic there was mass incidence of 'spying and reporting on neighbours', with the Board of Health and the police receiving letters informing on people suspected of having smallpox or acting suspiciously. Such people were often interred in the Quarantine Station or confined to their homes for weeks on the least suspicion of having come into contact with smallpox (1985: 116).

Canada and the United States were also late in experiencing the ill-effects of industrialization, and concern about the relationship between urbanization and the health of the population was therefore not engendered until the late nineteenth century (Fee and Porter, 1992: 254). These factors, in concert with the North American tradition of concern for the freedom of the individual and its sheer geographical size and dispersed populations, meant that there was greater resistance to the development of public health policing activities and less centralization of government

(Duffy, 1990: 138–9; Turner, 1990: 8). Various reports by American public health reformers emulating Chadwick appeared in the mid-nineteenth century, but it was not until a series of yellow fever epidemics in the southern states that the first permanent American state board of health was set up in Louisiana in 1855. The outbreak of the American Civil War in 1861 ensured that the creation of a permanent national public organization was delayed until the 1870s (Duffy, 1990: ch. 7). By the late nineteenth century there was a proliferation of government agencies and professional specializations set up to deal with public health issues, and the American Public Health Association was formed in 1872 (1990: 130). Voluntary movements committed to social reform began to flourish, many of which included middle- and upper-class women, who were actively involved in campaigns for such issues as improved housing, temperance and maternal and child health (Fee and Porter, 1992: 256). Fee and Porter (1992: 256–7) note that in the United States, '[p]olitically, public health reform offered a middle ground between the cut-throat principles of entrepreneurial capitalism and the revolutionary ideas of the socialists, anarchists and utopian visionaries'. Reform stopped short of radical restructuring of society, and as in other countries, focused not only on the humanitarian benefits of public health reform, but also on their financial benefits.

The vaccination debate

In addition to such techniques as quarantine, involving forcible removal of people from their homes, direct government intervention into the bodies of individuals was associated with the strategy of vaccination against smallpox. However, just as quarantine was often resisted by citizens, attempts by governments to introduce compulsory vaccination met with opposition on the part of vociferous anti-vaccination groups and individuals in most countries. In Britain in 1853 a compulsory vaccination act was passed which made it obligatory for parents to have their infants vaccinated within three months of birth. Parents were fined if they did not conform and the act made it possible for them to be imprisoned for non-payment of the fine (Wohl, 1983: 133). A series of smallpox epidemics in the state of New York inspired the state department of health to appoint a team of health inspectors to go from house to house in working class areas in New York City to check that inhabitants were vaccinated (Duffy, 1990: 140). In Australia, an outbreak of smallpox in New South Wales in 1881 occasioned the government to issue instructions that all police, government boatmen, health workers, ambulance men and all inmates of public institutions should be vaccinated (Curson, 1985: 110).

In all these countries, attempts by the state to enforce vaccination were achieved in the face of political indifference and hostility on the part of the general population. For example, during a series of smallpox outbreaks in the American city of Milwaukee in 1894, some parents refused to allow their children to be vaccinated and hid those sick with the disease. The city council responded by dismissing the health commissioner and reducing the powers of the health department (Duffy, 1990: 179–80). When a county in North Carolina attempted to introduce compulsory vaccination of school children in 1905, anti-vaccinationists forced the health authorities to go to court to have the order upheld, while in Washington state following pressure from anti-vaccinationists and Christian Scientists a bill was passed prohibiting compulsory vaccination (1990: 201). Although there was a furious debate between pro-vaccinationists and anti-vaccinationists in Sydney in 1881, all agreed that the Chinese should be compulsorily vaccinated and they were subsequently forced to submit to the procedure (Curson, 1985: 110). In Britain the anti-vaccination movement did not oppose vaccination on the grounds of efficiency, but on the grounds of violation of personal liberty and the 'unnaturalness' of vaccination, as well as religious principles, centring around the belief that it was sinful to inject impurities into the blood: 'it was argued that the rights of the individual had to be defended against this new menace of a doctoring state' (Wohl, 1983: 134).

In Australia and North America, debate also raged against the side-effects of smallpox vaccination, with some opponents, including physicians, arguing that vaccination stimulated the emergence of latent diseases in the body as well as introducing new diseases. One leading Sydney doctor, who gave evidence before a Committee of Inquiry established in 1881 to decide whether compulsory vaccination should be introduced, declared 'I would rather be shot than have anyone of my family vaccinated' (Curson, 1985: 111–12). The efforts of public health authorities in Canada were frequently challenged by the population, especially the working class, who found public health laws costly and intrusive. The courts often agreed, dismissing prosecutions brought against citizens by the Health Officers. A Canadian anti-vaccination movement was created in 1885, which continued to campaign vigorously against compulsory vaccination into the early twentieth century (Bilson, 1988: 171–2).

The turn towards personal hygiene

The doctrine of personal hygiene was central to the practices and ideology of the public health movement from the early nineteenth century onwards. Hygiene at that time was a term used to describe the collection of practices and knowledges which were believed to preserve health, including the use of soap and warm water to remove dirt to 'purify' the body and let it 'breathe' (Vigarello, 1988: 170–2). The emphasis was on monitoring the passage of exterior elements, such as air, water, earth and food into the body and the passage of interior elements, such as faeces, urine, sputum, sweat and semen, out of the body and into the environment. It is during this time that there emerged the contemporary obsession with hygiene and dirt, with purity and cleanliness, with the bowels, the skin, the mouth and the sexual organs (Armstrong, 1993: 396–8). The dead body posed a particular problem, for it marked the site at which the boundary between environment and body threatened to blur. Thus new regulations were instituted to maintain definite distinctions between places of burial and dwellings, including rules about disturbing buried bodies and the prohibition of the erection of buildings upon disused burial grounds (1993: 399–400).

In the Victorian era in Britain, 'public health, like so many other social reforms and endeavours, took on the form of a moral crusade': epidemics were seen as evidence of neglect, as undermining other areas of social progress (Wohl, 1983: 6). These ideas predated Darwin, but gained even more support with his emphasis on the survival of the fittest and the role played by the environment in adaptation and survival (1983: 7). Cleanliness was indeed considered next to Godliness for the Victorians, and rhetoric around the need to defeat dirt and disease verged on the zealous, as evidenced by the text of this advertisement for Hudson's soap that appeared in 1891:

> PUBLIC HEALTH. DIRT HARBOURS GERMS OF DISEASE. The source of Danger removed by Washing everything with HUDSON'S EXTRACT OF SOAP. Dirt cannot exist where HUDSON'S SOAP is used for all Domestic Washing, Cleaning and Scouring . . . Home, Sweet Home! The Sweetest, Healthiest Homes are those where HUDSON'S EXTRACT OF SOAP is in Daily use. (reproduced in Wohl, 1983: 71)

Wohl also quotes from the treatise of Sir Benjamin Ward Richardson, who wrote in 1875: 'Let us cleanse our outward garments, our bodies, our food, our drink and keep them cleansed. Let us clean our minds, as well as our garments, and keep them clean' (1983: 72). One British doctor wrote a pamphlet published in 1854 expressing the view that 'there is a close affinity between moral depravity and physical degradation'. Cholera 'respects cleanliness, sobriety and decent habits. It seldom intrudes where industry and good morals prevail. Hence, in regard to this dreadful pestilence, man is, in no small degree, the arbiter of his own fate' (quoted in Bilson, 1988: 165).

As these texts suggest, the theories of cleanliness that became dominant in the eighteenth and nineteenth centuries had an ideological function; they ensured social order and bolstered hegemonic moral values. As Corbin (1986: 5) notes: 'Abhorrence of smells produces its own form of social power. Foul-smelling rubbish appears to threaten the social order, whereas the reassuring victory of the hygienic and the fragrant promises to buttress its stability.' A technology of the self had emerged which linked the cleanliness of the body to the purity of one's moral standing, and urged that care be directed at the former so as to improve the latter. By the latter half of the nineteenth century, people were viewed as having certain 'constitutions' which determined the extent to which they would be willing to engage in personal hygienic behaviour (Armstrong, 1993: 402).

The notion of quarantine had become elaborated under the concept of sanitary science, which was concerned with the natural and built environments and their relationship with the human body. Certain social groups were set apart as those most susceptible to lack of hygiene and therefore needful of public health interventions: in particular, the poor, members of the working classes and immigrant groups were constituted as sanitary problems, as sites for the breeding of disease and contagion that continually threatened to spill out into other, respectably 'clean' groups in society. More discrete groups such as prostitutes, Jews, ragpickers, domestic servants, sewermen, drain cleaners, prisoners, knackers and garbage workers were also signalled out for especial attention as unclean and malodorous (Corbin, 1986: 145). For the public health reformers, the conditions in which such groups lived and their lifestyles rendered them susceptible to contagion: 'Pauperism is no longer simply the source of a moral contagion but both the cause and effect of disease' (Dean, 1991: 206).

The problem of sexuality as it was expressed in the context of the working-class family also emerged as a dominant problem for public health reform. Since the emergence of Christianity the sexual body has been conceptualized as a source of disorder and contagion, requiring a high level of control and the stringent maintenance of body boundaries. Sexual urges and acts threaten the cherished notion of the modern, rational, controlled body. Subsequently, much public health literature since the nineteenth century has been devoted to outlining norms and conventions of sexuality, identifying, categorizing and labelling varieties of sexual 'deviance' and pronouncing on the differences between 'normal' and 'abnormal' sexual acts and desires (Foucault, 1979; Mort, 1987). At the time in which sexuality was emerging as a construct needful of surveillance and control, the working class was also emerging as a social category requiring regulation, given its propensity for disorder. Members of the working class insisted on drinking to excess, blasphemed and swore both in private and in the public domain, refused to keep their persons clean, let their children run wild on the streets, engaged in licentious sexual behaviour such as incest and prostitution, and seemed unable to control their urges in the manner deemed to be appropriate of 'civilized' humans (Finch, 1993). As such, it was believed that it was the duty of hygienists to influence all areas of human activity, at all levels, ranging from personal cleanliness and everyday habits to the political level. Their efforts were devoted towards 'civilizing' the poor and members of the working class, ensuring that both their material circumstances and their morals were improved. The hygienists believed in teaching these groups to become more middle-class by example and education programmes, so as to achieve the vision of an orderly society which was productive and lawful (La Berge, 1992: 18).

Thus the goal of 'cleaning' up underprivileged social groups in the interests of the nation's health expanded from the actual state of cleanliness of individuals' bodies to a concern with their morals, education and conduct: 'Hygiene was seen as part of the process by which the poor were civilized, disciplined and made into rational economic actors' (Jones, 1986:

11). The family continued as a prime site for the interventions of the public health movement to be translated into individuals' everyday lives. The working-class family in particular, and the child in that family, were represented as 'at danger' from their own ignorance, lack of cleanliness and morality. People deemed to be members of the working classes were categorized as either 'respectable' or 'disreputable', based on the bourgeoisie's assessment of such factors as the arrangement of sleeping quarters in their homes and the observable behaviour of women in relation to the family (Finch, 1993).

The birth of the microbe

In the closing years of the nineteenth century a new regime of public health developed in concert with the discovery of microbes. The rising dominance and respectability of the new science of bacteriology ensured that the status of medical practitioners working in public health improved. Public health, formerly dependent on the age-old miasmic and contagionist models of disease causation, had become legitimated as 'scientific'. Its protagonists were now able to cite a tangible reason for infectious disease, and it gave many in the medical profession the opportunity for a flourishing and authoritative career (Bilson, 1988: 170; Fee and Porter, 1992: 265; Sears, 1992: 69). In the United States, and somewhat later in Britain, the bacteriological laboratory became the new dominant symbol of a new, 'scientific' public health, the province of professionals, differentiated from the old, amateur and superstitious public health (Fee and Porter, 1992: 266). The discovery of microbes served to support the contagionist theory by revealing the process by which contagion was passed from individual to individual. The 'enemy' had now been rendered visible, and a logical sequence of events could be outlined to link the causes of illness (Latour, 1988: 45). Science now promised a golden new future for public health reformers, in which disease could be virtually eliminated. As one hygienist wrote in 1894: 'If we could know the microbe at the source of each disease, its favourite haunts, its habits, its way of progressing, we might, with good medical supervision, catch it in time, stop it in its tracks, and prevent its continuing in its homicidal mission' (Emile Trèlat, quoted in Latour, 1988: 45–6).

As a result of the discovery of the microbe, the great problems of hygiene were reinterpreted or dissipated. In North America, the discovery of bacteria as the cause of major diseases such as tuberculosis drew attention away from the broad social causes of disease and ill-health such as poverty and inadequate housing, narrowing public health problems to those that could be identified under the microscope (Fee and Porter, 1992: 267). It seems that in Britain, however, public health reformers were slower to take up bacteriology, preferring to emphasize lifestyle and sanitarian changes up to the mid-twentieth century (Weindling, 1992: 309).

By the early decades of the twentieth century, the principles of *laissez-faire* government became superseded by a belief in greater regulation. The social hygiene movement reflected this change, advocating that the state should consciously control and manage the population (Jones, 1986: 161). This era marked a change in public health, from an emphasis on the environment to an emphasis on the individual. It was realized that environmental bad smells were not necessarily harmful, even though they irritated the olfactory glands, that quarantine was useful only if infected bedlinen was also controlled and that cemeteries posed no threat to the living (Latour, 1988: 48). While it became accepted that bad smells did not necessarily denote contagion, it was still believed that odour was a sign of the presence of disease. Thus, the demand for social segregation of the 'dirty' and the 'clean' continued, albeit in more subtle form, based on the systematic medical surveillance of the whole population (Corbin, 1986: 227).

The concern with personal hygiene developing in the late nineteenth century was coupled with national concern about the health and fitness of the population, especially that of the infant and child. Once the focus on 'dirt' had changed from the visible to the non-visible, the focus of the sanitarians turned from the state of cleanliness of the larger environs to that of individual bodily cleanliness and the domestic environment. While personal cleanliness and bodily odour continued to be a dominant theme of public health discourses as well as popular culture, these concerns constructed bodies and the categories of 'healthy' and 'unhealthy' in somewhat different ways. It was no longer enough to gauge a 'healthy' body or home simply by looking or smelling, for 'dirt' and 'disease' had now become invisible (Vigarello, 1988: 214). The poor continued to be stigmatized as 'unclean', and their dwellings considered to be the breeding places of disease, 'but now because they harboured "microbe factories" instead of filth and bad smells' (La Berge, 1992: 325). By the 1930s, advertising in the United States was extolling the sanitary ideal of the clean body and home: 'Popular magazines were full of faces (male and female) contorted with disgust over everything from "sneaker smell" to "smelly hands"' (Lears, 1989: 57). Advertisements for antiseptics used 'surgical cleanliness' as selling points for one's body and home, offering total control over the vagaries of nature (1989: 58–60).

In concert with the new imperative of hygienism, individuals, especially school children, were exhorted not to pick their noses, place their fingers or any other objects apart from food and drink in their mouths, to keep their hands clean and not to cough or sneeze in a person's face. Thus the space that was policed was that between individual bodies rather than between groups of bodies and the environment (Armstrong, 1993: 404). 'Modern' public health became viewed as 'the province of the pathologist and the physician rather than the sanitary engineer' (Lewis, 1992: 211). Theories of cleanliness also had an impact upon the architecture of housing and cities: washrooms and bathrooms became common, with doors protecting against the invasion of private space, sewage systems and water conveying systems were built so that water was available to all for washing (Vigarello, 1988: 230).

Armstrong (1983: 8–9) describes the development of the philosophy of the Dispensary as a new apparatus for diffusing the medical gaze into the community. In Britain, from the late nineteenth century onwards, the dispensary as a building was introduced as a means of delivering and monitoring health care for out-patients. The 'Dispensary' (as concept rather than physical building), was a new way of organizing health care, locating disease in the community rather than in the individual body; in the spaces between people, in their relationships and contacts with each other: 'In that the Dispensary required the social body to be monitored, it extended its gaze over the normal person to establish early detection, to advise on appropriate behaviour and relationships and to enable the potentially abnormal to be adequately known' (1983: 9). Under this new medical gaze, a new form of patienthood was generated: everyone, regardless of their actual state of health, became 'at risk', potentially ill, the subject of medical surveillance (1983: 740). Health became a duty, a goal after which people should strive rather than a private, inherent possession of individuals. It became a social state, influenced by one's relationships with others rather than one's relationships with the natural environment.

Hence the surveilling gaze of public health moved from the environment to the minutiae of social life (Armstrong, 1983: 10–11). Armstrong (1983: 11–12) provides the example of tuberculosis, which had previously been conceptualized and dealt with as a disease of individual bodies and environmental neglect, but by the early twentieth century had become a disease of social contact, requiring notification of all cases and their contacts to the state. The tuberculosis bacillus was the link between individuals, invisibly bridging the space between infected individuals' mouths and noses and those of their contacts. So too, the increasing attention paid to tracing the contacts and social relationships of people with venereal disease served to construct a newly medicalized map of social space. Hence, venereal disease 'changed from being used as a means of forbidding certain relationships to a mechanism for observing them' (1983: 13).

The late nineteenth-century public health movement became more concerned with maintaining the boundaries of populations, preventing contamination of those within from those without. Immigration was especially seen to pose a threat to the health of nations (Sears, 1992: 70–1). Like bacteria, immigrants were conceptualized as foreign agents seeking entry into the social body, requiring a vigilant defence to protect boundaries from invasion and occupation (Lears, 1989: 60). In photographs of public health work taken in the early nineteenth century, doctors and nurses were shown examining the poor and immigrants as they arrived in the United States, including measuring, weighing and recording the details of patients and listening to patients' chests with their stethoscopes. These representations were striking for several reasons: such encounters were depicted as occurring not in private clinics or hospital wards, but in large open spaces, often including many onlookers. The patients shown being examined were usually children and immigrants, and the underlying subtext of such photographs was the use of medical examination in the interests of the public good rather than the good of the individual patient (Fox and Lawrence, 1988: 52). Medical workers were performing the service of checking stigmatized outgroups for the potential they might harbour in spreading contagion to dominant groups.

Advertising focusing on bodily hygiene and appearance around this time and well into the post-Second World War era had a claustrophobic quality, representing the self as trapped within a decaying body threatening betrayal (Whorton, 1989). In a world in which external events seemed out of the individual's control, anxiety and attempts at regulation retreated within the body. For example, a preoccupation with 'auto-intoxication' emerged in American advertisements in the first three decades of the twentieth century. This condition was believed to be caused by the build-up of proteins in the bloodstream, which was considered debilitating of the body and even threatening of life (Lears, 1989; Whorton, 1989). As one advertisement for a remedy published in a 1928 issue of *Literary Digest* magazine announced:

> Auto-intoxication – a form of self-poisoning . . . the most common ailment of the hurried times . . . Sluggish bodily functions permit food to remain within us too long, fermenting and setting up poisons. The result is intestinal toxaemia, or Auto-Intoxication – the most common Twentieth Century ailment . . . [it] weakens the body's resistance to disease. It robs nearly every one of some part of health, some portion of vitality. (reproduced in Whorton, 1989: 103)

The construction of this condition was influenced by the epistemology of bacteriology, for it was unheard of before bacterial flora that broke down protein residues in the intestinal tract had been discovered. It also harkened back to the miasmic discourse, in representing the intestine as a sewer, releasing dangerous gases. One physical educator wrote at the time: 'One cannot live over a cesspit in good health. How much more difficult to remain well if we carry our cesspit about inside us – especially when, as so often happens, the cesspit is unpleasantly full' (F.A. Hornibrook, 1934, quoted in Whorton, 1989: 102). Significantly, an obsession with this new condition developed at around the same time as the United States was experiencing a moral panic over communism and immigration. Both anxieties concerned the threat of alien invaders into the body, harbouring the potential of silent destruction from within.

In the early twentieth century, the ideology of the social hygiene movement in Britain combined the concerns of social Darwinism and its eugenic stress on heredity, fitness and racial progress with the governmental activities of the early public health movement, which emphasized the relationship between social class and disease (Jones, 1986: 5–6). The eugenicists had been among the first medical commentators who noted the prevalence of chronic degenerative diseases such as tuberculosis, alcoholism and venereal disease, yet warned against prevention and treatment among groups they considered to be 'genetically poor' (Weindling, 1992: 309). This branch of public health reform actually criticized environmental changes for allowing the less fit to survive for longer, resulting in 'race decay' (Wohl, 1983: 334). As one writer of the day described this perspective, poor housing conditions were viewed as 'the natural environment of an unfit class and the means whereby such a class prepared the way for its own extinction' while high infant mortality 'weeded out the sickly and the weaklings' (L.T. Hobhouse, 1922, quoted in Wohl, 1983: 335). Reformists therefore advocated the techniques of birth control, segregation, sterilization and new legislative measures to regulate birth rates (Jones, 1986: 160).

Exercise and education for health

During this time great attention was also paid to education concerning such areas as disease transmission and personal hygiene, for ignorance about such matters, particularly on the part of the poor and the working class, was viewed as the source of ill health (Sears, 1992: 72–5). The prevailing belief was that education campaigns would effectively bring the message to the masses; the motto of the Ontario Board of Health in 1920 was 'Let not the people perish for lack of Knowledge' (quoted in Sears, 1992: 73). In 1928, the British Chief Medical Officer to the Board of Education and the Ministry of Health, Sir George Newman, published a book in which he claimed that public health should no longer be concerned with such issues as sewerage, the notification and registration of disease and the suppression of nuisances, but should instead be directed towards the provision by physicians of health education to the people to improve their 'domestic, social and personal life' (Lewis, 1992: 211).

The Boer War sparked concerns about the physical fitness of Britain's young men in maintaining the Empire and providing the labour force, and concentrated public health efforts towards infant mortality and the falling birth rate evident at the turn of the century (Wright, 1988: 308–9). Similarly, in Australia, the declining birth rate at the turn of the twentieth century and the seeming threat posed by the Asiatic 'yellow hordes' to Australia, especially the emerging power of Japan, incited the emergence of the infant welfare movement (Lewis, 1988: 304–5). The doctrine of *mens sana in corpore sano* (a healthy mind in a healthy body) had emerged by the mid-nineteenth century and was articulated in social relations, particularly in British public schools, where sporting activities were viewed as contributing to a 'moral education' by training individuals to be determined in the face of adversity, to exert control over the emotions, to accept authority, fit in with peers, take decisions, lead subordinates and accept responsibility (Hargreaves, 1987: 143). Conversely, for working-class men sporting activities were used to 'improve' them, to render them more 'rational' and amenable to discipline, to learn to follow rather than lead. The ideal male, according to dominant discourses of the time, possessed the following physical and moral attributes:

> An upright posture with no hands in pockets, short hair, a clean well-washed body, a simple neat and tidy appearance, teetotalism, no smoking, no 'self-abuse', no sex outside marriage, active participation in organized sport, frequent and regular physical exercise, fitness and good health, and above all, a 'hard' body – constituted the God-fearing, obedient, hard-working, respectable individual. (Hargreaves, 1987: 146)

Emphasis was placed on improving the 'stock' through focusing on individuals' general physique and wellbeing by paying attention to physical exercise and diet, particularly at the school level (Wohl, 1983: 338). In their history of physical education in Victorian government schools between the 1880s and the early 1900s, Kirk and Spiller (1993: 105), note that such education 'was concerned with disciplining children by working primarily on their bodies . . . the problem which faced Australian educators was the taming of the body as a site of unruly passions, and the channelling of intellectual power into productive work'. As a result, such practices as drill and gymnastics 'came to be constituted by other, related though less specific, discourses such as militarism, nationalism and economism', schooling docile bodies: (1993: 113). In Britain and the United States, photographs were common portraying individuals engaging in the disciplined exercise believed necessary as the 'cure for national enfeeblement' including British photographs showing children exercising at school in military fashion (Fox and Lawrence, 1988: 52). In 1901, a British Fabian, Sidney Webb, argued that the prime duty of the government for the future was 'the prevention of disease and premature death, and the building up of the nervous and muscular vitality of the race', in the achievement of which education was a vital strategy (quoted in Donald, 1992: 28).

With the increasingly eugenicist approach to regulating the reproduction of bodies came a focus on sex education, directed at preserving the modesty of young girls and controlling the urges of young boys and men. Several recent revisionist histories of sexuality have claimed that the idea that the Victorian era was characterized by sexual repression and an all-abiding disgust for sexual expression is a myth (see, for example, Foucault, 1979; Seidman, 1991). They have argued that, on the contrary, Victorians elevated sex to a central part of their lives, investing sex with an enormous importance. Sexology, or the 'science of sexuality', developed as a field of knowledge directed at documenting and providing advice upon the sexual government of the body. A series of popular medical and advice texts proliferated, giving guidelines of how to conduct oneself sexually and warning of the dangers of spermatorrhoea (loss of semen), masturbation and sexual congress outside the marital bed, but also describing the pleasures and beneficial aspects of sex within the right context (that is, marriage). By the late 1890s, marriage advice manuals were responding to a perceived collapse of clear marital norms, with the crisis being perceived as being rooted in sexual discontents based on lack of sexual knowledge and expertise. Marriage manuals positioned themselves as guides to achieving sexual fulfilment, thus making marriage more successful (Seidman, 1991: 74–6).

In the early twentieth century mothers were encouraged to discuss sex with their children, especially their daughters, so that they might be instructed and warned by knowledge (Finch, 1993: 140). It was argued by reformers that sex education was too important to leave to parents and should become a public responsibility, introduced into schools (Brandt, 1985: 25–6). 'Plain' and 'honest' speaking about sex was declaimed as the only means to contain the spread of licentious behaviour and disease. For example, Finch (1993: 141) quotes from a social hygienist text written in 1918, entitled *Sex Hygiene and Sex Education*, which warned that: 'In this book we speak plainly about matters connected with sex. Public opinion, for a time at any rate freed from false modesty and prudish sentiment, recognizes that something must be done to check immorality and sexual disease, and we propose to strike while the iron is hot.'

There was particular concern around venereal disease as a threat to the family unit and to reproduction levels. Venereal disease in the early twentieth century became redefined from a 'carnal scourge' to 'family poison' as a greater emphasis was placed on the susceptibility of innocent wives and children to disease passed on to them by the head of the household (Brandt, 1985: ch. 1). Public education was considered a panacea for the ills of venereal disease; for example, physicians and reformers who were members of the American Society for Sanitary and Moral Prophylaxis (founded in 1905) called for the education of the American people as the only means of eliminating venereal disease. It was believed that once the people knew how venereal disease was spread, they would realize their moral duty to remain chaste in the interests of their health (1985: 25).

The mother as moral guardian

The emphasis on the health and wellbeing of the child in the context of the family unit continued into the twentieth century, bringing with it a focus on the behaviour of mothers. The death of infants became viewed in western societies as a problem 'about which something ought to be done' rather than as an inescapable fact of nature (Wright, 1988: 302–3). Infant mortality was viewed as 'one of the greatest social problems of the day . . . "Preventable infanticide!" became a battle cry for reform' (Levenstein, 1988: 128). The solutions proposed were medical rather than simply moral; national systems of trained health visitors and domiciliary midwives were developed to institute charge over the family domain, milk treatment and bottling was developed, classes and information were provided for mothers, improvements in sanitation were made and infant welfare and antenatal classes began to be offered (Wright, 1988; Levenstein, 1988: ch. 10). In the early twentieth century, British mothers were encouraged, and in some cases, paid, to bring their children to milk depots, where the latters' state of health and growth were closely scrutinized, including regular weighing, and individual dossiers of this information made up for each child to keep account of their progress. Maternity benefits were introduced and services for the medical inspection and screening of children were introduced in schools (Armstrong, 1983: 14–15).

As the web of surveillance grew around the infant and child, new conditions and illnesses were constructed, requiring medical or social welfare attention: 'Nervous children, delicate children, neuropathic children, maladjusted children, difficult children, over-sensitive children and unstable children were all essentially inventions of a new way of seeing childhood' (Armstrong, 1983: 14). The germ pathogeny theory gave added scientific authority to the encroachment of medicine and the infant welfare movement into the family domain. Mothers were warned to guard against illness caused by bacteria by imposing strict control over family hygiene, and were urged to take responsibility for the moral standards of their family members for the sake of the nation's health. For example, Sears (1992: 72) quotes from a Canadian public health document written for new mothers in 1921, in which it was claimed that: 'No national service is greater or better than the work of the mother in her own home. The mother is the "First Servant of the State" .' The discourses and practices of dentistry also constituted the mother as the agent of discipline in the family unit. Beginning with the initial reports commissioned by the British Dental Association in 1892 to gather statistics on the state of children's teeth, surveys were regularly carried out in the quest for the effective management of dental care. The school, the dental surgery and the home were the three main sites for the surveillance of children's teeth. By the early decades of the twentieth century, children's mouths came to be regarded as a mirror of their mothers' skill at child-rearing, with dental decay viewed as a pointer to mothers' level of ignorance and degree of concern about their children's welfare (Nettleton, 1991).

This new focus upon the problem of infant and child health and welfare was reflected in both American and British photographs representing medical and public health practice as taking responsibility for the social and physiological wellbeing of the family. The photographs represented efforts to improve the health of mothers and babies, including showing babies and children being examined, vaccinated and weighed to monitor their growth (Fox and Lawrence, 1988: 188). Thus, the marker of public health intervention into the health of the population changed from images of forcible evacuation, quarantine, the collection of refuse and the disinfection of homes to a more intimate, interpersonal concern with young children's health and that of their parents. Health reformers focused increasingly on domestic hygiene rather than public sanitation, portraying themselves as educators rather than regulators (Rogers, 1992: 66–7). This approach combined elements of contagionism, with its concern about isolating infectious bodies from the well, with humoral theory, which recognized the importance of an individual's disposition and everyday activities in contributing to good health, and emphasized individuals' responsibility to preserve their own health status.

Despite this new representation of the caring, non-interventionist public health worker, intent more on helping individuals to help themselves rather than forcing them to improve their health against their will, older, more overtly coercive methods of dealing with disease continued to be employed. Decades after the germ theory of disease had been developed, public health officials tended to revert to the age-old methods of quarantine, fumigation, lime-washing and street cleaning when epidemics struck and public panic levels were high. At the turn of the twentieth century, tuberculosis patients were isolated in special sanatoria by American state and federal governments. State laws were introduced to permit enforced treatment of the 'careless consumptive' and to prohibit patients from discharging themselves from care without medical approval (Musto, 1988: 76). In the polio epidemic in New York City in 1916, even though a virus believed responsible for the disease had been isolated seven years earlier, the city's public health authorities decided to take no chances, and embarked upon a hygiene campaign, flooding the streets with millions of gallons of water daily, removing piles of refuse, collecting all stray cats and dogs, issuing flyscreens and urging people to keep their homes spotless, cover their garbage bins and take daily baths (Risse, 1988: 51). Due to the emphasis on dirt, the finger of blame, as has been common with many epidemics, was pointed at the poor and ethnic minorities, in this case Italian immigrants, who were deemed ignorant, unhygienic and apathetic. As one editorialist at the time wrote in the *New York Times*; 'If we could get rid of ignorance and the filth and superstition that go with it, there would be little need to hunt down the mysterious germs that no filter can stop and no microscope disclose' (quoted in Risse, 1988: 51–2).

While coercive measures of public health continued to be employed in times of emergency, the trend towards education rather than enforcement of public health principles dominated in the twentieth century. The traditional rationale for health education was that disease and illness are largely preventable, that human behaviour is strongly linked to the aetiology of many diseases and conditions and the management of others, that therefore, people should be encouraged to adopt a 'healthy' lifestyle, follow medical advice in a rational and sensible manner and use health services wisely (Tones, 1992: 33). As the British Minister of Health commented in 1943, 'education is the instrument of reform, the giver of hope, the guide which directs the conscious individual effort without which health cannot be attained' (quoted in Tones, 1993: 138). In the United States, health education developed from 'medical social workers' at the turn of the century who were trained to teach impoverished and working-class women the principles of personal hygiene and child care. By 1925, school health programmes involving education and physical examinations for students were under way, and in the 1930s and 1940s public health nurses moved into the area of community health education. Publicists were employed to write health education pamphlets and press releases explaining correct health practices for schools and the public. Health educators were also used to inform people about appropriate services in the attempt to reduce utilization of medical resources (Brown and Margo, 1978: 4–5).

Health education was viewed as a 'promising handmaiden' for preventive medicine, serving to support rather than supplant biomedical practice (Tones, 1993: 127). Consequently, health education materials well into the middle of the twentieth century relied on instructing individuals on the best way to 'maintain' the machinery of the body, with doctors portrayed as the 'body engineers', or the experts with the technical knowledge required to preserve good health. Little cognizance of the socio-cultural restraints to taking up the 'sensible' advice of doctors was demonstrated in most of the health educational literature (Amos, 1993: 145). These sentiments were well evident in an American textbook on health education first published in 1937, which was dedicated to 'the doctor, whose title really means teacher' (Bauer and Hull, 1942: 10). The text went on to state that the aims of health education were as follows:

1   To instruct children and youth so that they may conserve and improve their own health.
2   To establish in them the habits and principles of living which thruout [sic] their school life and in later years will aid in providing that abundant vigour and vitality which are a foundation for the greatest possible happiness and service in personal, family, and community life.
3   To promote satisfactory habits and attitudes among parents and adults thru [sic] parent and adult education and thru [sic] the health education program for children, so that the school may become an effective agency for the advancement of the social aspects of health education in the family and in the community as well as in the school itself.
4   To improve the individual and community life of the future; to ensure a better second generation, and a still better third generation; to build a healthier and fitter nation and race. (1942: 13)

It would seem that health educators in the 1930s and 1940s were highly aware of the use of the mass media in conveying information about health issues, for there follow chapters on using radio, the exhibit, the meeting, pamphlets, the newspaper, the motion picture, slides, magazines and books for disseminating information, including detailed instructions on the writing of texts, the sort of paper and type of font to choose for pamphlets, the best use of visual material, writing for newspapers and magazines, producing films, making slides and the way to present a talk effectively. The authors recognized the importance of dramatizing health information, of avoiding over-exposure on radio and of presenting visual material in an interesting manner to capture the attention of the audience. They remark that:

There is so much to be overcome of ignorance, prejudice, superstition, perversity, suspicion, laziness, inertia, and procrastination. Racial customs and family habits take a strong hold upon the individual, and it may take much time and patience to create the acceptance and the motivation to desired conduct which is the health educator's objective. (Bauer and Hull, 1942: 294–5)

By the 1960s, this model of health education had changed little. As one British textbook published in 1962 claimed, health education involves providing people with an understanding of medical principles, doctors' work and health care delivery, knowledge of human physiology and of hygiene (Pirrie and Dalzell-Ward, 1962: 18–19). The obsession with personal and domestic cleanliness and the moral sub-text of health education as it was practised in the early decades of the twentieth century remained evident in this text:

The aims of hygiene are not only to prevent the spread of infection, but also to promote well-being. Good housekeeping, with an insistence on tidiness, cleanliness, ventilation, and the maintenance of the dwelling in a good state of repair and decoration, goes much of the way to preserving a healthy domestic environment. (1962: 23)

Concluding comments

This chapter has discussed the continuities and discontinuities in the discourses and practices of public health from the Middle Ages until the mid-twentieth century. As shown, some central problems constructed and regulated by medieval measures of public health have remained stable: epidemics, disease, dead bodies, dirt, the policing of space, the maintenance and defence of boundaries around bodies and populations. While organized attempts to control disease outbreaks were originally somewhat ad hoc and reactive, since the Enlightenment a vast network of rationalized governmental activities, dispersed amongst an array of sites, has grown around the central problems of public health. These activities have reflected wider social ideologies and concerns, including the belief in scientific method and calculation and of good health as a right of citizens emerging in the Enlightenment, a concern about social order arising from the massive social changes wrought by industrialization and urbanization in the eighteenth century, and the problems of reproduction of the population, including sexuality, the child and the family which characterized the nineteenth and early twentieth centuries.

The discourses and practices of public health have carried with them moralistic and discriminatory meanings disguised under their utilitarian logic. When disease threatens to rage out of human control and science and medicine appear to be ineffective in containing it, notions of blame draw upon fears which can be traced back to medieval notions of sinfulness and punishment, purity and contagion, cleanliness and dirtiness. Conceptions of Self versus Other, inside versus outside and order versus disorder, and, in more recent times, eugenic principles around the survival of the fittest, have been integral to the definitions of those groups deemed 'dirty' and 'contagious' and therefore requiring extra surveillance, and those elite groups deemed at risk of contagion and needful of protection. For centuries, the poor, the working class and immigrants have routinely been constructed as the Other in public health discourses and practices.

Definitions of dirt and those things or people who are considered 'unclean', are highly suggestive of symbolic anxieties, fears and repulsions. As Douglas (1980: 35) notes, '[i]f we can abstract pathogenicity and hygiene from our notion of dirt, we are left with the old definition of dirt as matter out of place' (see also Kristeva, 1982). At the deeper level of meaning, then, public health has been directed at attempts to police body boundaries, to guard the integrity of the public body against the disorder threatened by dirt. In public health discourses, dirt, whether visible or in the invisible form of microbes, equals disease, and the hygienist ideology thus supports the most overt attempts at social regulation. The dirty body is a horror, a source of loathing and disgust, a thing whose boundaries are leaky and uncontrolled and threaten to contaminate others; its apotheosis is the corpse (Kristeva, 1982: 3–4). The rituals of hygiene, directed both at the private body and at the body politic, have remained vital in maintaining the distinction between spaces and bodies. On the inside of the boundary lies social order, 'Us', while the outside is 'a twilight place of outcasts, danger and pollution' (Armstrong, 1993: 394).

As the following chapters demonstrate, these deep anxieties around disorder, dirt, bodily control and the Other have remained central to public health and health promotional discourses and practices in the late twentieth century, albeit usually expressed in more subtle ways. The next phase of public health was to move in the 1970s from health 'education' to health 'promotion'. The claim of health promotion was that it eschewed the individualistic and moralistic approach of health education for a renewed focus on the environmental conditions giving rise to ill-health. Chapter 2 discusses in detail the ideologies, discourses and practices of contemporary public health and health promotion, seeking to examine the extent to which the 'new' public health may be considered a novel and more progressive approach to the quest of improving the public's health.

2

Technologies of Health: Contemporary Health Promotion and Public Health

Within the field of health promotion, there is a continuing debate concerning how exactly the field should define itself. What is health promotion? What should it attempt to do? What should its politics be? Despite this debate, the disputes around what is health promotion have rarely been grounded in critical social theory. Debates around public health which balance the utilitarian good of measures taken to improve and protect the public's health against the restriction of individual liberty enforced by public health measures represent the individual as distinct from the social. The social is viewed as having the potential of intruding into the individual, while the individual is viewed as having the potential to affect the health of others. What this debate fails to recognize is that there is a symbiotic relationship between the social and the individual; the subject is constituted in and through social processes, and subjects, in turn, influence the character of the social.

As noted in the Introduction, the political economy critique of public health and health promotion generally positions the state as coercive, intent on repressing individuals' rights in the interests of perpetuating the capitalist economic system. Critics from the right also represent public health and health promotional activities as emerging from a state that is too concerned with regulation, hindering personal autonomy, but their concern is that the economic system is not allowed free rein. Each position fails to recognize the liberal nature of contemporary government, in which free choice is actively encouraged, and there is no clear opposition between public and private, state and civil society, coercion and consent (Rose and Miller, 1992: 174). Indeed, contemporary, 'progressive' health promotion represents a neo-liberal approach to the authority of the professions, an approach which is 'constantly suspicious of its own authority; one which seeks to establish grounds of responsibility both within itself, as a profession, and to its constituency without seeking to govern either professionals or their clients in a straightforwardly directive, or "sovereign" manner' (Osborne, 1993: 346).

The endeavours of health promotion are easily recognizable as the strategies of liberal governmentality. That is, they are directed at the level of the population, they constitute individuals and groups as 'problems' and domains of governance needing the assistance of health promotion 'experts', they are systematic, calculated and directed at defined ends, they emerge from the state but are also articulated by associated independent institutions and agencies, they are constantly subject to evaluation and revision, they are not crudely repressive of rights but are directed at productive purposes (the health and happiness of the population). Public health and health promotion depend on knowledges to effect governmentality. Here knowledge refers not simply to 'ideas' but to 'a vast assemblage of persons, theories, projects, experiments and techniques' (Rose and Miller, 1992: 177). A critical approach to health promotion should involve an explicit questioning of whose voices are being heard and privileged, the alliances and conflicts involved, what body of expertise is cited in support, 'what counts as knowledge', how it is organized, controlled, authenticated and disseminated, who has access to knowledge and how this knowledge is taken up, justified and used by health promotion practitioners (Colquhoun, 1991: 17; Fox, 1993: 134).

This chapter discusses in detail the governmental nature of contemporary health promotion. It begins by looking at health promotion in the context of the emergence of the 'new' public health and goes on to examine several dominant discourses, knowledges and practices of health promotion, including health, rationality, empowerment, community, demography, epidemiology and health economics.

Health promotion and the 'new' public health

Most accounts of the development of the health promotion movement portray it as superseding the outdated health education phase of public health and forming part of the 'new' public health movement which is represented as spearheading public health endeavours into the next millennium (for example, Bunton and Macdonald, 1992: 10–11). The origins of the 'new' public health movement are generally located by commentators in the 1970s, a time when the writings of critics calling into question the efficacy and social cost of medicine were attracting attention and when other social movements championing improved living conditions and human rights were under way. Proponents of the 'new' public health took up Thomas McKeown's claim in his book *The Role of Medicine: Dream, Mirage or Nemesis?* (1976), that decreases in mortality rates in western countries over the past two centuries have largely been due to the control of infectious diseases, and that therefore the attention of health authorities should be paid to environmental conditions rather than progress in medical or surgical treatment or immunization measures. Ivan Illich's (1976) assertions that the drug therapies and surgical intervention of biomedicine were more likely to result in iatrogenesis (medically caused illness) than improvements in people's health were also influential in constructing a vision of the 'cultural crisis of modern medicine'. As a result, public health reformers began to argue that resources should be directed away from curative technologies to the prevention of illness and disease.

The 'new' public health is typically represented as a reaction against both the individualistic and victim-blaming approach of health education and the curative model of biomedicine. It is heralded as a return to the concern with environmental factors that first generated the public health movement of the nineteenth century (Bunton and Macdonald, 1992; Young and Whitehead, 1993). Proponents of the 'new' public health argue that during the early to mid-twentieth century the public health movement lost its direction in narrowing the focus upon the individual, by championing preventive medicine rather than community health-oriented strategies to improve population health, and by being disease-focused rather than health-focused. They routinely refer to the time between the original public health movement of the mid- to late-nineteenth century and the 'renaissance' of public health in the 1970s, when therapeutic medical services took over and the emphasis on 'holistic' and 'preventive' health was lost (for example, Ashton and Seymour, 1988: 19–21). Proponents often refer back to the original public health movement of the nineteenth century as an exemplar for remodelling the 'new' public health, recalling its imputed interest in environmental conditions and improving living standards rather than the emphasis upon the individual which it seems obtained in mid-twentieth century public health; for example, Lewis (1986: 3) refers approvingly to the 'broad vision of the nineteenth-century public health pioneers'. There is an irony in such appeals, for as discussed in Chapter 1, the interest of reformers in the early public health movement was in the main pragmatically oriented towards ensuring the continued supply of able-bodied workers for burgeoning industry and suppressing discontent among the working classes that threatened to lead to revolution, rather than attempting social change for the sake of humanitarian ideals.

Health promotion is a central plank of the 'new' public health. 'Health promotion' as a term and concept is extremely broad, and could conceivably encompass any enterprise directed at 'promoting' 'health'. It is a relatively recent term in public health, having been first introduced in 1974 in a report by the then Canadian Minister of National Health and Welfare, Marc Lalonde. Lalonde's argument was that the public's health could best be ameliorated by avoiding curative treatment of illness for prevention, adopting a combination of paying attention to the environmental factors affecting health and individuals' lifestyle choices related to health states (Bunton and Macdonald, 1992: 8–9). Lalonde's report was hailed as a turning point for public health activities and as marking the beginning of a new era in public health (Minkler, 1989: 19). The Report was followed in Britain by the Department of Health and Social Security's consultative document *Prevention and Health: Everybody's Business*, published in 1976, and in the United States by the Surgeon General's report *Healthy People* in 1979. All three documents placed a high degree of emphasis upon the individual's responsibility for maintaining health; the *Healthy*

People report argued that 'we are killing ourselves' through 'our own careless habits' and allowing environmental pollution and inequitable social conditions to exist (Minkler, 1989: 18), while the British document stated that '[m]uch of the responsibility for ensuring his [sic] own good health lies with the individual' (Pattison and Player, 1990: 69).

The term 'health promotion' is now generally used to describe specific activities directed at particular goals, with a strong focus on the 'rational' management of populations' health. Much emphasis is placed in the health promotion literature upon planning and coordination, assessing needs, consultation with the appropriate individuals and groups, piloting and evaluating programmes. The major focus in health promotional rhetoric is on fostering 'positive health', preventing illness and disease rather than treatment, developing performance indicators based on specified objectives, the use of mass media to 'market' health-enhancing behaviours and attitudes, and a focus on working with 'communities' to develop health-enhancing environments (Tones, 1986: 3). Health promotion adopts a range of political strategies along a continuum from the conservative to the extremely radical. At its most politically conservative, health promotion is presented as a means of directing individuals to take responsibility for their own health status, and in doing so, reducing the financial burden on health care services. More radical versions of health promotion view it as effecting 'fundamental shifts in the relationship between the state and citizens' through avoiding institutionalized medical forms of care for a focus on public policy and multi-sectoral action (Bunton and Macdonald, 1992: 2). At its most radical, health promotion is represented as a means of facilitating major social change, adopting the rhetoric of 'community development' and seeking to encourage and 'empower' citizens to group together to challenge the state (Minkler, 1989; Grace, 1991).

Health promotion is thus directed not only at those who are sick, as is medical care, but at all individuals at all levels of the population. In health promotion, with its interest in 'multi-sectoral' collaboration, preventive health care has moved from the dispensary, clinic and hospital out to all major social sites and urban spaces, including schools and other educational institutions, workplaces and shopping centres (Bunton, 1992). Most social issues have become subsumed under the rubric of health, and therefore have been rendered appropriate problems for health promotional intervention (Stevenson and Burke, 1991: 286). There is thus a shift from viewing ill-health as caused by an infective agent such as a bacterium or virus, to ill-health as a product of society, in which illness is viewed as expressing the condition of a group as a social entity (Figlio, 1987: 79). Ill-health is conceptualized as 'a symptom of the pathology of civilization', an outcome of the stresses and poor lifestyle choices of the members of modern societies, a sign that modern life is inherently damaging to health (1987: 81). To deal with the complexity of disease causation in modern societies and the need to maintain continuing surveillance of all members of the population, health promotion has engendered a 'vast network of observation and caution' throughout society, involving the participation of all citizens in the generation and regulation of anxieties around public health (Armstrong, 1993: 407).

The break between earlier public health and biomedical endeavours of the twentieth century and the approach of the new public health is by no means decisive. While there is much emphasis on the 'new' nature of the contemporary public health movement, evidence of previous approaches is still very much evident in public health rhetoric and practice. Indeed there are at least five identifiable approaches which merge 'old' and 'new' perspectives in the championed strategies for preserving the public's health. They include health protection (related to the concerns of contagionism and social hygienicism, using the strategies of quarantine and isolation), preventive medicine (the use of medical procedures to treat illness early in its development), health education (drawing upon the humoral understanding of the interaction between lifestyle and health), healthy public policy (associated with the concerns of the welfare state and directing the focus towards the structural determinants of ill-health) and community empowerment (a focus on organization and decision-making in the context of social groups) (Holman, 1992). There is a continuing debate in the public health literature around which of these approaches are most appropriate for the contemporary public health movement. This debate seems unlikely to be reconciled easily: Beattie (1991: 194) sees health promotion activities as directed by conflicting political philosophies that are split between the binaries of paternalist versus participatory and individualist versus collectivist, with conservative (health persuasion techniques), reformist (legislative action for health), libertarian (personal counselling for health) and radical pluralist (community development for health) strategies all falling within these axes.

While criticizing both biomedicine and the earlier health education approach, most mainstream health promotional literature acknowledges the need for public health practice that incorporates elements of both. The term 'health promotion' superseded the term 'health education' in the 1980s (Beattie, 1991: 162), when it was thought that the use of the term health 'education' continued to carry resonances of individualistic approaches to the enhancement of health status and the notion of the passive individual requiring 'facts' to defeat ignorance, and was thus avoided by some practitioners. The traditional rationale for health education has been criticized because it is considered both ineffectual and unethical, taking no account of environmental and structural issues (Tones, 1992: 33; Bunton and Macdonald, 1992: 10). Health promotion is viewed as progressing from health education in being more humanistic and fostering 'positive health' and personal growth rather than adopting a purely didactic role (Tones, 1992: 31). However, the term 'health education' continues to be used in the 'new' public health literature, sometimes interchangeably with health promotion, and is generally viewed as an essential component of the multi-tiered health promotion project. Therefore, while the 'new' public health has been viewed as going beyond the health education model, it may be more a shift in title than a true paradigm shift (Rawson, 1992: 203). Contemporary health education has been defined as:

> any activity which promotes health-related learning, i.e. some relatively perma-
> nent change in an individual's capabilities or dispositions. It may produce
> changes in understanding or ways of thinking; it may bring about changes in
> belief or attitude and facilitate the acquisition of skills; or it may generate
> changes in behaviour and lifestyle. (Tones, 1986: 6)

Health education is now directed at providing information to individuals not only about body maintenance and lifestyle change to prevent disease but to facilitate 'voluntary' decision-making and educate people about the appropriate use of health services – indeed, in the United States, health education units are attached to some hospitals' marketing divisions and play a part in 'selling' the hospitals' services (Minkler, 1989: 21). The idea is to persuade people to change their behaviour en masse, even if they might be at low risk, rather than identifying those at high risk, or displaying symptoms, for treatment or preventive measures. The emphasis, at least in the rhetoric of health promotional literature, is on protecting 'free will' by fostering 'informed' health choices rather than attempting persuasion or coercion (Tones, 1986: 7).

The 'new' public health is defined as an approach which considers environmental change as well as personal preventive measures and 'appropriate therapeutic interventions' (Ashton and Seymour, 1988: 21) with a renewed focus on public policy and intersectoral cooperation. Although proponents of the 'new' public health insist that their movement is directed towards prevention rather than curative therapies, the notion of 'prevention' in health promotion and the new public health is somewhat elastic. In addition to health promotion efforts directed at the individual level and the community level, emphasis is also placed on the prevention of 'preventable conditions' such as genetic defects, infectious diseases, accidents and obesity, as well as rehabilitation and health services for those who escape the net and the provision for earlier diagnosis of conditions before they become serious (Ashton and Seymour, 1988: 22–3). There is a hierarchy of action, in which self-care and responsibility for one's health are at the top, as the most desirable strategies for improving the public's health, and the 'safety net' of health care delivery is at the bottom, as the most costly and least desirable approach. 'Preventive' health is said to incorporate three levels of prevention: primary, secondary and tertiary, where primary prevention refers to preventing illness before it occurs, secondary prevention to early detection of disease and tertiary prevention to the treatment of illness and rehabilitation (thus 'preventing' illness and disease from worsening or causing death or permanent disability). The term 'health promotion', therefore, is often inconsistently used, including strategies directed at disease prevention and medical treatment as well as the active preservation of good health.

An attempt to draw a distinction between the 'old' and the 'new' public health is thus somewhat difficult to justify, as the 'new' public health continues to be characterized by some approaches that date back centuries as well as those that can be more readily identified with contemporary concerns. Just as the early public health movement was mobilized by economic concerns, the objective of health promotion in ensuring productive citizens still dominates public health discourse. The bottom-line of the logic of all these 'preventive' actions is not simply human happiness achieved through the minimization of illness and pain, but preserving and redirecting the limited resources available for health care. For example, Ashton and Seymour quote the goal of the World Health Organization's (WHO) *Health for All by the Year 2000* report issued in 1981, which stated that 'the main social target of governments and WHO in the coming decades should be the attainment by all citizens of the world by the year 2000 of a level of health that *will permit them to lead a socially and economically productive life*' (Ashton and Seymour, 1988: 8, emphasis added).

Although the current emphasis is upon self-management, the strategies of forcible isolation and even incarceration of individuals considered a contagious threat are still drawn upon at times, especially in the face of a life-threatening illness. For example, as recently as January 1994, Australian police officers in the state of Victoria handled the case of a man who had been alleged to spread HIV in a small town. He was arrested and charged with three counts of 'reckless conduct endangering life' after several women made allegations against him for engaging in sexual intercourse with them without using safer sex procedures. Some years previously, public health authorities in New South Wales enacted the Public Health Act of 1902 to incarcerate for a time a prostitute who had appeared on television claiming that she was HIV positive and did not enforce safer sex procedures with her clients. In March 1993, the New York City Health Department adopted strict regulations for detaining tuberculosis patients who failed to continue to return for treatment, including the possibility of confining them at a clinic for more than a year.

'Theory' in health promotion

Some commentators within the field have identified an existential crisis over the lack of a unified theory for health promotion. They argue that there is too much eclecticism, leaving health promotion open to assimilation or dismissal on the basis that it is not a 'real' discipline (Rawson, 1992: 218). It is argued that health education/promotion must 'come to know itself' and stop borrowing indiscriminately from a jumble of social science approaches to understanding human behaviour (Caplan, 1993: 148). Such critiques imply that a 'true' theory should be developed, a corpus of knowledge peculiar to health promotion so that it may be deemed a 'discipline'. There is evidence of a desire here for legitimacy and academic respectability as well as a sense of unification. This impetus is somewhat naive, given the blurring of boundaries that has productively occurred between the traditional disciplines in the social sciences and humanities over the past decade.

While health promotion is often said to be multi-disciplinary, incorporating perspectives from fields as diverse as epidemiology, sociology, education, economics, marketing and communication, the predominant models used to explain behavioural change in health promotion are primarily based on understanding of behaviour within the paradigm of social psychology. Although the term 'theory' is commonly employed in the health promotion literature, that use is generally limited to explaining links between attitudes and behaviour, adopting a cause-and-effect model, rather than an overarching attempt to construct an epistemology of public health. As one article published in a health education journal argued, 'our theories can be regarded as being essentially statements identifying factors that are likely to produce particular results under specified conditions' (Hochbaum et al., 1992: 296). The dominant concern has been instrumental, directed at providing a model of explanation for the effects of a planned intervention, with the objective of more effectively influencing individuals or groups (Bunton et al., 1991).

The term 'model' is often conflated with 'theory' in the health promotion literature. As Rawson (1992: 212) contends, for health promotion, 'model construction appears to be the only basis of core theoretical development thus far'. Furthermore, the models in use tend to describe forms of service delivery rather than health education principles (1992: 210). There are many models of health behaviour currently circulating, several of which are confusingly reiterated with different names, and few of which have been demonstrated through analytical or empirical research to 'work' (1992: 207). The multiplicity of models of behaviour used in health education and health promotion, each employing different terms to describe similar processes, means that fundamental differences are rarely acknowledged and the precise definition of health education and promotion is rendered elusive. The models are mostly derived from American mass communication models first developed in the 1950s and 1960s. Individuals' beliefs about their perceived susceptibility to a condition or disease feature prominently in these models. A great fondness in the health promotional literature is demonstrated for reifying the models graphically, using figures with arrows pointing to the direction of change, or showing 'feedback loops', or plotting 'adopters' of behaviours on graphs. The quasi-scientific discourse of 'norms', 'phases', 'stages', 'forces', 'targets', 'locus of control', 'barriers', 'resources', 'knowledge gap' and 'self-efficacy' dominates. The very names of the models of behaviour – the Health Belief Model, the Theory of Reasoned Action, Subjective Expected Utility

Theory, Protection Motivation Theory – denote a focus upon rationality, the weighing up of costs and benefits, conscious thought which progresses in a linear fashion from A to B.

The assumptions of health promotion that underlie these models of behaviour include that its primary goal is behaviour change and that beliefs and attitudes mediate this behaviour change. It is assumed that at least in some instances, health behaviours are mediators of health status, that health behaviours are the results of knowledge, beliefs and attitudes, and that specific behaviours, when changed, improve health (Lorig and Laurin, 1985: 232). As I noted in the Introduction, western thought since the Enlightenment has valued knowledge, reason and rationality, viewing these as central to human development, happiness, progress and the promotion of social order. Knowledge is a term used frequently in health promotion/education and health care settings: medical knowledge, patients' knowledge of their illnesses, the lay public's knowledge of health risks and the causes of illness and disease. The concept of knowledge forms an integral basis for virtually all models of health education and health promotion. The so-called Knowledge–Attitude–Behaviour (KAB) model, for example, is a mainstay of health education, expressing an essentially linear relationship from the acquiring of knowledge leading to the changing of attitudes, subsequently leading to the changing of behaviour. The Health Belief model and its variants predict that the likelihood of individuals taking recommended action to ameliorate their health status is based on self-perception of individual susceptibility, perceived threat of disease, perceived benefits of preventive action and the perceived barriers to preventive action. These stages all involve the weighing up of acquired knowledge. The Theory of Reasoned Action argues that behaviour is governed by the individual's attitudes towards that behaviour and its outcomes and the individual's perceptions of what important others will think of their behaving in certain ways. These combine to form an 'intention' to behave. The Precaution Adoption Process asserts that the propensity to engage in risk-taking is related to a person's stage of belief about susceptibility to harm: an individual must know that something is potentially hazardous to act in a preventive manner, and must acknowledge personal susceptibility (Lorig and Laurin, 1985; Salt et al., 1990; Bennett and Hodgson, 1992).

Models of behaviour which seek to empower individuals also rely upon knowledge as the central means by which people are encouraged to make choices, as do community action models of health promotion (Kemm, 1991: 291–2). So too, the importance of individuals' perceptions of personal risk with regard to behaviours said to predispose them to illness is commonly accepted in most public health research and practice. Education is seen as the key to behaviour change: if people are informed about the dangers of indulging in certain activities, it is argued that they will then rationally use this information to weigh up the risk to themselves and act accordingly. Such uses of the term imply a neutral, fully objective and progressive knowledge. It assumes that knowledge is a good: the more knowledge one has, the better, whether it be as a patient in the medical encounter, 'empowered' by improved knowledge of his or her condition, or as an individual requiring greater knowledge of the causes of an illness so as to act in a rational manner to avoid contracting or developing that illness. Likewise, health promotion/education literature routinely argues that lack of knowledge is always negative. Yet, in the context of the late twentieth century, more knowledge does not ensure a greater degree of certainty or less ignorance, but may incite the proliferation of doubts (Smart, 1993: 105).

These models construct the individual as a rational actor who is motivated by a number of different stimuli – cues, perceptions, information – to behave in a logical manner. A degree of intentionality is assumed, thus implying that non-compliance with health advice may be unintentional (Salt et al., 1990: 70). Hindess describes what he calls the 'portfolio' model of the rational actor as follows:

> Imagine that actors each carry with them their own distinctive portfolio of beliefs and desires. (The image is that of an artist or illustrator, not an investment manager.) Given a situation of action, an actor selects from its portfolio those elements that seem to be relevant, and it uses them to decide on a course of action . . . Rational choice analysis modifies the portfolio model in assuming that the actor's desires are such that an optimal outcome can be defined in most situations. (1989: 112)

This model understands rationality as both the individual's capacity to follow a chain of reasoning and the inherent coherence of the chain of reasoning itself, and seeks to explain departures from rationality by a variety of internal and external obstacles (1989: 116). It reflects the belief in contemporary western society that views the very essence of humanity as being based on the notion of the ideal self as autonomous from the body.

Such representations conform to the 'deficit' model of human behaviour, which explains behaviour in terms of the individual 'lacking' attributes such as knowledge and self-efficacy (Daykin, 1993: 96). Furthermore, the models, based as they are on psychological tenets, narrow behaviour to the micro-level of the cognitive functioning of the individual, who is represented as behaving almost in a social vacuum. While some models recognize the importance of 'social norms' in shaping behaviour choices and attitudes, this overwhelming concern with the individual fails to account for the complexity of the socio-cultural world in which subjectivity is constructed and reconstructed. In their obsession with personal skills and self-efficacy, the models over-simplify and provide facile solutions to the problems they identify. They suggest first that lifestyle habits are amenable to change, and secondly, that most people, if rationally told the 'risks', will make efforts to do so. Alternatively, individuals who possess knowledge about the health effects of behaviours but continue on as before are represented as requiring further assistance to help them resist temptation and change their ways.

For example, an article by Solomon and Cardillo on smoking argued that '[m]any people know that smoking is bad for them, want to quit, and yet are unable to do so. They simply lack the skills required to become and remain a non-smoker such as resisting peer pressure to smoke' (1985: 63). This view of individuals represents them as empty vessels, needful of the 'right' kind of socialization, persuasion and skills in order to live their lives well. Another example is found in an article published by Peterson and Stunkard (1989) on 'personal control and health promotion', where they discussed high personal control as being characterized by 'intellectual, emotional, behavioural, and physiological vigour in the face of challenging life situations and events', while low personal control was associated with 'maladaptive passivity and poor morale' (1989: 819). The authors assert that the concept of personal control provides a perfect unifying 'theory' for health promotion, explaining why it is that some people or groups respond positively to health promotion and others resist. The solution to groups such as 'racial minority groups' and 'lower class men' failing to respond to health promotion interventions is therefore to deal with their 'diminished sense of control' by using psychological techniques to 'instill' self control in those who do not possess it: 'People must possess or be taught outcome expectancies (that certain behaviours lead to reduced morbidity and mortality) and efficacy expectancies (that they can perform these behaviours)' (1989: 823).

Community development and the discourse of empowerment

As the above discussion suggests, the emphasis on 'lifestyle' factors in promoting or debilitating individuals' health statuses remains a central feature of health promotion, albeit often modified by references to 'intersectoral approaches' in which government and other agencies work together to 'improve social and economic conditions which influence choice of lifestyle' to 'make the Healthy Choices the Easy Choices' (Ashton and Seymour, 1988: 22). The 'active participation' of everyone in health promotion is encouraged, as is the use of many different approaches and the entry of health promotion into all areas of social life, from the home to the school to the workplace. The role of health professionals is to 'nurture' health promotion by helping people to develop 'personal skills' to make 'healthy choices' by providing information and education, thus 'enabling' people to 'exercise more control over their own health and over their environments' (1988: 26).

The 'new' public health movement is strongly associated with the notion of 'community' and its development, with slogans such as 'Health for All' emphasizing the participatory nature of the movement. By the late 1980s, the terms 'community development', 'community participation' and 'community empowerment' became central to health promotion discourses (Farrant, 1991: 424). The Ottawa Charter for Health Promotion, drawn up in 1986 and quoted often in health promotional literature as providing the tenets of the field, asserts that:

> Health promotion works through concrete and effective community action in setting priorities, making decisions, planning strategies, and implementing them to achieve better health. At the heart of this process is the empowerment of communities, their ownership and control of their own destinies. (quoted in Farrant, 1991: 432)

Based on these tenets, Ashton and Seymour (1988: 26) claim that health promotional professionals should thus 'learn new ways of working with individuals and communities – working for and with rather than on them' (1988: 26). The Enlightenment project, privileging progress and control of one's destiny, is evident in such rhetoric. This is not surprising, given that the discourse of empowerment as used in health promotion draws upon the critical pedagogy movement that emerged in the late 1960s, calling for more autonomy and responsibility on the part of the individual, who was constructed as an agent of historical change (Peters and Marshall, 1991: 123).

The vexed relationship between the state and those it seeks to act for becomes apparent in the paradoxes in community development activities. While the discourse of community development sets out to 'empower' the underprivileged, allowing them a voice, the role of the health promotion bureaucracy is itself challenged in the context of wider challenges to the structure of the state generated by 'successful' community development (Beattie, 1991: 178). While the 'health from below' approach privileges community action, there is usually direct collaboration with officials 'from above', and demands for resources are made by community groups for resources on state health services (Sears, 1992: 32). Public health officials are typically represented as dispassionate and politically neutral, rising above vested interests to serve the community (1992: 34). When health promoters attempt to act both as mediators between underprivileged groups and health care providers and as advocates for the former, there is inevitable conflict. Health promoters often act as facilitators of co-option rather than enhancing the agency of community groups (Brown and Margo, 1978: 8; Grace, 1991: 331–2). Public health sees the community from the perspective of the state, which is privileged as the facilitator for shaping the health of the community (Sears, 1992: 67).

Radical activists have rarely gone so far as to challenge the orthodoxies of health promotion that insist, for example, that high blood pressure, obesity or the propensity towards eating junk foods are 'health problems'. Although much progressive health promotion is directed at the 'community', notions of 'empowerment' and collective action, there is often still an emphasis on encouraging individuals to behave in certain ways deemed appropriate by public health professionals. For example, Brown and Margo (1978: 20) describe in approving terms a hypothetical programme set up to work on obesity and poor eating habits which runs educational programmes 'to explain the consequences of obesity and teach proper nutrition', small-group discussions encouraging people to discuss their eating habits and 'how they may use food in ways that parallel tobacco or alcohol use' and problem-solving groups that 'encourage their members to examine their personal lives for sources of dissatisfaction, stress, and other factors that may contribute to their compulsive or otherwise destructive food consumption'. They also promote action groups designed to work for the provision of a food stamp programme to enable people to afford 'adequate diets' and to call on local supermarkets to remove their displays of junk foods. A moralism associated with interrogating individuals' lives for the reasons they choose to eat certain foods in certain quantities, an acceptance that certain diets are 'unhealthy' and must be changed, and the pathologization of eating as a health risk and enjoyment of food as an 'addiction' is evident in this description.

There is a contradiction inherent in the use of the term 'empowerment' in relation to community development, a word which suggests individualistic meanings of rationality, autonomy and responsibility. The term also implies that 'someone more powerful or vested with greater authority empowers another, who is lesser' (Peters and Marshall, 1991: 124). The rhetoric of empowering and enabling thus serves to mask the investment and intervention of public health professionals in persuading groups to develop 'skills' and 'exercise control' over their lives (Grace, 1991: 331). For example, Tones (1993: 149) defines empowerment as people not only believing that 'they were capable of influencing events but [they must] also possess a repertoire of skills which would enhance their capacity to do so'. Such skills, he believes, can be taught by use of face-to-face teaching, simulation, gaming and role play. He sees this approach as avoiding victim-blaming. But there is a didactic and somewhat paternalistic emphasis here. The emphasis on personal learning activities such as role play still focuses on the individual acquiring skills to go out and influence events. The model used is still that of the health education approach, devoted to training people in the 'appropriate' ways of thinking and doing but with little emphasis on enhancing the opportunities for collective action born of conflict and tensions between subcultures (Caplan, 1993: 154).

The rhetoric of community development as it has been embraced by the new public health bureaucracy has rarely been translated into action: 'Health promotion priorities continued to be professionally, specifically medically, defined, with "community participation" being used to describe what often amounted more to community manipulation' (Farrant, 1991: 425). The nebulous meaning of the word 'community' itself resists attempts more precisely to define what exactly 'community development' is. It fails to recognize that individuals may be part of many different 'communities', depending on the types of subjectivities they favour at the time, the interests of which may contradict each other. The use of the term 'community' as an identifiable entity assumes that a 'community' is a united group sharing the same interests, thus obscuring differences within the group itself. The term is often used in bureaucratic rhetoric as a synonym for a 'target group' identified for management (H. Rose, 1990: 211–12; Petersen, 1994: 109). Indeed, it could be argued that the demand for greater participation has been absorbed into state management strategies, using the term for its own purposes: 'The seductive promise of "community" is revealed by the frequency of its use within political and policy discourses' (H. Rose, 1990: 211). While community 'development' has taken place, the term has been most commonly used to describe the decentralization of services rather than challenges to the power relations obtaining in regions (Petersen, 1994: 110–11).

In its reliance upon scientific expertises and emphasis on neutrality, public health discourse conforms to other social policy governmental activities of capitalist states, which are founded on the notion of the neutral and beneficent state acting in the best interests of the majority and standing above vested interests (Sears, 1991: 34). While health promotion shares the rhetoric of other social movements such as feminism and gay liberation, unlike other social movements the origins of health promotion lie within the state rather than directly challenging the state. As such, attempts to encourage empowerment and political action tend not to be committed to the long term, framed as they are by the demands of the state and constructed as they are as projects rarely lasting more than a few years (Peters and Marshall, 1991). This fundamental paradox ensures that health promotional activities, for all the rhetoric about social change and challenging the status quo, will inevitably be limited in their political scope and objectives (Stevenson and Burke, 1991: 281).

Throughout the rhetoric of community development and empowerment there is a strange tension between the pastoral ideal and the notion of active citizenship, between the concept of the client and that of the active agent, between the vision of the rational, active, responsible citizen and the citizen who needs much encouragement, assistance and persuasion on the part of state agencies to 'do the right thing'. The self that is being privileged and normalized in such discourses is that of the enterprising and entrepreneurial self, the individual who is interested in and willing to take action to improve his or her health status. It is assumed that all individuals have the potential for such social action in the name of good health, and that it is simply up to the health promotion officer to encourage or 'facilitate' the realization of this potential. The discourse assumes a 'free subject' who has a number of choices of action, but also constructs health promotion as working to shape and make use of the kinds of choices that are made for its own governmental ends (cf. Dean, 1994: 161–3). There is thus a dual construct involved in discourse of liberal health promotion: 'on the one hand, "we" provide according to "their" needs, yet on the other hand "we" tell "them" their needs' (Grace, 1991: 339).

Epidemiology and health economics: technologies of rationality

Like other caring professions associated with liberalism and the welfare
state (for example, social work and health care visiting), the ideologies and
practices of health promotion are strongly underpinned by economic
rationalities. Such activities involve techniques of alignment, where 'governmental strategies try to link individual aspirations with collective goals'
(Stenson, 1993: 60). This is particularly evident in health promotion.
Health promotion is legitimized both by its idealistic search after improved
health for all and its promise of reducing the amount of resources spent by
the state for medical treatment and the loss of human-power due to days
spent off work because of illness.

The contemporary western valorization of rationality is challenged by
the social and physical disorder posed by disease and death. In medieval
times, mortality rates fluctuated wildly. As a result, people were highly
aware of the unpredictable and ephemeral nature of life and thus favoured
a value system that emphasized the metaphysical and collective survival
strategies (Imhoff, 1992: 374). Death was once believed to be random and
unpredictable, able to strike anyone at any time; all individuals were
believed to be equally vulnerable to the fickle finger of fate. Since the end
of the eighteenth century, death rates have stabilized and are no longer
characterized by periods of high mortality. The current trend towards slow
deaths at a later age has led to secularization and individualization (1992:
374). In the late twentieth century, death has become viewed as 'the
ultimate failure of rationality . . . the scandal of reason' (Bauman, 1992:
1). Because early death is not as common now as it once was, there has
developed a great fear around it. Dying has become viewed as a
humiliating failure. The modern era demands vigilance, a high degree of
self control: reason is dominant and death is a paradox (1992: 4). As a
consequence, Bauman argues:

> Our own death cannot be thought of as instrumental. It invalidates the discourse
> of instrumentality as it spells the termination of purposeful action. This is where
> its horror resides in the modern world of instrumental rationality: the world
> where deeds are lived as means to ends and justify themselves by the ends which
> they serve as means. There is no way in which this horror could be argued away.
> It can be only barred from consciousness, tabooed as a topic, heaved out away
> from current concerns; or, in the typically modern way, split into small-scale
> worries, each one separately removable – so that the fearful finality and
> irremediability of the original worry can be never scanned in its totality. (1992: 5)

In modern medicine, each death has an individual cause, as determined
by a doctor, coroner or pathologist. The format of the death certificate,
which must be filled in by a medical practitioner when someone dies,
implies several rules: death is a product of pathology and is a physical
event; the cause of death is visible at post-mortem, is always a singular
event, is proximate to the event of death and makes sense in the context of
assumptions about natural and normal death (that is, it should be a likely

event given the person's age, medical history and so on) (Prior and Bloor, 1993: 363). Hence an 'unexplained death' is impossible to conceptualize, for death is not recognized as inevitable and universal, but is seen as unnatural (Shilling, 1993: 192). Yet it is often the case that causes are imprecise, or multifactorial, and doctors are aware of the social need to cite, for example, liver disease rather than alcoholism as a cause of death (Prior and Bloor, 1993).

Death, in its physical form (the dying person and the corpse) has been removed from the public eye at the same time as public and private discourses constantly discuss the ways of guarding against death. For example, funerals are ways of excluding the dead, marking them as abnormal and to be shunned, separating them as if they are contagious (Bauman, 1992: 2). Consequently, the idea of one's own death, or that of a friend or loved one, seems almost incomprehensible for the contemporary self (Mellor and Shilling, 1993: 417–19). As a result, the search for causes of death is inevitable, for it is believed that people cannot die of mortality, they must die of something (Bauman, 1992: 5). As many people in contemporary western societies no longer hold any convictions concerning spirituality and the afterlife beyond the flesh, the death of the body signals the emphatic death of the self. Hence the paradoxical contemporary obsession with and repression of the ageing and death processes:

> the presence of death appears especially disturbing in this context of reflexively constructed self-narratives which have at their centre a concern with the body. After all, what could more effectively signal to the body-conscious individual the limitations of their reflexive ordering of self than the brute facts of their thickening waistlines, sagging breasts, ageing bodies and inevitable deaths? (Mellor and Shilling, 1993: 413)

Featherstone and Hepworth (1991) have commented on the disgust and fear held for the ageing body in contemporary western societies. They refer to the 'mask of ageing', or the physical signs of decay, such as wrinkles, grey hair and flabby flesh, from which people dissociate themselves – they feel that their true selves are hidden behind this mask. As they note, '[s]uch a conception of ageing sets great store on the belief that ageing is a potentially curable *disease*' (1991: 379, emphasis in the original).

Illness flies in the face of the ideology of human progress and rationality for it threatens social life, exposes the fragility of social order and erodes individual self control. Epidemic disease that strikes a large number of people, in particular, may be viewed as 'a medical version of the Hobbesian nightmare – the war of all against all' (Strong, 1990: 249). In such a situation, humanity's ability to command authority over nature appears threatened. Hence the ability of 'rational' and 'scientific' biomedicine to deal with sickness is valorized (Kirmayer, 1988). Public health practices similarly rely on 'rational' methods of ordering disease, including the constant monitoring of patterns and cases of disease, surveillance of the movement of bodies in space and the recording of medical information on the population by means of mass screening programmes and the survey

(Armstrong, 1983). Public health and health promotion activities are directed at staving off the thought of physical decay and death. Just as life-tables and medical causes of death recorded on death certificates tend to reduce death to an organic function divorced from the socio-cultural context in which the individual died, health promotion texts often discuss death in a manner which skirts around the issues, using euphemisms, metaphors and metonyms: 'weight problem' or 'smoking habit' as meto-nyms for 'the dying body', 'reduce your risk' and 'exercise for life' as euphemisms for 'warding off death'.

In their very attempts to contain, control and deny the reality of death, such representations have the paradoxical effect of locating death every-where, requiring constant attention to keep it away. Because the causes of death have been refined, they have proliferated, and therefore the individual must be ever more vigilant: 'Death is watching when we work, when we eat, when we love, when we rest. Through its many deputies, death presides over life. Fighting death is meaningless. But fighting the *causes* of dying turns into the meaning of life' (Bauman, 1992: 4, emphasis in the original). All these activities serve to push the reality of death away, to deal with its inevitability by fighting it in its localized form. Religious survival strategies are now replaced by the policy of self-care, in which the health and fitness of the body are integral aspects. Anxiety around physical decay and death is subsumed under the obsession of maintaining the body, of guarding against the discrete causes of death and illness identified by medicine and public health such as heart disease or cancer, and thus avoiding the thought that death is inevitable in the end (Mellor and Shilling, 1993: 425).

The human sciences set up around public health, such as demography and epidemiology, are instrumental in categorizing death in ways that avoid direct confrontation with its reality. In concert with increasing rationalization, death has become linked to new notions of chance, cause and determination, located not in the individual, but in the population. In the nineteenth century, statistical principles began to be applied to tame death, to render it controllable and predictable, to give it the semblance of order, to make it calculable (Prior and Bloor, 1993: 353–5). The super-natural and religious explanations of death prevailing in the Middle Ages were therefore replaced by a form of 'fatalistic rationalism' to explain death (1993: 360–1). While demography is interested in death, it does not speak of death overtly, but instead uses terms such as 'mortality', broken down into finer and finer categories and measured through ever more complex instruments. Demography then does not refer to the fate of the dying person or the individual but the fate of the species (Prior, 1989: 7–8). Demography also serves to obscure the links between death and socio-economic status. For example, in his study of Belfast records of death, Prior noticed a distinct change from the nineteenth to the twentieth century in the explanations recorded for causes of death by the coroner. Where once the social context of death was recorded – for example, 'want of the common necessities of life' or 'died from cold and whiskey' – causes of death are now restricted to sanitized pathological categories, limited to individualized physical malfunction or damage that is located to an anatomical site and devoid of the social setting in which individuals died (Prior, 1989: ch. 2). Prior observes that 'in Belfast, as in most other parts of Western Europe, one dies from one's diseases rather than say of old age, malfeasance or misfortune' (1989: 26).

Like demography, the relatively new field of epidemiology employs statistics to serve as a modern, rationalized technology to counter epidemics. The word 'epidemiology' originates from the same etymological roots as 'epidemic'. To label a collection of cases of an illness or disease an 'epidemic' or 'outbreak' is to give a certain meaning to these cases. The word 'epidemic', in particular, connotes a highly contagious disease, spread invisibly and without warning; its most potent exemplar is the Black Plague, a disease which still has cultural resonance for its sheer magnitude of destruction, its association with fear and panic, divine retribution and evil (Herzlich and Pierret, 1987: 3). 'Epidemic' suggests the potential for sudden, exponential spread, for societal disorder, the need for harsh and decisive measures to be taken to keep the disease in check. An 'epidemic logic' takes over, which seeks immediate action to the threat, including the proliferation of regulatory practices which both construct and seek to contain the object of fear: 'Under the logic incited by epidemics, forms of regulatory intervention into the lives of bodies and populations which might, in other circumstance, appear excessive can now appear as justified forms of damage control and prophylactic protectionism' (Singer, 1993: 30). This is especially the case when mysterious epidemic disease is the focus, for concern about the source of disease, and its mode of spread, inspire irrationality, suspicion and stigmatization, in which 'personal fear may be translated into collective witch-hunts' (Strong, 1990: 253). Central to epidemic logic is the identification of Other, the source of infection, who is then problematized as an object of exclusion or confinement (Frankenberg, 1992: 74).

Since the Middle Ages, the enumeration of deaths believed to be caused from a single disease has been a major element in the construction of an epidemic, transforming an illness from an individual plight to a collective disaster (Herzlich and Pierret, 1987: 4). This remains central to definitions of epidemics today. Because epidemiology is treated and viewed as a 'science' it conforms to the post-Enlightenment privileging of rationality. It offers a way of countering anxiety and fear, of re-establishing social order. An outbreak of epidemic disease is accompanied by three other types of psycho-social epidemics: an epidemic of fear, an epidemic of explanation and moralization, and an epidemic of action or proposed action (Strong, 1990: 251). The generation of exact numbers is considered an important means of action in taking control of an outbreak of disease, and is integral to the endeavours of epidemiology. Epidemiology is directed towards identifying patterns in diseases at a population level, seeking to discover reasons for certain groups developing diseases over other groups. It operates on a network of surveillance, drawing data from diverse sources such as medical records and case studies, hospital data and sociological and population surveys. Just as other forms of government require the continuous collection of data as a basis for the legitimacy of expertise, the statistical documentation of epidemiology serves to reify problems, making them calculable and real, and hence subject to diagnosis and intervention (cf. Rose and Miller, 1992: 185–6).

Epidemiological knowledge is constructed from a multitude of sites and methods. For example, the epidemiological knowledge of HIV/AIDS has relied upon such sources as retrovirological and immunological experiments, statistics from broad populations, HIV testing data from populations as diverse as army entrants, pregnant women, newborns, haemophiliacs and attenders at sexual health clinics and anthropological and sociological small-scale studies of the beliefs and cultural practices around sexuality and drug use (see Fujimura and Chou, 1994). Epidemiological techniques are taught in public health and medical training programmes as a quasi-scientific method, replete with hypotheses, risk ratios, statistical formulae and control groups. A book on the principles of epidemiology, published in Britain in 1957, describes it as the 'science of epidemics' and goes on to claim that the epidemiologist's principle task is to 'describe patterns of disease in communities': which diseases are present, their relative importance, their frequency and distribution, the types of individuals they affect, when they occur, where they are located. The authors assert that:

> Armed with the answers to these questions . . . the epidemiologist may postulate theories of the mode of spread in the diseases he [sic] finds, and these theories may be put to the test by clinical, field or laboratory studies . . . having made his epidemiological diagnosis, he may be able to put forward logical ideas for the control of those diseases he describes. (Taylor and Knowelden, 1957: 1)

The analogy used in this description is that of the epidemiologist as physician to the social rather than the individual body: carefully observing the 'symptoms and signs' of disease as it is manifested in a population, diagnosing the cause and then developing a solution for its amelioration. This analogy also appears in a textbook on epidemiology for medical and other health care students published in Australia three decades later: 'As a physician assesses a patient's health by clinical history and physical examination, so an epidemiologist tries to assess the "health" of a community' (Christie et al., 1987: 8). Indeed, epidemiology is routinely taught to medical students as part of their course, and academic epidemiologists are generally located within medical schools.

Such practices cast the state as the unique agency responsible for protecting health at the level of the population, enforcing the borders of a community, and 'keeping disease out' (Sears, 1992). Just as the rules for the sterilizing of instruments and equipment in the hospital setting are, in part, bureaucratic rituals to protect the institution from blame should something go wrong (Rawlings, 1989: 289), the public investigations of epidemics by public health personnel, and the accompanying rhetoric of haste and urgency and the emphasis on efficiency serve to demonstrate that all that *can* be done, *is* being done, that the rationality of modern public health is taking command. The processes of defining and counting 'cases' provides a sense of progress, of re-ordering disorder, reconfirming modern humanity's control over its destiny (Oppenheimer, 1988: 270). Like demography, the discourses and practices of epidemiology serve to distance practitioners from their subject material. Individuals' deaths are rendered as statistics, numerators, cases, mathematical calculations, contributing to incidence and prevalence and mortality rates, classified under cause of death in tables: for example, the 'proportional mortality rate for cancer' is described as an equation which divides the number of deaths ascribed to cancer by the total deaths from all causes and multiplying by 100 per cent. By this process, '[d]iseases and their causes are seen as having a life of their own for which communities, bodies social and bodies physical, merely provide a frame' (Frankenberg, 1994: 1329).

The rationalized mathematical logic and rhetoric of the discourse of epidemiology serves to obscure moral judgements about individuals' or groups' behaviour. The epidemiological survey acts as a technique of normalization, focused as it is on measuring the continuum of bodily states evident in populations, as well as a device for individualization, through measuring the differences between people (Armstrong, 1983: 51–3). It enables a 'double alliance' on the part of public health experts, in which on the one hand they ally themselves with state objectives and concerns about regulation and surveillance of populations, and on the other, seek alliances with individuals themselves in the role of adviser on the successful maintenance of personal good health (Rose and Miller, 1992: 188). •Epidemiology has developed a 'multi-causal' model to explain the advent of disease in certain individuals – causes may be drawn from lifestyle, occupation, environment, personality type, age, gender or ethnicity. This very wide net means that some causes may be emphasized over others, depending on the social values held by the epidemiologist, yet '[w]hen included in the model, embraced by professionals, and published in the scientific press, such value judgements appear to be objective, well-grounded scientific statements' (Oppenheimer, 1988: 269).

The notion of the 'candidate' for an illness, both among epidemiologists and members of the general population, conforms to a particularly moralistic explanatory framework. The word implies choice, putting oneself forward for selection, 'allowing' a disease to happen (Davison et al., 1991: 10; see also, Frankenberg, 1994: 1330). While epidemiological language is commonly accepted as politically neutral because of its medico-scientific context, it often uses explicitly discriminatory language. As one study of Australian medical textbooks dealing with HIV/AIDS found, injecting drug users were commonly described as 'drug abusers' or 'drug addicts', and several references were found to 'promiscuous' homosexual men and a certain sensationalization of gay men's 'perverse' sexual practices (Waldby et al., 1994).

The 'science' of epidemiology not only acts as a means to take control of epidemics, but has been used more and more in the larger bureaucratic endeavour of rationalizing the resources of health care services. By 1987, according to the contemporary textbook on epidemiology quoted above, the purpose of epidemiology was not only to study 'the distribution and determinants of disease in human populations' but to 'help us with the ordering of priorities of resource allocation in health care' (Christie et al., 1987: 1). The need to rationalize the rising costs of health care has been a dominant feature of community and public health policy in Australia since the 1970s. In the past two decades the participation of economists in most areas of government and social policy has grown rapidly. The emergence and growing dominance in public health of the sub-discipline of health economics reflects these changes, with its economic and managerial discourse of 'cost–utility' and 'cost–benefit' analysis and 'quality adjusted life years' (QALYs) seeking to impose values and statistical measurements upon moral and ethical questions. In Britain, in particular, where the government-sponsored National Health Service (established in 1948), has experienced difficulties in containing costs in the climate of political conservatism, health economics has enjoyed a boom (Ashmore et al., 1989: 2).

Health economics uses its access to quantification and scientific measurement to support its claims to truth, arguing that it is far more rational than the decision-making processes of medical practitioners, which are 'biased' by internal divisions, political infighting and vested interests (Fox, 1991: 718). For health economists, health care systems are characterized by irrationality, waste, political self-interest and emotional decisions, neglectful of the considered weighing of pros and cons of resourcing various health care strategies and evasive of 'hard' decisions. They are therefore considered to need the 'disinterested', 'neutral' and 'value-free' advice of health economists (Ashmore et al., 1989: 82–3). The model of consumer sovereignty used in the health economics paradigm is that of the rational actor, seeking to maximize his or her objectives through conscious efficient choices. The QALY measurement, for example, seeks to discover to what extent people are willing to trade years of life for quality of life. Participants are given hypothetical scenarios involving serious pain, physical distress or disability such as paralysis or kidney failure and asked to make a choice about which they would prefer, or upon whom they would like to see resources being expended. Alternatively, a health state is broken down into numerous 'dimensions' such as 'physical functioning', 'socio-emotional functioning' and 'health problem' which are then scored on a scale (Richardson, 1992). The measurements derived from people's responses to these scenarios, as well as indices of costs related to treating conditions, are then used to support policy decisions concerning the use of resources in health care delivery. The technique assumes that choices made hypothetically are applicable to real-life situations, and reduces immensely complex human experiences and problems to numerical equations. As a result, '[o]nce complex administrative decisions have been reduced to simple, and usually quantified, comparisons of cost and benefit, it comes to seem irrational (or improper, if individuals choose to pursue their private ends rather than the public good) not to act in accordance with the numbers' (Ashmore et al., 1989: 90).

Fox (1993: 127) sees the popularity of the use of measurements such as QALYs as representing the bureaucratic model of action and managerial philosophy pervading health care delivery, which 'fail to offer any guarantee of the morality of the care deriving from this effort at rationalization. Indeed, it is all too easy to see how a substantive rationality which has a very doubtful morality (from another interest perspective) might be adopted.' As Fox (1991: 719) argues, however, any attempt to calculate and evaluate costs and benefits in health care ignores the socially constructed nature of economic values and the power relations inherent in any assessment of the utility of commodities. For example, the relationship between consumers and commodities is not simply based on use-value: 'not only are goods consumed according to agents' substantive rationalities, they are constitutive of those rationalities' (1991: 720). Rationalities are not generalizable but are local, highly contextual on the social setting in which they are constructed and exercised. Fox's (1991) own ethnographic study of surgical routines in an English hospital found that the power struggles between clinicians and management and their often oppositional vested interests around clinical autonomy and authority and the definition of surgical 'success' and efficiency meant that the striving of management towards rational efficiency (in terms of processing patients through surgery as quickly as possible) was constantly confounded.

'Health' and healthism in health promotion

In contemporary western societies the concept of 'health' has become central to the construction of subjectivities. 'Health' has become a way of defining boundaries between Self and Other, constructing moral and social categories and binary oppositions around gender, social class, sexuality, race and ethnicity (Crawford, 1994: 1348). The epistemology, ontology and discourse of 'health' is, of course, a mainstay of public health and health promotion. Most health education, promotion or communication documents begin by attempting to define 'health'. The current favoured definition is that posed by WHO: health as 'a state of complete physical, mental and social well-being, not merely the absence of disease or infirmity' (Better Health Commission, 1986: 1). Yet, as Figlio points out (1989: 86), the term 'health' itself is not necessarily a directly oppositional term to disease, for health refers to either good, bad or indifferent health. There must be a countervailing quality, such as 'perfect health' to provide an opposite to disease or illness: 'On its own, health does not refer to an active defence against disease, but to a kind of commonweal of the person, as public is a commonweal of the group.' The term 'health', as it is commonly used in both public health and lay discourses, therefore serves as a gloss for 'good health'. If something is 'healthy' it is implied it promotes the state of good rather than ill health. Likewise, 'health targets' or 'health goals' are those directed at achieving good health. 'Health' therefore denotes more than a medical condition, disease, or lack thereof, but comprises a group of knowledges used to assess different populations for different governmental strategies. These knowledges are developed and deployed not only by medical doctors and health promoters, but by teachers, social workers, bureaucrats, parents, economic advisers and so on.

Under the prevailing discourse of 'healthism', the pursuit of good health has become an end in itself rather than a means to an end. Healthism insists that the maintenance of good health is the responsibility of the individual, or the idea of one's health as an enterprise (Crawford, 1980; Greco, 1993: 357). Healthism represents good health as a personal rational choice, 'a domain of individual appropriation' rather than a vagary of fate (Greco, 1993: 357). This discourse, as it is employed in public health and health promotion, serves to separate health from the individual. 'Healthiness' is constructed as being carried 'within' the individual, a potential needful of release by virtue of engagement in certain behaviours or attitudes deemed 'promoting' of good health: 'There is a dissociation between the person and her/his health: they are constructed in a dialectic' (Fox, 1993: 135). Each entity may have an impact on the other. This conception underlies the emphasis on individual responsibility for health status: 'the person is the victim of her/his health turned nasty, but also the agency responsible for this state of affairs' (1993: 135). The social epidemiological model of health views health states as arising from interaction of the human body with its environment. Health in both models is primarily biologically defined and viewed as the absence of illness.

As noted in Chapter 1, the contemporary ideal body is that of the civilized body, subject to highly conscious and rational control. The practices of the self are strongly linked to the ideal of good health and longevity (bordering on the desire for immortality). Now that the body has come to represent the inner self, to speak of its capacity for self-hood, the pressures on individuals to conform to contemporary imperatives concerning the ideal external appearance of the body have often been translated into activities such as dieting, watching one's weight and exercising (Bordo, 1990; Crawford, 1994). Indeed, one can explain current norms around the government of the body in terms of taste; it is now considered poor taste to be overweight, to eat unhealthy foods (especially junk foods), to have an unfirm body, to smoke. Poor health itself is a 'distasteful' state.

There are echoes in the contemporary understanding of health of the ancient humoral theory of disease (discussed in Chapter 1), in its emphasis on individuals' constitutions, the importance of maintaining the delicate balance of health that is threatened from without, the conceptualization of health as the harmonious integration of body and mind. Under this model, such factors as stress, diet, sleeping patterns and exercise serve either to bolster or undermine the strength of a person's constitution and hence his or her ability to withstand illness. The notion of a 'predisposition' to illness which is to some extent subject to the control of individuals, a notion central to the humoral model of disease causation, remains important in contemporary understandings of health. This humoral approach is overlaid with a more recent mechanistic model of the human body which conceptualizes good health as perfect working order. A breakdown of the body/machine is rectified through attention to the faulty part. Under this concept, ill-health has one or more identifiable causes, which may then be dealt with, producing good health (Kelman, 1975: 628–9). The concept of health as it is employed in contemporary public health and health promotion thus tends to individualize health and ill-health states, removing them from the broader social context. Thus, heart disease is understood to arise from an individual's lifestyle 'choices' such as lack of exercise, stress, over-weight or a diet rich in fats, and the 'cure' for heart disease is the addressing of these factors.

All medical conditions are subject to moral judgements, based on such concepts as personal responsibility for illness and the patient's compliance with medical advice. The moral judgements made of people in medicine are translated to public health. Just as illness 'makes the patient's stewardship of the body suspect' (Kirmayer, 1988: 62), placing oneself at risk of disease, or developing a medical condition related to lifestyle factors denotes a certain laxness towards one's body. As Coward (1989: 43–6) notes, in contemporary western societies we are expected to attain health, to release the potential of health lying inside us. Disease is no longer misfortune, for all of us have the potential to be 'totally healthy'. Total health is not just the absence of disease or illness, but a higher state of being, a state of harmony between spirit, body, mind, society and the environment, which is achieved through personal transformation. All of us have a 'will to health' which is dependent upon achieving a 'natural state', a state in which the body is allowed to take control and fight off illness: 'an essentially innocent body, born with wholesome impulses but gradually worn down by the hostile world' (Coward, 1989: 50). The triplex 'exercise =fitness=health' dominates understandings of the ways in which bodies should be maintained and should look in the interests of good health (Kirk and Colquhoun, 1989). Good health has become a visible sign, demonstrated by the lean, taut, exercising body. The holistic model expands the definition of health to include feelings of self-empowerment and autonomy, a potential for self-improvement, and spiritual equilibrium. Such a philosophy of health, encompassing all dimensions of a person's life, is evident in the literature of alternative therapies but is also pervasive in health promotional discourses.

The official definitions and interpretations of 'health' thus attempt to impose a version of health upon those they describe. They rarely allow for individuals' own definitions of health, which are relative, dynamic and strongly linked to personal experience and observation. These definitions also serve to represent those whose bodily states do not in some way conform to the accepted notion of health as Other, exemplar of the worst-case scenario. For example, according to the WHO definition, people who are permanently disabled are not healthy, even though they may require little medical care or ongoing treatment. People living with cancer or HIV/AIDS are certainly not defined as healthy, using the above definition, yet many such individuals view themselves as healthy. Anglo-Americans and Japanese-American patients interviewed by Kagawa-Singer (1993), for example, almost all perceived themselves as 'healthy', even though at the time of the study they were all receiving treatments for cancer. One woman with metastatic breast cancer asserted that 'I don't consider myself sick. I just have this problem, but it doesn't necessarily make you sick. I just can't get around like everyone else, and I'd like to. Otherwise, I think of myself as healthy!', while another man who had been on continuous chemotherapy for four years said 'I don't feel ill and I don't consider myself, ah . . . actually I feel quite healthy' (Kagawa-Singer, 1993: 301). Kagawa-Singer argues that these individuals' notions of health 'was based upon their ability to maintain a sense of integrity as productive, able, and valued individuals within their social spheres, despite their physical condition' (1993: 295). So too, people with a disability do not think of themselves as walking exemplars, as helpless 'cripples' or 'invalids' nor even necessarily unhealthy. As one woman with a mobility disability commented when shown advertisements warning that lack of seat-belt use could end in being confined to a wheelchair, 'You know, frankly, I'll look at an advertisement like this and say what's so bad about using a wheelchair?' (Wang, 1992: 1089; see also, Hevey, 1992). While others might consider such people seriously ill, the individuals themselves have reconceptualized notions of health and illness to cope with their condition. Such research demonstrates that notions of health are changeable and are highly contingent upon context.

As noted above, the dominant representation of health in contemporary health promotion has been the notion of health as a personal responsibility. One prime example of this representation is an article written for the journal *Science* by John Knowles, president of the American Rockefeller Foundation, in 1977. In his article, entitled 'Responsibility for health', Knowles asserted that the 'temptations' and 'hedonism' of everyday life are destroying people's health. He argued that the habits people 'enjoy', which he described as 'overeating, drinking, taking pills, staying up at night, engaging in promiscuous sex, driving too fast, and smoking cigarettes' are preferred over those that 'require special effort', such as 'exercising regularly, improving nutrition, going to the dentist, practising contraception, ensuring harmonious family life, submitting to screening examinations'. He thus set up a dichotomy between behaviours people like to indulge themselves in (as 'unhealthy'), versus those that require a degree of will power and asceticism (as 'healthy'). Health status is represented as a sign of self-control, the degree to which temptation can be resisted. Not only does hedonistic behaviour invite ill-health, it affects others by draining public resources: 'one man's freedom is another man's shackle in taxes and insurance premiums'. As a result:

> The next major advances in the health of the American people will be determined by what the individual is willing to do for himself [sic] and for society at large. If he is willing to follow reasonable rules for healthy living, he can extend his life and enhance his own and the nation's productivity. (Knowles, 1977: 1103)

The underlying concern is thus the drain on the health dollar provided by people's self-indulgence, while the rhetoric draws upon the utilitarian ideals of improved health for all. The discourse of healthism is also explicit in this argument. Given the continuing prevalence of such discourses, it is not surprising that an American physician recently wrote a piece for the journal *Tobacco Control* entitled 'Why I don't treat cigarette smokers' (Jameson, 1993). In the article, he argued that:

> People have a right to smoke cigarettes and people also have a right to health care. However, these two rights are incompatible; a person cannot claim both rights . . . Should physicians ignore patients' personal behaviours that are harmful to the public? I think not. Physicians have a duty to the public as well as to their patients. Traditionally, physicians are trained to be patient advocates. However, advocating for cigarette smokers is advocating for irresponsible behaviour and endangerment to others. (1993: 236)

While the piece by Knowles and the article above are overt in their denunciation and 'victim-blaming' of people who display little self-control and an unwillingness to engage in 'rational' health-preserving activities, recent documents concerning preventive health are complex, in that they combine discourses of individual freedom and liberalism with economic rationalism and utilitarianism. One example is the *Looking Forward to Better Health* final report, published in 1986 by Australia's Better Health Commission, which was established to consider national preventive health policy. The report describes health as a 'resource for everyday life, not the object for living' (Better Health Commission, 1986: 2); in other words, a state that facilitates enjoyment of life rather than as something to be achieved for its own sake. Recognizing the need to avoid 'blaming the victim' for ill-health, the document recognizes that health choices are not made entirely freely, and are constrained with the socio-economic environment (1986: 4). It goes on to assert that '[p]eople usually "choose" a behaviour that is least costly in terms of convenience, money or time, this being balanced against the pleasure and perceived benefits of such behaviour' (1986: 4), employing the discourse of economic rationality in its use of 'cost–benefit' terminology.

Yet the notion of individuals as rationally employing consumer sovereignty is counteracted by the simultaneous positioning of individuals as
weak, requiring support and encouragement to make personal changes: 'all
of us are beset by human frailties. Supportive and enabling mechanisms are
therefore necessary' (1986: 4). While the Better Health Commission report
goes on to list such mechanisms as legislation, price incentives and
disincentives, community involvement and the provision of screening
procedures, the emphasis on personal change is still evident:

> The aim of preventive programs is to encourage and help people to feel and
> function better by making the following choices: to be non-smokers; to eat a diet
> lower in fat and salt; to be aware of their blood pressure and blood cholesterol
> levels; to be lean and active. As with all efforts to prevent disease, the process
> involves providing people with information, motivation, and opportunity. (1986:
> 117)

In concert with an increasing use of managerial discourse since the late
1980s, a more recent Australian report, entitled *Goals and Targets for
Australia's Health in the Year 2000 and Beyond* (Nutbeam et al., 1993), as
its name suggests, seeks to take a systematic approach to reviewing the
progress of the Better Health strategies by identifying goals and targets to
facilitate 'good management practice' in health promotion. Good management includes the governmental aims of the bureaucratic apparatus of
health promotion and public health, and also the management of the self.
The report goes on to discuss the need for individuals to develop skills in
resilience and coping, including self-esteem and problem-solving skills, 'to
enable them to cope with and adapt to life stresses, and to achieve mental
wellbeing'. Health literacy is defined as 'the ability to gain access to,
understand, and use information in ways which promote and maintain
good health' and it is stated that 'personal health literacy enables people to
make informed health choices' (Nutbeam et al., 1993: 151). As a result, the
report outlines proposed targets and priority populations deemed as
needing more information about specific aspects; for example, adolescents
are singled out as needing to 'correctly identify the physical and psychological changes they are likely to experience with the onset of puberty' (1993:
153).

As these documents suggest, like medical discourses, public health and
health promotional discourses continually seek to emphasize and reproduce the divisions drawn between 'healthy' and 'unhealthy' states and
social groups. In health promotional discourses, members of the population, or 'consumers' as they are often referred to, are represented as
experiencing a lack. Notions of the 'healthy' self are constructed not only
through comparison of one's internal state, but comparison of oneself with
'unhealthy' others who embody the characteristics falling outside the
'healthy' self (Crawford, 1994: 1348). As such, those individuals who do
not achieve a permanent state of 'good health' are constructed as
abnormal, requiring the attention of the health care or health promotion
system. Health status becomes something that consumers must continually

monitor and evaluate, so as to be aware of their needs and wants and to take the appropriate steps to satisfy them. This discourse draws upon the rhetoric of marketing: 'clients' or 'consumers' are provided with health promotional services, just as the ill are provided with biomedical services. There is no coercion involved: consumers are 'free' to make their own choices on the information provided them, and change because they 'want to' (Grace, 1991: 334–40).

Concluding comments

The nineteenth-century emergence of biomedicine as a highly rationalized, 'scientific' body of knowledge supported the view of the body as subject to the will of humans. Given the shared project of biomedicine and public health to improve health status, to rid the body (both individual and social) of disease, and to promote the perception of disease and illness as irrational, chaotic, a failure of human control, it is not surprising that the logic and discourse of public health continues to reproduce the ideal of the highly rationalized body dominated by the conscious will. Just as the germ theory of disease represents the body as an armed fortress, protecting itself against invasion by microscopic enemies (viruses and bacteria), or even from self-destruction via auto-immune disease (Haraway, 1989), health promotional discourse often represents the enemy as the failure of self-control, the invasion of weakness, lack of self-discipline, against which the individual should be ever-vigilant. The moralism that is extended to people who become ill because they have allowed themselves to be 'invaded' is also extended to those who allow the entry of disease by failing to regulate their 'lifestyle' with sufficient discipline. Similarly, the notion of the individual body as besieged by self-destruction is expanded in public health discourse to the concept of the social body, the health of which must be protected by its individual members acting responsibly to keep out disease: 'It is as if disturbing social events can be controlled by individuals imposing upon themselves regimes of discipline and healthful living' (Seidman, 1991: 192).

The identification and stigmatization of marginalized groups who are considered to be 'unhealthy' or 'risk takers' serves to allow ingroups to project their anxieties concerning chaos, forbidden desire, lack of control, death and disease (Frankenberg, 1992: 74; Crawford, 1994: 1363–4). As discussed in Chapter 1, members of the working classes have historically been represented as the archetypal 'uncontrolled' body in public health discourse, as lazy, dirty, immoral, incapable of resisting their urges. So too, in contemporary health promotional discourses, members of the middle class are commonly represented as capable of the valued qualities of self-denial and self-efficacy, while working-class individuals are typically portrayed as those who frequently fail to take up the exhortations of health promoters, who deliberately expose themselves to health risks rather than rationally avoiding them, and therefore require greater surveillance and regulation. Other stigmatized or underprivileged groups, such as immigrants, prostitutes and gay men, are similarly commonly represented as subject to less personal control.

Public health workers may be described as 'serving' the public, by assessing its needs, providing it with assistance to meet its health goals and evaluating consumer satisfaction, but do so within the context of a bureaucratic structure that is funded by the state and conforms to its own set objectives. In the case of the 'new' public health, individuals are largely governed through inciting them to exercise personal autonomy and political awareness. The discourses of freedom, of collective action, of empowerment as advocated by radical critics have been absorbed into the complex bureaucratic network of public health. Thus the 'new' public health, in concerning itself with the political as well as the environmental aspects of public health, demands an even wider hygienic strategy than that of the 'old' public health movement (Armstrong, 1993: 405). Every individual is now involved in observing, imposing and enforcing the regulations of public health, particularly through the techniques of self-surveillance and bodily control encouraged by the imperatives of health promotion.

3

Taming Uncertainty: Risk Discourse and Diagnostic Testing

Contemporary societies have become more and more aware of risks, especially those caused by technology and 'lifestyle' habits. Health risks seem to loom around every corner, posing a constant threat to the public: modern individuals are afraid of '[n]othing much . . . except the food they eat, the water they drink, the air they breathe, the land they live on, and the energy they use' (Douglas and Wildavsky, 1982: 10). Risk disputes receive a great deal of public attention, engaging and polarizing a variety of groups: scientists, company doctors, lawyers, government administrators, journalists, health and consumer bodies and policy experts. Their interests in risk stem from such divergent factors as economic imperatives, professional ethics, bureaucratic routines, personal concern about health, concern about the environment, career pressures and ambitions and political predilections (Nelkin, 1989: 95–6). Risks constantly make headlines in the news media and are increasingly the subject of health promotion campaigns. Associations of risk have been made between such diverse characteristics and conditions as male-pattern balding and heart disease, breast implants and immunosuppression, lack of sleep and 'sleep-deficit syndrome' and amalgam dental fillings and mercury poisoning. Risk assessment and risk communication have become growth industries. In short, the word 'risk' itself has acquired a new prominence in western societies, becoming a central cultural construct (Douglas, 1990: 2). This chapter explores the use and socio-cultural dimension of a dominant discourse, 'risk', and a related practice, diagnostic testing, in public health and health promotion.

Risk discourse in public health can be separated loosely into two main perspectives. The first views risk as a health danger to populations which is posed by environmental hazards such as pollution, nuclear waste and toxic chemical residues. In this conceptualization of risk, the health threat is regarded as a hazard which is *external*, over which the individual has little control. The second approach to health risk focuses on risk as a consequence of the 'lifestyle' choices made by individuals, and thus places the emphasis upon self-control. Risk in this sense is *internally* imposed, a function of the individual's ability to manage the self. Individuals are subsequently exhorted by health promotion authorities to evaluate their risk of succumbing to disease and to change their behaviour accordingly. A third, less common use of the term, refers to social groups rather than individuals as being 'at risk' through not having sufficient access to health care services. Here, risk refers to social disadvantage, which depending on the political stance taken may be represented as a function of external factors such as income or internal factors such as lack of motivation, or a combination of both.

The strategy of diagnostic testing has been adopted to deal with both externally and internally imposed health risks. The logic of testing is that patterns of risk must first be ascertained, by identifying those who harbour the potential to develop a certain condition or disease (for example, those who possess the antibodies to HIV and who may then be expected to develop the symptoms associated with AIDS) and then rationally dealt with. It is believed that diagnostic screening allows disease to be identified before symptoms appear, providing time to treat or prevent it, or alerts people to their potential to pass on a disease or condition, such as HIV or a genetic illness. Having a test, of any kind, is conceptualized as offering control, of being a way of 'doing something' in the face of the incipient disorder created by the presence or potential of disease. It is assumed that individuals must have 'knowledge' of their hidden disease, or its pre-cursors, to be able to act to protect themselves against it. The relationship between the discourse of risk and the strategy of diagnostic testing is therefore synergistic: individuals are exhorted to attend for a test because they are deemed to be 'at risk' of developing a disease or condition, and the statistics produced from testing data serve to support or rephrase assessments of patterns of risk in the population.

The meanings and measurement of risk

Given its centrality in both public and private discourses around health, surprisingly little has been written about the epistemology of risk in general, or how notions and knowledges concerning risks are developed, understood and embedded in the social world (Hayes, 1992: 402). The concept of risk has different meanings according to who is using the term. The proliferation of usages of the term in both vernacular and professional applications means that its meanings are both complex and confusing. In its original usage, 'risk' is neutral, referring to probability, or the mathemati-cal likelihood of an event occurring. Used in the more mathematical areas of the burgeoning field of risk analysis, this strict sense of the term is adhered to. Risk discourse depends on its calculability, and quantification and measurement are integral to the discourse and philosophy of risk. Risk depends upon a belief in law-like mathematical regularities in the popula-tion, itself dependent upon the collection of data and its tabulation (Hacking, 1990: 3). Thus, risk analysts speak of the statistical likelihood that an event may occur, and use the mathematical model produced to assist in decision making in such areas as economics and management. The likelihood of an event happening is calculated to numerical odds: one in fifty chance, one in a hundred, one in a million, as is the magnitude of the outcome should it happen. However, as it is commonly used, the term 'risk' has taken on more ominous overtones. Risk now signifies danger and any risk is now negative; it is a contradiction in terms to speak of something as a 'good risk' (Douglas, 1990).

Most industries devoted to the quantification of risk place a great deal of importance in measuring risk assessment, risk perception and risk evaluation on the part of individuals in the general population. Psychologists in the field of decision analysis employ laboratory experiments, gaming situations and survey techniques to understand risk perception, attempting to arrive at a quantitative determination of risk acceptance. Risk perception research tends to represent the individual as lacking the ability to unemotively respond to risk, based on research which has revealed that the higher a risk is seen as 'dread', the more people want to see its current risks reduced and strict regulation enforced. These perceptions are contrasted with those of 'experts', who understand risk using statistical measures. For example, one study using psychometric measures defined risk perceptions as 'intuitive risk judgements' (Slovic, 1987: 280), contrasting them with 'technologically sophisticated analysts [who] employ risk assessment to evaluate hazards'. These determinations of risk acceptance, based on characteristics of the risk itself, largely fail to account for the socio-cultural contexts within which risk perception takes place. The influence of meanings and messages conveyed by a shared cultural experience, or the symbolic nature of risk, is little recognized by such individualistic models of risk perception.

Yet, as Ewald (1991) has pointed out, the category of risk is purely socially constructed, for nothing is a risk in itself until it is judged to be a risk. The 'philosophy of risk' incorporates a secularized approach to life where things do not simply happen without warning, but can be predicted. It is an extension of the idea of one's life as an enterprise, and the belief that individuals should plan for the future and take judicious steps to ensure protection against misfortune, retaining responsibility for their affairs. To protect oneself against risk is to 'master time, discipline the future' (1991: 207). The philosophy of risk assumes that risk is collective: 'Whereas an accident, as damage, misfortune and suffering, is always individual, striking at one and not another, a risk of accident affects a population' (1991: 202–3). The concept of risk further assumes that each person is 'a factor of risk', is exposed to risk; that is not to say, however, that each person is exposed to the same *degree* of risk, for '[t]he risk defines the whole, but each individual is distinguished by the probability of risk which falls to his or her share' (1991: 203). The concept of risk, therefore, may be viewed as integral to a rationalist understanding of reality, in which unfortunate events are deemed to be both predictable and avoidable. Risk discourse is an attempt to tame uncertainty. There is thus a contradiction inherent in the concept of risk; there are laws of risk that may be identified and applied to individuals and groups, but risk may also be avoided, as long as one is aware of these laws and willing to act rationally to avoid being a casualty of risk.

The risks which are selected by a society as requiring attention may therefore have no relation to 'real' danger but are culturally identified as important. One example is the contemporary panic around asbestos placed in buildings such as offices, schools and houses to provide protection against fire and as insulation. In several countries, large sums of money have been expended to remove the asbestos in such buildings because of a concern about its association with the serious diseases asbestosis, lung cancer and mesothelioma. Yet while there has been a link established between these diseases and workers who were exposed to asbestos fibres over a long period of time, there has yet to be determined a link between spending time in a building with undisturbed asbestos insulation and such illnesses. Indeed, the removal of the asbestos from buildings, requiring that it is broken up and therefore releasing fibres into the air, poses more of a threat to those in the vicinity, and does not guarantee the 'safety' of the building. However, because the substance has been labelled as a health risk and has received wide publicity engendering public anxiety, particularly around school children's health, the expensive removal of asbestos continues (Sapolsky, 1990: 86–8). The imperative to *do* something, to remove the source of a health risk, however tenuous, impels action. The discourse of risk becomes a political strategy, a way of negotiating the dialectic between private fears and public dangers. Using the word 'risk' instead of 'danger' has the rhetorical effect of providing neutrality, bearing with it as it does the 'aura of science' and the 'pretension of a possible precise calculation' (Douglas, 1990: 5).

For the sociologist Ulrich Beck, a heightened and critical consciousness about risk is a condition of the late twentieth century. In his book *Risk Society* (1992), Beck describes risk as a paradox of late modernity, in which the drive for human progress and industrial development has resulted in an increasing number of hazards threatening the ecosystem and the health of humanity, which in turn have prompted heightened anxiety and cynicism on the part of citizens about the claims for progress made by government and industry. Instead of contemporary society being characterized by the production of wealth, goods and commodities, as it was in early or classical modernity, Beck argues that it is marked by the production of more and more hazards and dangers, emerging from industry and science out-of-control. According to Beck, in the early days of industrialization, risks and hazards were evident to the senses, while risks today are invisible and escape human perception; for example, toxins in food, the nuclear threat, radioactivity, air and water pollution (1992: 21–3). These dangers are no longer limited in time, but face humanity at a global level now and in the future. Thus, Beck argues, '[s]tatements on risk are the moral statements of scientized society' (1992: 172). Danger, rephrased as 'risk', has become viewed as emerging from human behaviour rather than from supernatural or divine influences. Beck's statements about risk society mainly focus on the concept of risk as an external danger. While such risks may have been politicized in recent years, the notion of internally imposed risk has yet to be fully critiqued for its political and moral dimension. It is this conceptualization of risk which is a mainstay of health promotional activities.

Risk discourse and health promotion

In the case of internally imposed risk, biomedicine and epidemiology, as 'objective' bodies of knowledge, make judgements on what behaviours are considered risky and which individuals are deemed to be 'at risk'. Their ability to define risk and to make pronouncements as to how people might avoid or minimize risk is central to the reinforcement of their standing as dominant, high-status institutions. In public health and health promotion, the word 'risk' as a synonym for danger is in constant use. A 'discourse of risk' has evolved with particular application to health issues. Individuals or groups are labelled as being 'at high risk', meaning that they are in danger of contracting or developing a disease or illness. Epidemiologists calculate measures of 'relative risk' to compare the likelihood that populations exposed to a 'risk factor' will develop an illness compared to populations which have not been exposed. In response to epidemiological predictions of risk, public health and health promotional texts identify discrete groups in the population requiring specific attention.

One example is the *Goals and Targets for Australia's Health in the Year 2000 and Beyond* report (Nutbeam et al., 1993), which uses the term 'targets' to gloss the specific sub-populations deemed to be especially 'at risk' from various illnesses or conditions. Priority populations are identified, based on their current level of morbidity and mortality, and given ideal target levels to aspire to; for example, women aged 50 to 69 years are identified as a priority population for the reduction of breast cancer mortality, with the target of a 10 per cent reduction by the year 2000. This document, and other public health texts of its genre, represent an attempt to take control over the contingencies of serious illness and death, by giving precise figures and statistical calculations to risk factors and proposed outcomes of intervention. For example, the *Goals and Targets* report notes in relation to cancer that: 'Overall, about one-third of cancer deaths can be attributed to tobacco and another 3% to alcohol. Risk factors associated with sexual behaviour and reproductive patterns account for a further 7% of deaths and about 4% may be due to occupational exposure' (Nutbeam et al., 1993: 36). By drawing up neat equations of risk and risk modification, the document implies that the rationality of health promotional discourse will eventually conquer sickness and premature mortality, if only the correct advice is taken.

As noted in Chapter 2, individuals' beliefs about their perceived susceptibility to a condition or disease figure prominently in models of health behaviour such as the Health Belief Model and the Theory of

Reasoned Action, which assume that perceived susceptibility to a risk is essential in motivating behaviour. To apprise target groups of the health risk it has been decided they are heir to, and to allow them to better 'manage' this risk, a network of strategies exists, ranging from individual attention such as risk assessment, counselling and case management, to involving family members, instituting prevention programmes in schools, workplaces and recreation sites, and community-wide programmes involving the use of the mass media or the enactment of legislation. Risk assessment related to lifestyle choices is formally undertaken by means of health risk appraisals and screening programmes in which the individual participates and is given a rating. These health risk appraisals are used to counsel individuals about prospective threats to their health which are associated with behaviours deemed to be modifiable. The objective is to promote awareness of potential dangers courted by lifestyle choices, and then to motivate individuals to participate in health promotion and health education programmes (DeFriese and Fielding, 1990: 403). The risk appraisal is calculated after an interview with a person which elicits details about personal health habits and risk factors. These data may be supplemented by biomedical measurements. Using this information, a quantitative or qualitative assessment is made of the person's future risk of death or adverse health outcomes from several specific causes. Counselling is then provided to the individual in the ways to avoid such outcomes by changes in personal behaviours. The process of undergoing a personal risk assessment is therefore like that of the religious confession. Individuals are incited to tell their 'sins' to the health worker, or else their bodies provide mute testimony to their self-indulgence (if found to be overweight or to have a high blood cholesterol reading, for example). Once the assessment is finalized, judgement is passed upon participants, and they are given appropriate 'penances' to perform to re-establish bodily, and moral, integrity.

Despite the aura of scientific calculability that surrounds them, personal health risk appraisals have been shown to have serious limitations in their predictive capabilities. These limitations include their use of epidemiological data produced from population research not designed to be applied to personal health risk. There are also problems with the available statistical methods for estimating risk as a quantitative score using disparate items of measurement (Fielding, 1982; DeFriese and Fielding, 1990). The health risk appraisal literature also fails to recognize that the experience of being labelled 'at risk' itself may be detrimental to people's health status, becoming a self-fulfilling prophecy (Oakley, 1992: 269). Critics argue that there is more to risk than the disclosure of technical information and the mathematical determination of probabilities, and more to the individual's perception of risk than the assimilation and rational weighing up of impartial technical information (Nelkin, 1989: 96; Douglas and Calvez, 1990). Despite these problems, little research has been undertaken into the practical and ethical consequences of health risk appraisals, including their capacity to arouse anxiety in the well and their appropriate use in patient counselling. Proponents of health risk appraisal continue to support it as a means of giving individuals 'knowledge' about themselves which they may then use to change their behaviour: for example, the comment that: 'While some . . . fear that pointing out even ameliorable risks may constitute "blaming the victim", we must blame ourselves as professionals if we do not do all we can to help individuals understand how much they (and frequently they alone) can do to improve their health' (Fielding, 1982: 338).

The incursion of health risk discourse into almost all areas and institutions of life, and the vested interests it supports, has rarely been challenged or questioned from within mainstream public health. The development of the new corporate health ethic, for example, is a two-edged sword. Ostensibly the introduction of such programmes signal philanthropic motives on the part of employers to improve the quality of their employees' health, as well as serving the function of containing health care costs (particularly in the United States, where many employers offer health care schemes to their employees and their families). However, the encroachment of appraisal and testing programmes into the workplace signals a new type of control over the worker's body. The measurement of health risks, fitness assessments and screening programmes at the work-place establishes the grounds to screen out 'undesirable' employees on the basis of such factors as their body weight, lack of adherence to a self-disciplined lifestyle and recreational use of drugs. The emphasis on physical fitness and no drug taking in effect serves to exhort workers to engage in certain activities and relinquish others in their spare time. The all-embracing concept of 'lifestyle', as measured in workplace pro-grammes, therefore encompasses the private as well as the public domain. Programmes such as drug screening enable employers to determine what workers are doing in their spare time, casting the net of corporate control ever wider (Conrad and Walsh, 1992: 97). The possibility is that such screening could be extended to testing for HIV infection, hypersusceptibi-lity to cancer, alcoholism and even genetic defects (1992: 98).

The precise mathematical calculation of risk as it is performed in health risk appraisals fails to recognize the complexity of risk relations across time and space, assuming the regular, stable and uniform nature of the cause–effect model (Hayes, 1992: 405). Similarly, the discourse of risk as used in epidemiology tends to obscure the complexity and social dimension of disease and illness and glosses over the debates in the medical and public health literature over the causes of disease (Oakley, 1992: ch. 2; Hand-werker, 1994; Frankenberg, 1994). Epidemiological and medical defini-tions of what behaviours constitute risky behaviours, and how these behaviours in turn affect health status, are subject to continual change. For example, there is currently confusion and controversy around the wisdom of regulating one's blood cholesterol level, yet health promotional docu-ments take the simple line, continuing to warn individuals to be vigilant about their cholesterol level for the sake of the health of their heart. Although the precise causes of breast cancer have yet to be identified and the degree of risk associated with specific lifestyle factors is subject to controversy, risk discourse continues to position certain behaviours and groups of women as being unambiguously at 'high risk' from the disease (Gifford, 1986: 217).

Yet another example is the current debate around the association of HIV with AIDS. Given that there have been identified cases of people with symptoms associated with AIDS who do not test positive for HIV antibodies, and there are also cases of people who have tested positive for HIV antibodies for many years yet have not developed any of the symptoms related to AIDS, some scientists are questioning the current widely accepted wisdom that HIV causes AIDS. They argue, instead, that HIV is a symptom rather than a cause of AIDS, suggesting that such factors as drug use, chronic parasitic infection and chronic malnutrition may cause the immune system to break down, rendering the individual more susceptible to infection by viruses such as HIV (Nicoll and Brown, 1994; Fujimura and Chou, 1994). This controversy calls into question the orthodox epidemiological categorization of 'at risk' groups in relation to AIDS, and the vast network of statistical surveillance, public policy, testing procedures and educational campaigns that have been established to minimize the spread of the syndrome. Yet because epidemiology has accepted the HIV causes AIDS thesis, dissenters who seek to challenge it are treated with hostility, and the advice given to the public about risk in relation to HIV has remained unchanged. The certainty of the advice given to the public about risk factors and risk relationships therefore obscures the continuing, complex and often very fraught medical and epidemiological debates around the 'truth' of this advice. That epidemiological knowledges are 'dialectical/undetermined/underdetermined and under continual (re)construction' (Fujimura and Chou, 1994: 1032) is little acknowledged in the public face of epidemiology and risk discourse.

Living with risk

There are fundamental differences between clinical and epidemiological understandings of risk and lay understandings. The epidemiological conceptualization of risk 'describe[s] relationships which are objective, depersonalized, quantitative, and scientifically measured' and reduces the causality of disease to a single factor or combination of discrete factors whose effects may be traced in a cause–effect relationship similar to the biomedical model (Gifford, 1986: 217). This conceptualization, expressing a statistical measure, when translated to clinical practice and lay understandings of health and illness takes on very different meanings, both intended and unconscious. Individuals become defined and labelled by risk discourse, with diverse aspects of their lives ranging from their marital status to their choice of lunch becoming markers of risk. The ways in which people interpret risk are highly contingent on the socio-cultural context. While epidemiologists refer to risk in the abstract as a measured property at the population level, when individuals attempt more specifically to assess risk calculations as they apply to themselves personally the concept becomes a subjective, lived experience. People do not conceptualize risk in terms of objective statistical probabilities but rather make subjective judgements based on ontological and cosmological assumptions: 'For the patient, risk becomes a lived or experienced state of ill-health and a symptom of future illness . . . it is internalized and experienced as a state of being' (Gifford, 1986: 215; see also Handwerker, 1994). Gifford's (1986) interviews with American women who had been designated as at 'high risk' of breast cancer found that being 'at risk' was experienced as a liminal state between health and illness. The women commonly drew on subjective experiences and emotions to describe their responses to risk, expressing their anxiety, uncertainty and fear.

Risk relations are derived from consideration of both genetic or biological factors ('nature') and those related to social and environmental factors ('nurture') (Hayes, 1992: 404). Models of risk factors relating to the disease are therefore a source of confusion, for they combine contradictory understandings of why people become ill or die prematurely: fatalism and lifestylism. Because they are deemed modifiable, it is lifestyle factors that risk reduction is directed towards, despite the evidence that genetic or biological factors may have more effect. In the vain attempt to lessen the vagaries of fate, health promotional discourse urges modification of factors related to lifestyle, such as diet, and in doing so, tends to obscure the factors that are not amenable to change, such as one's gender. For example, being male or having a history of heart disease in the family are prime risk factors associated with early death from heart disease, yet attention is rarely drawn to these risk factors by health promoters when discussing the causes of heart disease. Risk discourse tends to assume universal experience and ignores social differentiations, such as ethnicity and social class. Yet there is a class difference in the manner that people are exposed to risk: wealth may buy safety from risk while poverty attracts risk (Beck, 1992: 26). This is particularly the case in relation to occupational risk, where workers often have little choice in the degree of exposure they may have to dangerous chemicals or hazardous activities, regardless of their knowledge of risk or their personal caution. In such situations, the threat of losing one's job is a greater risk than is the danger of exposure to workplace hazards (Nelkin and Brown, 1984).

The social processes by which a risk is judged 'acceptable' or otherwise are revealing of broader concerns and the role of 'experts' in making knowledge claims around risks. A detailed account of a public school controversy over the risks posed by a school child with HIV to other children demonstrates the difficulties associated with defining and judging acceptable risk in such a case, as well as the moral implications of risk assessments and disputes (Nelkin and Hilgartner, 1986). The authors describe the arguments used in a lawsuit in New York, when two school boards sued the city of New York in an attempt to prevent a seven-year-old child with HIV/AIDS from attending school. The hearings revealed a wide range of issues, including: How is the risk of HIV/AIDS defined? How much scientific uncertainty surrounds the subject of HIV transmission? What constitutes adequate evidence? Whose judgement is to be considered in evaluating the acceptability of risk? Who should be involved in decisions about controlling risk? The use of 'what if' risk scenarios on the part of the school boards forced the court to confront the difficulties of extrapolating from epidemiological data to make inferences about rhetorical situations.

As noted above, epidemiology is a probabilistic field of inquiry in which outcomes and associations can never be said to be sure to occur. When the lack of certainty of epidemiological prediction was dealt with in the context of the courtroom, confusion thus reigned 'between evidence and proof, between facts and theories, between findings and explanations, between probable judgements and unassailable conclusions' (Nelkin and Hilgartner, 1986: 126–7). This confusion between laypersons and epidemiologists' understandings of risk made it difficult for the court to decide upon acceptability of the risk. As the authors state, this case, and other risk disputes, demonstrates the symbolic and political issues bearing upon risk perception and acceptability (1986: 139).

Another example is the issues around those parents who refuse to allow their children to be immunized with the usual vaccines. Such parents are often represented in the medical and public health literature as neglectful, ignorant, overly anxious or not fully cognizant of the risks to their children of contracting childhood illnesses. However, when New and Senior (1991) interviewed women in the North West of England who had not taken their children for the full series of immunization they found that the participants' decision not to have their child immunized was often made for fully considered and 'rational' reasons relating to their everyday knowledge of the associated risks of vaccination. Several women knew or had heard of children who had had serious side-effects following pertussis vaccination (for whooping cough) or had observed side-effects in their own children such as severe hair loss. They recounted instances of vaccinated children contracting whooping cough or unvaccinated children whose state of health was far better than that of their vaccinated peers: 'If this was so, to have one's child immunized was to take an unnecessary risk for no apparent benefit' (1991: 514). Some women mentioned their belief that if their child caught whooping cough it would be a stroke of fate, and out of their control, but if their child were to suffer a serious side-effect of vaccination such as brain damage, then they would feel responsible. 'It was no comfort to be told that the risk was slim, as "my child might be the one in a thousand" ' (1991: 513). The findings showed that the majority of women had carefully considered the relative risks and benefits of vaccination for their child and had decided against vaccination. Their reasons for not having their children vaccinated were not based on ignorance, but rather on their heightened awareness of the risks involved.

Since the advent of the HIV/AIDS epidemic, sexual behaviour has been colonized by the discourse of risk, which has attempted to construct new ways of expressing sexual desire. Health promotion undertaken to prevent the spread of HIV has relied heavily upon the social psychology models of behaviour referred to in Chapter 2. The dominant understanding of sexual behaviour in much health promotional literature is that it is rational, considered, comprised of conscious decisions and the weighing-up of alternatives. For example, an 'AIDS Risk Reduction Model' recently developed rests on the premise that 'to avoid HIV infection, people exhibiting high risk activities must typically perceive that their sexual behaviour places them at risk for HIV infection and is, therefore, problematic' (Catania et al., 1990: 54). The model identifies three conditions as being vital for people to label their sexual behaviour as being problematic: knowledge of sexual activities associated with HIV transmission; believing that one is personally susceptible to contracting HIV; and believing that having AIDS is undesirable. Related to this belief in rational behaviour is the approach taken in campaigns directed at preventing the spread of HIV that are frequently redolent with notions of 'punishing' people for their ignorance, apathy or behaviour (see Chapter 4 for a detailed critique of the use of media in education campaigns for AIDS and other health risks).

The privileging of rationality in much scientific and public health literature about behaviour related to AIDS ignores the role of the unconscious, desire and pleasure in sexual expression. It fails to acknowledge that for some, risk-taking itself is pleasurable, enhancing the notion of sex as an escape from the humdrum of everyday existence and the danger of the forbidden (Bolton, 1992: 199). The discourse of safer sex makes the underlying assumption that pleasure and desire can be reorganized in response to imperatives based on health risk. It also assumes 'the capacity of regimentary procedures to construct a body capable of taking pleasure in this new form of discipline' (Singer, 1993: 122). A further assumption is that sexuality is 'contained' within the individual, and that safer sex must therefore be imposed on this inherent sexuality. What the epidemiological construction of risk often fails to recognize is the ways in which 'real' sexuality is constructed as involving certain behaviours, such as penetrative sex in heterosexual encounters, without which the activities are not seen as 'sex'. If the dominant ways in which people understand sexual desire emphasize the 'uncontrollable' nature of passion, its irresistibility, then insisting on stopping to use a condom introduces a self-consciousness to the activity. Once the 'irrationality' of sexual passion takes over, the 'rationality' of condom use is allowed no space to enter (Miles, 1993: 501). Condoms signify lack of trust, dirtiness, sleaziness, homosexuality and the Other (Gamson, 1990; Miles, 1993: 501; Lupton, 1994b: 137–8). They also act as symbolic as well as literal barriers between sexual partners, reducing the desired level of intimacy, drawing an invisible line between 'getting close' to one's partner and merging with them on both the physical and emotional levels (Wilton and Aggleton, 1991: 155).

The discourse of risk and safer sex also largely fails to take into account that sexual behaviour, like any other behaviour, is not atomistic but highly socially contextual. The ways in which people appraise their partners, their desired level of trust and intimacy are all integral to their assessment of risk and their use or non-use of safer sex techniques. Little attention is paid in AIDS health promotional literature to the issues of trust and danger that accompany arousal and sexual pleasure. Should a gay man who chooses not to insist on condom use during penetrative homosexual activity necessarily be viewed as 'relapsing' or 'irresponsible' for 'deliberately' exposing himself to risk? These terms bring together the discourses of health preservation on the one hand, and admonition for lack of self-control on the other. Perhaps men who choose to 'relapse' have complex reasons for accepting the risks that are more important to them than avoiding HIV infection, such as expressing love or trust, or being coerced or paid for the activity. The context of the relationship, or the particular occasion of sexual activity itself, may change, resulting in the individual judging the risks differently. Yet the frequent use of the term 'relapse' to describe the activities of gay men in the epidemiological and medical literature, while emerging from well-intentioned researchers and practitioners intent on preventing further infections, largely ignores these complexities and conveys the ideologies of addiction, uncontrollable sexual appetites, morality, deviance and otherness (Hart et al., 1992). It also fails to acknowledge that very few heterosexual men have even taken the first step of adopting safer sexual practices from which they could 'relapse', and are not as subject to the same level of moralizing discourse around giving up penetrative sex as are gay men (Watney, 1991: 11–12).

The epidemiological categorization of 'risk groups' and 'risk behaviours' in relation to HIV/AIDS implies that individuals' sexuality and sexual practices are unidimensional and fixed rather than fluid. Such a taxonomy has difficulties dealing with the fact that drug users may also be homosexual and vice versa, that many men who have sex with other men do not identify themselves as either gay or bisexual, that self-identified lesbians sometimes have sex with men, and that men may be the active partner in one experience of anal penetration with a partner, and the receptive partner in another (see also Schiller et al., 1994). Even within the identified subcultures built around such characteristics as gender, social class, sexual identity, ethnicity and nationality, individuals derive pleasure from different acts: 'Even identical genital acts mean very different things to different people . . . Sexuality makes up a large share of the self-perceived identity of some people, a small share of others. Some people spend a lot of time thinking about sex, others little. Some people like to have a lot of sex, others little or none' (Sedgwick, 1993: 249). These differences are often ignored or minimized in discourses about human sexual behaviour in the medical and public health literature. Instead, universal norms of behaviour are put forward as typical of certain subcultures: gay men, for example, are typically represented as enjoying multiple casual sexual encounters, always involving anal penetration; heterosexual men are positioned as experiencing uncontrollable sexual urges, constantly frustrated by their female partners in their attempts to have sex as often as possible. Such stereotypes of behaviour linked to subgroups work to constrain subjectivity within defined boundaries, to pose conditions of normality, not accounting for wide variability both between individuals and within individuals. Hence, those men who may not necessarily be very often interested in sex, come to view themselves as aberrant, needing therapy or medical treatment. Or individuals who sometimes experience intense sexual desire for men, while at other times experiencing similar attraction to women, may perceive themselves as worryingly unpredictable, lacking a 'whole', coherent and definable sexual identity. The members of western societies, particularly those trained in the quasi-sciences of medicine and epidemiology, have been acculturated to distrust and feel uncomfortable about such ambiguities.

Risk as moral danger

Risk, in contemporary societies, has come to replace the old-fashioned (and in modern secular societies, now largely discredited) notion of sin, as a term which 'runs across the gamut of social life to moralize and politicize dangers' (Douglas, 1990: 4). Although risk is a much more 'sanitized' concept, it signifies the same meanings as sin, for 'the neutral vocabulary of risk is all we have for making a bridge between the known facts of existence and the construction of a moral community' (1990: 5). Douglas believes that 'being at risk' is the reciprocal of sinning, for the emphasis is placed upon the danger of external forces upon the individual, rather than the dangers afforded the community by the individual. She argues that the modern concept of risk, like that of taboo, has a 'forensic' property, for it works backwards in explaining ill-fortune, as well as forwards in predicting future retribution: 'To be "at risk" is equivalent to being sinned against, being vulnerable to the events caused by others, whereas being "in sin" means being the cause of harm' (1990: 7).

Douglas' analysis of the concept of risk is closely tied to the term as it is used in politics, especially with reference to the risks placed by environmental hazards upon individuals who have little personal power to deal with them. However her distinction, while enlightening, is accurate only when applied to risk which is believed to be *externally* imposed. The theory is less apt when viewed in the light of health risks which are considered to be the responsibility of the individual to control. So too, Beck's (1992) reflections on the 'risk society' refer mainly to externally imposed risks, those generated by industry such as pollution and toxins. Many of his arguments are not quite so relevant in the context of the second source of risk: internally imposed risk. Public health and health promotional discourses have introduced a new moral meaning around risk. Just as a moral distinction is drawn between 'those at risk' and 'those posing a risk', these institutions routinely draw a distinction between the harm caused by external causes out of the individual's control and that caused by oneself. Lifestyle risk discourse overturns the notion that health hazards in contemporary society are out of the individual's control. On the contrary, the dominant theme of lifestyle risk discourse is the responsibility of individuals to avoid health risks for the sake of their own health as well as the greater good of society.

Risk discourse in public health focuses on the biography of individuals, the trajectory of their movements within and between social spaces. It is part of the 'pathologizing' of life, the obsession with making every part of one's life 'healthy', the assumption that one's life is not healthy to begin with, that there is a lack (Greco, 1993). According to this discourse, if people choose to ignore health risks they are placing themselves in danger of illness, disability and disease, which removes them from a useful role in society and incurs costs upon the public purse. Should individuals directly expose others to harm; for example by smoking in a public place, driving while drunk or spreading an infectious disease, there is even greater potential for placing the community at risk. When risk is believed to be internally imposed because of lack of will-power, moral weakness or laziness on the part of the individual, the symbolic relationship of sin and risk is reversed. Those who are deemed 'at risk' become the sinners, not the sinned against, because of their apparent voluntary courting of risk. They are described as 'risk takers', who insist on ignoring their categorization into the 'high risk' group. Such people are represented as irrational, self-deluding and irresponsible if they challenge health risk assessments. Failure adequately to control risk through strength of will has become a form of irrationality, or evidence of the inability to master the self. Disease has become linked to the state of one's moral qualities rather than the individual's constitution (Greco, 1993: 359–60). For example, people who are deemed likely candidates for heart disease are viewed as overweight, lazy, smokers, self-indulgent, or conversely workaholics, worriers, people under stress: all are commonly described as bringing the disease on themselves and even 'earning it' (Davison et al., 1991: 10–13).

In the case of pregnant women, the woman's choice to engage in behaviours such as smoking and the consumption of alcohol, or even her use of prenatal health services, has become directly associated with the health of another: the foetus *in utero*. The pregnant woman is constructed as the 'container' for the foetus, charged with the responsibility of monitoring her own activities for its sake to the exclusion of her own needs. The rights of the foetus thus are seen to take precedence over the rights of the mother. Under this discourse, any defect or problem in the child may be located as the mother's responsibility, and the woman's body is constructed as a potentially 'hostile' environment for the foetus. Women have been described as 'unnatural' and 'criminals' for allegedly endangering the health of their offspring by engaging in 'at risk' behaviours (Petchesky, 1987; Tsing, 1990). The ideology of motherhood is central to this brand of risk discourse, in which it is expected that women should be self-sacrificing and obsessive about preserving the health of their children. Recently the responsibility of women for guarding the health of their offspring has been extended to that of their *grandchildren*. A British study reported in the *Sydney Morning Herald* in February 1994 argued that the non-smoking daughters of women who smoked during their pregnancies were more likely to miscarry their foetus than were the non-smoking daughters of non-smoking mothers. According to the study's director, the development of the daughters' reproductive organs was 'disturbed' in the womb by the effects of cigarettes on their mothers (Larriera, 1994).

People's fears about risks can be regarded as ways of maintaining social solidarity rather than as simply reflecting 'objective' health or environmental concerns: 'definitions of risk are an expression of the tensions inherent in given social and cultural contexts' (Nelkin, 1989: 96). As Hacking (1990: 3) notes, the idea of statistical regularities has its roots in 'the notion that one can improve – control – a deviant subpopulation by enumeration and classification'. Individuals are commonly categorized into risk groups based on social factors such as their ethnicity, race, social class or sexual identity, regardless of their personal behaviours or state of health. This results in 'a stratification of "goodness" ', especially in studies linking social class with patterns of ill-health and behaviours such as smoking (Figlio, 1989: 87–8). Definitions of risk serve to identify Self and Other, to apportion blame upon stigmatized minorities, or as a political weapon. Figlio (1989: 88) gives as an historical example the identification of chlorosis, or the 'green sickness', a disease related to anaemia commonly diagnosed in young European women in the nineteenth century. He suggests that the epidemiology of chlorosis was used as evidence that young women from the working class and the aristocracy indulged in bad habits such as idleness. The disease was thus 'in' the social groups differentiated from an upwardly mobile middle class seeking to distance itself from both the working class and the aristocracy.

Handwerker (1994) provides a contemporary example of the categorizing of pregnant women in an American clinic as being at 'high risk', 'medium risk' or 'low risk' of experiencing an adverse outcome of their pregnancy based solely on race and ethnicity. She observed that Asian, Caucasian and Hispanic patients were frequently labelled as 'low risk', while African-American patients were more frequently categorized as 'high risk', regardless of other factors such as diet and the pregnant woman's health status. Another contemporary example is the case of HIV/AIDS, where those individuals initially defined as 'at high risk' by epidemiologists have been subject to opprobrium because of the causal factors associated with the spread of HIV believed to be purely voluntary: male-to-male anal intercourse, multiple sexual partners and injecting drug use. Yet it was only because epidemiologists noted that most individuals in the United States becoming ill with AIDS-related conditions (although not in other areas such as sub-Saharan Africa) identified themselves as homosexual that the syndrome became known as a 'gay plague' and a sexually transmitted disease, even though HIV is also spread by routes other than sexual contact (for example, blood transfusions, needle-prick injuries, from mother to foetus *in utero* and injecting drug use). Indeed, the condition was first dubbed 'GRID', an acronym for Gay-Related Immunodeficiency Syndrome, by American researchers, who chose to ignore the other, non-gay-related characteristics of the condition in their choice of name.

It is clear that risk discourse provides a powerful rationale, cloaked in the 'neutral' language and practice of public health and health promotion, to cast blame upon stigmatized minority groups for their state of health. Figlio draws on psychoanalytic theory to suggest that 'the discovery of discrete pathology in a distinct group of patients externalizes – in an attempt to master – primitive terrors for a society, and that this externalization is facilitated by subdivision of a population into actuarially based risk groups' (1989: 90). He argues that the fragmentation of society in health-risk groups achieves a sense of 'healthiness' by the projection of anxieties about the body onto these marginalized groups (1989: 94; see also, Frankenberg, 1992; Crawford, 1994). Just as clinical medicine locates disease in certain parts of the body, which are then targeted for punitive action, public health identifies disease in specific social groups. Both strategies externalize and de-centralize the threat of disease from the Self. The central strategy then, to deal with health risks, is externalization; either the externalization of the threat itself, or that of the individual or group deemed to be most susceptible to it. The rhetoric of risk therefore serves different political functions, depending on how personally controllable the danger is perceived as being. Douglas (1986: 59) has pointed out that 'blaming the victim is a strategy that works in one kind of context, and blaming the outside enemy, a strategy that works in another'. Both types of attributions of risk serve to maintain the cohesiveness of a society; the first in protecting internal social control, and the second in bolstering loyalty.

The diagnostic test and the danger within

The current popularity of testing and screening procedures to diagnose disease in its early stages is a modernist response to the threat of disease and death, especially that which lurks invisibly in the body. The ill or diseased body often no longer announces its condition in luridly visible ways: pathology has become reduced to the invisible workings of cells, lymphocytes, bacteria and viruses. To detect this silent illness, a diagnostic test is put forward as the solution. Concordant with the ideology of rationality which permeates biomedical discourses and practices, it is believed important to have 'knowledge' of the presence of a hidden illness within rather than remain ignorant, for such knowledge is viewed as allowing medical science the opportunity to step in (Herzlich and Pierret, 1987: 94; Nelkin and Tancredi, 1989). The discourse of diagnostic testing and screening represents these procedures as 'scientific' and objective, value-free determinations of a reality uncontaminated by social processes: 'The test is seen as an isolated event in which objective *technical* data rationally persuades patients of their normality thus *determining* the benefit, reassurance' (Daly, 1989: 100, emphasis in the original).

However a diagnosis based on a medical test is not a purely objective, technical event, but relies upon the social context of both doctor and patient, and may or may not be beneficial for the patient. Human error is also a factor which is ignored: in some diagnostic tests, the margin for human error is rather large, beginning from when the doctor or other health professional takes the sample of tissue/urine/blood or an X-ray. Test results are then constructed by laboratory technicians, who must carry out the test and, more importantly, *interpret* the result using subjective criteria often based on a continuum, such as colour change, shape of cells, degree of 'abnormality' and so forth. The possibility of receiving a false positive or false negative result, therefore, is quite high for some diagnostic tests, but this caveat is rarely conveyed to those undergoing the procedure (Edwards and Hall, 1992: 267). When the potential for false results is revealed to members of the public, they often react with anger and cynicism, having been assured that the process of undergoing the test would protect them from harm. One example is the controversy initiated in the Australian news media in late 1992 concerning the efficacy of Pap smear tests (used to detect the early stages of cervical cancer). News media reports drew attention to the advertising of the New South Wales Cancer Council, which had distributed posters of smiling women saying, 'Cancer of the cervix. It can't happen to me. I have a regular Pap test', suggesting that regular participation in the testing programme would ensure that women would never fall victim to the disease. The media reported several case studies of women who had undertaken regular Pap tests which gave negative results, but yet were later diagnosed with cervical cancer, some of whom had subsequently died. These stories provoked such front-page headlines as 'Revealed: Pap smears give the all-clear to many with cancer' (*Sydney Morning Herald*, 19 September 1992).

The experience of undergoing a diagnostic screening test is primarily an emotive one. Health promotion campaigns, in their efforts to persuade as many members of the target group as possible to attend for testing, attempt psychological manipulation by appealing to people's emotions, fears, anxieties and guilt feelings. They often focus upon the central notion of risk around which dramatic imagery of doom, death and fear are constructed (as will be shown in Chapter 4, anti-smoking and AIDS education campaigns have often adopted this approach). Anxiety about the disease is deliberately engendered by the inducements used to persuade individuals to attend such programmes, where previously none may have existed. Symptomless people are forced to consider the possibility of harbouring a serious disease. For example, in the attempt to recruit women for breast cancer screening programmes, health promotion literature tends to make the misleading suggestion that 'no woman needs to die of breast cancer if she reads and heeds the leaflets of the cancer societies and has her breasts examined regularly' (Skrabanek, 1985: 316). The poster used to promote Pap smears discussed earlier used a similar strategy. Such exhortations often imply that not to do so is to let both the woman herself (that is, her body), as well as society, down. It is the woman's responsibility to attend for screening, and to attend regularly, or otherwise be held responsible for allowing the unchecked spread of cancer in her body. Women are invited to participate in breast cancer screening programmes without being given adequate information about the uncertainties and risks involved, and without being informed that their participation is required for further testing of the hypothesis that mammography works (Skrabanek, 1989: 428). Skrabanek (1985: 316) points out after an extensive review of the literature that the medical evidence is overwhelming that most forms of breast cancer are incurable, and that early detection therefore only adds years of anxiety and fear (see also, Roberts, 1989; Skrabanek, 1989). Healthy women are exhorted to attend mammographic screening programmes or to conduct breast self examination, only to be faced with a diagnosis which changes their lives but does not necessarily ameliorate their state of health.

Such emotional manipulation has also been taken up by commercial services attempting to attract customers. In Australia, a print media advertisement for a medical insurance fund advertises its mammographic screening service by asserting that: 'For many women early detection can mean a complete cure. Early detection is your best protection from the consequences of breast cancer. It can save your life, often without the need for a mastectomy.' The bright assurances of the value of mammographic screening in such advertising does not reveal the medical uncertainties around the efficacy of mammographic screening and subsequent treatment of breast lesions referred to above. In the United States, medical services are marketed to healthy women (who would otherwise have no need for medical services) using a language and style that mimic that of the women's health movement by emphasizing the demystification of medical technology and the right of all women to have access to health care services and to be actively involved. Thus the discourse of prevention, although positioned by women's health groups as a way of reducing women's dependence upon medical services, is often cynically used as a marketing device to attract female clients to such services as mammography screening, stress management courses, bone density screening for osteoporosis and hormone replacement therapy, most of which involve participation in expensive medical services rather than the prevention of ill-health (Whatley and Worcester, 1989: 200).

While screening is often promoted as a means of providing reassurance for individuals, this is not necessarily the case. Screening for any disease invariably engenders psychological costs among those screened in terms of the generation of high anxiety levels (Marteau, 1990: 26). Participants are told that the procedure is 'low risk', but they are not told of the high risk of psychological distress (Fentiman, 1988: 1042). In the clinical context, a false negative is more serious than a false positive result, for an individual who has been reassured that they have no signs of disease may be lost to the health system at a critical point, while false positive results can be rectified through follow-up tests. However, for the individual involved, a false positive result has potentially damaging psychological costs (Nelkin and Tancredi, 1989: 46–7). For some participants, receiving an invitation to be screened is enough to induce anxiety. Some participants may be more anxious after screening than before, even if they have received a normal test result. For those whose test is uncertain and requires further investigation, distress is an understandable reaction, and anxieties 'may remain for months or even years after a false positive result' (Marteau, 1990: 26). These observations of stress and anxiety in symptomless patients who are encouraged to attend screening raise serious doubts concerning the desirability of such programmes.

Daly, for example, examined the use of an echocardiology (cardiac ultrasound) test given to patients to 'reassure' them that their hearts were normal. She notes that echocardiology does not resolve uncertainty, for it requires 'interpretation of a complex moving image according to sometimes uncertain professional criteria' (1989: 104). Clinical diagnosis can contradict the test result; it is up to the cardiologist to decide what credence should be placed on the test. The cardiologist's decision may be coloured, consciously or subconsciously, by a number of factors, including his or her dependence upon insurance referrals and the training he or she has received in interpreting test results (1989: 109). Thus, while patients subscribe to the notion that technological investigation of symptoms provides an objective diagnosis, the medical discourse obscures the social forces shaping the test result. For example, when patients have cardiac symptoms, the result of the test is used as a placebo to reassure them that there is nothing wrong, obscuring the lack of skill in directly diagnosing or treating cardiac symptoms with no clear organic cause (1989: 114). Unfortunately, rather than being reassured, many patients are left with considerably more doubts about their hearts as a direct result of having the test done.

Prenatal screening tests have become extremely popular as a means of alleviating prospective parents' fears about the normality of the foetus, and as such have largely been accepted as accurate and harmless. The routinization and wide acceptance of prenatal screening methods such as amniocentesis and ultrasound, however, have not taken into full account the relative risks and benefits of the techniques. For example, there is an almost 1 per cent risk of spontaneous abortion following an amniocentesis test, compared with a 2 per cent chance that there will be a genetic abnormality (Rapp, 1988). Such techniques serve to individualize the reasons for chromosomal abnormalities, locating them on the individual or couple and ignoring the wider social reasons that may have caused genetic changes, such as exposure to environmental tetragens (Hubbard, 1984). There is also a risk of irradiation of the foetus using ultrasound, the effects of which have not yet been fully studied because of its popularity. There is no evidence that routine ultrasound screening is beneficial to the health of infants, while some studies have suggested that there may be possible harmful effects such as the restriction of growth after multiple ultrasounds (Rowland, 1992: 69–70; Saul, 1994). Furthermore, having the procedure is not necessarily reassuring for potential parents: there have been several occasions in which ultrasound screening has provided false positive results, so that women have been told that the foetus is dead, or has a malformation, when in fact there has been no such problem. The implications of such results for mental anguish in pregnant women and their partners are obvious (Saul, 1994: 14). Such screening procedures also serve to construct the mother–foetal relationship in certain ways, representing the foetus as separate from the mother, and placing pressure on the mother to undertake as many medical procedures as possible to ensure the health of the foetus.

One British study (French et al., 1982: 619) found that both attenders and non-attenders of a breast screening programme were anxious about the screening examination. A high percentage of non-attenders said that they felt that 'one should not go looking for trouble' and that they were afraid of cancer being found. A study of Scottish women (Maclean et al., 1984) found that the invitation to attend screening provoked worries on the part of the women they interviewed. Deep fear and concern about possible breast cancer were voiced by almost 40 per cent of their sample. The authors report that for their sample 'the entire philosophy of screening was foreign and they could see no point in searching for hidden, invisible ills within their bodies' (1984: 281). As these findings suggest, there is a difference between medical and lay definitions of the experience of a medical test such as a mammogram, ultrasound, amniocentesis or Pap smear. Medical and public health discourse argue that people benefit from having the peace of mind that comes from knowing that 'all is well', and adopt the rhetoric of evangelism to encourage people to 'come forward' to be 'saved' (Posner, 1991: 172), yet people attend for screening in the hope that there will be no sign of disease.

When there is an abnormal finding, the result is a psychological shock as the individual changes identity from a well person to a person harbouring disease. In two studies of British women undergoing screening for cervical cancer (Posner and Vessey, 1988; Quilliam, 1990), it was found that if there is occasion for further diagnostic procedures, waiting for and undergoing colposcopy (a surgical procedure to aid diagnosis of cervical cancer) can entail several months of agonized waiting for the woman and her family before she is told whether or not she really does have the disease. During this time, the women interviewed experienced a variety of emotions and thought processes including self-blame, sexual guilt, feeling dirty, creating links with past sexual traumas such as rape or abortion, fears of infertility, fear of death, dependency on health professionals and guilt about emotions. The fear of cancer, for many women, was debilitating: women expressed a feeling of defilement, alienation and loss of control of their own bodies, and were anxious waiting for their treatment. These feelings are created by the cultural meanings of cervical cancer, produced partly from health education messages, surrounding the sexually transmitted nature of the human papilloma virus which, it is currently believed, is associated with cervical cancer. Added to this medical definition of the cause of cervical cancer is the fact that the cancer occurs at the site of female reproduction and sexual activity, a bodily organ considered dangerous, unclean and mysterious. The interviewed women described cervical cancer in extremely negative terms. For example, one woman spoke of a 'vision of a dirty, horrible festering growth festering inside you', while another described the disease as 'a black fungus, creeping, mouldy' (Posner and Vessey, 1988: 56). The lack of clarity surrounding diagnosis of a pre-cancerous condition of the cervix is confusing and distressful for women. There are no certain explanations for the causes of a positive smear, so women cannot come to terms with why it happened to them. Furthermore, the alleged link with sexual activity may create doubt about their partner's fidelity, or incur hostility on the part of their partner.

These issues are also highly relevant to HIV antibody testing. The current irrational discrimination, fear and prejudice levelled against people with HIV/AIDS is a prime example of the way in which being 'at risk' becomes the equivalent of sinning. Research undertaken by McCombie (1986) illustrates the moral meanings around risk assessment and HIV antibody testing. She studied the counselling given by health workers to individuals deemed either 'high risk' or 'low risk' after an HIV test had been performed. McCombie noticed that 'high risk' individuals, whether HIV positive or negative, were treated differently from 'low risk' individuals: 'the high risk person is chastized, admonished and warned, while the low risk person is consoled and reassured' (1986: 455). She evaluated this behaviour in the context of taboo violation, pollution and punishment for sin. 'High risk' individuals were being punished for their deviant behaviour and were held responsible for their own behaviour if positive. By contrast, individuals deemed at low risk were looked upon more as innocent victims. The blood test itself was a ritual, acting as an anxiety-reducing measure for those who were concerned that the virus was getting out of control as well as implicitly acting as a tool for detecting social deviance.

Goldstein (1989: 89) views the process of having an HIV antibody test as an act 'of enormous courage', and asserts that in taking the test, people 'pass through a psychic rite that has less to do with fear of death than with the consequences of a positive result: guilt over the past, rage at the present, fear of the future. That fear must include not only the disease but disclosure – and the range of rejections that might ensue.' The experience of being identified as HIV positive can be personally destructive and almost inevitably emotionally harrowing (Grimshaw, 1987). Individuals who test positive will probably have to struggle with the imminent threat of death for the rest of their lives (notwithstanding the current controversy over the thesis that HIV is the cause of AIDS, discussed earlier in this chapter). Furthermore, there is a strong stigma associated with seropositivity and many members of the population are less sympathetic towards people living with HIV/AIDS than they are towards people with other conditions or illnesses. People living with HIV/AIDS are open to discrimination in the workforce, health care setting and other areas of life. For women who are pregnant or planning pregnancy there are associated anxieties, including the likelihood of transferring infection to the infant and the possibility of being abandoned by the father of the child should seropositivity be identified (Almond and Ulanowsky, 1990).

There has been very little research conducted into the reasons why people decide to participate in medical tests such as the HIV antibody test which throws light on the symbolic use of testing. In a study carried out by myself and colleagues (Lupton et al., 1995; Lupton et al., in press), people living in Sydney who had had at least one HIV antibody test were interviewed concerning their reasons for having a test and their experiences of the testing procedure. It was found that although the majority of the respondents had not engaged in the highest risk activities for contracting HIV, according to epidemiological orthodoxies current at the time (for example unprotected anal sex or sharing needles to inject drugs), many were using the test as a way of protecting their body boundaries from invasion and re-establishing subjectivity and feelings of self-containment after having sexual encounters. As one of the participants (a 26-year-old male) put it: 'I think if you're going to be sticking parts of your body into someone else or letting someone stick parts of their body into you, then you've got every right to make sure that the bits they stick in aren't going to leave something when they're gone.' For some interviewees, the test represented a disciplinary procedure, in which participants punished themselves for their lack of control over their bodies. The test was also used to punish others (one's unfaithful sexual partners) when the revelation of their infidelity came to light, or as a way of establishing purity, before launching into another relationship. People spoke of the need to 'clean the slate' at the end of a relationship and justified it in terms of their responsibility to protect themselves or their prospective partners from any diseases that may have been transmitted by the previous partner. They explained that having the test to confirm their HIV status at the end of a relationship was the last phase in the closing process that accompanies many relationships and, subsequently, heralded a new beginning for them. For many participants, offering to take the test was a way of demonstrating their sense of responsibility and commitment to their partner. Others, particularly men, had the test only because they were under duress from their partner, or wanted to dispense with condom use, while some people seemed to see the HIV test as part of a general health care maintenance programme, in which one had a regular test along with screens such as Pap smears or cholesterol tests. The assumption was that a positive result, indicating the presence of a condition or disease, was very unlikely. For many of the participants, therefore, the HIV antibody test was symbolically acting as a preventive rather than a diagnostic measure.

As these findings suggest, the discourses and meanings surrounding the experience of taking a diagnostic test may be very different for participants compared with the 'official' interpretation of the process. Those individuals whose anxiety is aroused by having a test will not always be reassured by the result, and may find the experience degrading and frightening, placing them in a liminal state where they are neither 'ill' nor 'well'. Others may seek testing for reasons other than wanting to discern the presence of disease. Diagnostic tests may be used symbolically as almost magical rituals, conceptualized as protecting individuals from the disease or acting as a purifying rite. Alternatively, they may be used for such purposes as proving commitment to a relationship.

Genetic screening: the new eugenics?

The newest means of testing for incipient disease is that using genetic screening to detect the presence or absence of a specific gene which it is believed influences the bodily expression of a disease or condition. Interest in genetic screening has intensified since the recently established Human Genome Project was initiated. The project is devoted towards mapping all the 100,000-odd genes that comprise human DNA. As more genes are identified from sequences of human DNA, the 'markers' or specific gene sequences, of the predisposition to mental illness, hyperactivity, alcoholism, diabetes, some forms of cancer and so on will be identified and used for diagnostic purposes. Since the project began, more and more behaviours have been mooted as being 'caused' by an individual's genetic makeup, even such seemingly solely socially determined behaviours as voting choice and social success.

The efforts to locate such genes have been greeted with much fanfare by the news media. The positive discourses around gene mapping hint of the promise of a world in which human suffering may be cleanly prevented through biotechnology (Lippman, 1992: 1469–70). For example, when a gene associated with the disabling condition Huntington's chorea was recently identified, an article published in the *New York Times* (24 March 1993) was headlined 'Team pinpoints genetic cause of Huntington's – 10-

year quest produces key to brain disease'. The article went on to claim
that: 'After 10 backbreaking years in a research purgatory of false leads,
failed experiments and long stretches of mordant despair, an international
team of scientists says it has discovered the most coveted treasure in
molecular biology, the gene behind Huntington's disease.' The *Wall Street
Journal*'s headline published the same day read, 'Huntington's disease
gene is found at last' and its lead sentence asserted that: 'The rapidly
advancing Human Genome Project, now identifying genes at the rate of
almost one a day, scored a long-sought victory.' These articles suggested
that the discovery of the gene would lead ultimately to a means of
treatment for Huntington's chorea. They positively represented biological
scientists as detectives, patiently solving a mystery and identifying the
'culprit' using forensic evidence, as winners in a hunt for 'treasure' finally
finding the 'key' to the treasure-chest, and also as victors in the 'battle'
against disease. The clear implication is that the painstaking work of the
scientists is rewarding humanity by moving one step closer to the
eradication of disabling disease.

Despite the largely positive representation of the futuristic possibilities
of genetic screening in the scientific and medical literature and the news
media, there are serious ethical and moral issues that require detailed
consideration. Critics have pointed out that for the individual who
undergoes a genetic test and is found to have the marker for the disease,
the knowledge of a potentially disabling or fatal illness can be debilitating
psychologically, and have implications for future employment (Nelkin and
Tancredi, 1989; Conrad and Walsh, 1992). In the discourse of genetic
screening, genes have become viewed as 'quasi-pathogens' and those who
carry the genes labelled as 'diseased', even if they do not physically express
the genes (Yoxen, 1982: 147–9). Differences between people have become
tied to their DNA codes, identifying some as 'normal' and others as
'abnormal' even though there is no outward sign of difference (Lippman,
1992: 1470). Indeed, the identification of genes leading to certain conditions has reshaped concepts of being 'at risk', fitting the wider epidemiological risk discourse that argues that individuals should be apprised of
their potential to develop illness so that they may take preventative steps
against the illness. Thus, according to the discourse of genetic screening, if
an individual is found to carry the gene that is believed to predispose
people towards a certain type of cancer, or to obesity or alcoholism, that
individual is given forewarning so he or she may take responsibility for his
or her health (Lippman, 1992: 1472). The marker for a genetic condition
has come to be reified as the disease; if you have the marker, you have the
disease. However, what tends to be ignored in the discourse of genetic
screening, particularly as it is portrayed in the news media, is that most
conditions require more than one gene to be expressed in bodily structures
and social or environmental factors can influence the degree to which traits
are biologically expressed (Nelkin and Tancredi, 1989: 43; Lippman, 1992:
1471; Billings et al., 1992). Thus, even if a gene for a trait is found to be

present in an individual's genotype, that trait may not necessarily show itself in the body.

Genetic disease is an issue that affects people at the most intimate levels of their lives: marriage, sexuality, parenthood (Yoxen, 1982: 154). The potential for racism and other forms of discrimination based on the 'objective', 'scientific' determination of an individual's genotype is obvious. Yoxen (1982: 149) gives the example of carriers of the gene of sickle-cell anaemia, who are almost invariably of African descent. Even though carriers of the sickle-cell anaemia gene may not have the condition themselves, and there is only a 25 per cent chance that their children will develop the disease, the carriers are classified as 'genetically diseased' and are frequently denied health insurance or employment (Draper, 1992: s16). In countries such as India and China where male children are more valued than female because of the economic liability associated with daughters or because of 'one-child only' policies, genetic tests such as amniocentesis have been used for some years to identify the sex of foetuses. Those foetuses pronounced to be female have been aborted simply because of their sex (Levidow, 1987).

There are political implications when a diagnostic test that has been developed for use in the clinical context is then adopted in institutions such as schools, insurance companies, prisons and workplaces. Employment, health insurance and other opportunities may be denied individuals on the basis of genetic tests. As I noted earlier in this chapter, in the United States corporations have tended to view occupational health problems as the responsibility of the individual worker. They have already begun to use genetic tests to predict who may be susceptible to future illness caused by workplace conditions and have used this knowledge to develop policies to exclude such workers or to increase control over their private lives rather than institute safer working practices (Nelkin and Tancredi, 1989: 83; Conrad and Walsh, 1992; Draper, 1992). It has been claimed that children diagnosed with having the genetic condition fragile X syndrome (related to intellectual disorders) have subsequently been discriminated against at school and not provided with the same opportunities because of their diagnosis. In one case, an American insurance company that found a child in one family had been diagnosed with the syndrome responded by withdrawing insurance cover from the entire family (Webb, 1993). The advent of litigation concerning 'wrongful birth' in the United States, where physicians have been sued by parents of children born with a serious genetic disorder that could have been identified prior to birth, has meant that failure to employ all possible diagnostic technologies constitutes implication of breach of duty on the part of physicians, hence placing pressure on the health care system to use screening tests as often as pos-sible rather than proceeding with caution (Nelkin and Tancredi, 1989: 57).

Genetic screening has the potential to reshape conceptions of bodies and subjectivities. The discourse of genetic screening constitutes an image of the human body as a collection of 'codes', a machine-like system that may be tracked, mapped and measured, thrown up on a computer screen to be viewed and interpreted by 'experts' (Nelkin and Tancredi, 1989: 15). Once individuals are identified as bearing a genetic disease, they are susceptible to stigmatization requiring a reconceptualization of subjectivity in certain contexts (Parsons and Atkinson, 1992; Richards, 1993). Diagnostic tests can constrain people's choices by making it appear as if there is only one reasonable solution based on scientific evidence. While, for example, counselling for parents facing the birth of a child with a genetic disorder is usually based on the non-directive philosophy, allowing the parents to make up their own minds, 'most people faced with the prospect of a defective child have, in fact, little choice. For their options are constrained by economic possibilities, social pressures, and therapeutic alternatives' (Nelkin and Tancredi, 1989: 171). When people are being counselled as to the appropriateness of undergoing genetic screening, the primary discourse is that of statistics and risk, which is central to establishing whether an intervention is required. Rapp (1988: 148) notes of communication in a prenatal counselling clinic, 'it is an axiom of good counselling that a patient must be told her risks before she can decide to take or refuse the test'. However, health professionals' understandings of the logic of risk and those of members of the lay population may differ significantly. Individuals may respond to the abstract mathematical rhetoric with reasoning based on personal experience that counters the technical calculation of risk (1988: 149). For example, in their interviews with women in families with Duchenne muscular dystrophy (a muscle-wasting disorder that, like hae-mophilia, is physically manifested only in men but is carried by women), Parsons and Atkinson (1992) found that all the women had been given a figure of probability to represent their 'carrier risk' which they interpreted in different ways to make it meaningful to their everyday experience. Some assumed that their carrier risk denoted a certainty that their sons would have the disorder, translating the mathematical figure into a binary descriptive category that enabled them to make decisions about reproduc-tion, such as the statement 'we can only have daughters'. Such translation was important for the women to resolve the existential state of being 'at risk'.

Any publicizing of a possible genetic link to a disease tends to encourage people to seek testing as a means of dealing with the uncertainty of the threat of developing the disease. Such individuals are not necessarily interested in predictive testing for late-onset diseases, as they are well aware that the disease 'runs in the family', but want the chance to undergo a test for traces of the disease. For example, while the gene predisposing individuals to ovarian cancer has been located, it is believed that only a minority of ovarian cancer cases are due to heredity. However, in Britain, considerable numbers of anxious women believing such cancer to 'be in the family' have approached genetic clinics, not because they wish to establish their 'genetic risk', but because they want screening and the chance to have prophylactic surgery (Richards, 1993: 574). Conversely, although know-

ledge of an invisible disease lurking within the body is generally represented as positive in health promotional discourses, uncertainty may be the
preferred option for some. The testing experience for people wishing to
know if they will have late-onset genetic conditions (such as Huntington's
chorea) affects those who find they have a low risk of carrying the gene as
well as those who are found to be at 'high risk'. Regardless of the outcome
of the test, the findings may challenge strongly held beliefs that individuals
may have constructed around the likelihood of having the condition. While
evidence of a positive result may obviously cause depression and anxiety,
those who test negative may experience feelings of 'survivor guilt' or of
'not belonging' to their family (Richards, 1993: 571; Davison et al., 1994:
353).

The expanding dominance of genetic screening also has implications for
the ways in which risk assessments are undertaken and their results
understood. Instead of basing predictions of the likelihood of disease
occurring on population aggregates, genetic testing allows for the construction of a risk profile that is peculiar to the individual. Understandings of
risk are therefore rephrased, individualizing risk to a far greater extent.
Because popular understandings of the relationship between genetic
susceptibility and the expression of the condition tend to assume that one
invariably leads to the other, the identification of being 'at risk' through
genetic screening is conceptualized as possessing that disease, and the
condition of being 'at risk' becomes the basis for intervention (Davison
et al., 1994: 343-4). The necessity to seek other causes and treatments for
illness, particularly those located in the social or physical environment, is
alleviated by placing the genome at the centre of the model of disease
causation. The social problem becomes a problem located at the level of
the individual. For example, spina bifida is treated as an exclusively
'genetic' disease, even though it is found in very high concentrations in
areas with high levels of industrial pollution (Draper, 1992: s17). As
Lippman (1992: 1472) points out, '[b]efore adopting the message of genetic
stories as a guide to health, we might consider whether preventable deaths
in the US are more likely to be associated with guns or genes'.

As more and more conditions are linked to specific genes, there will be
raised questions concerning ways of 'treating' or 'preventing' the genetic
'disease' that deal with eugenic issues around the types of people that are
considered desirable to reproduce. The eugenic implications of discourses
around genetic screening are often quite overt. References to the 'pollution of the gene pool', 'genetically healthy societies' and 'optimal genetic
strategies' are frequently made in the medico-scientific literature discussing
genetic screening (Nelkin and Tancredi, 1989: 13). As Nelkin and Tancredi
argue, with the increasing focus on the genetic predisposition for disease,
'[w]e risk creating a biologic underclass' (1989: 176). The use of amniocentesis to determine the sex of foetuses so that females might be aborted,
discussed above, is a prime example of the construction of femaleness as a
genetic 'defect'. The recent identification of a gene that has been claimed

to predispose people to homosexuality, or the 'gay gene' as it has been dubbed in the news media, is a forewarner of the further eugenic purposes to which genetic screening may be put. The very fact that researchers have considered it important to identify such a gene demonstrates the extent to which homosexuality is considered deviant, a condition requiring correction. It assumes that once such a gene is identified, then action should be taken to prevent its expression so as to reduce the numbers of people identifying as homosexual. Homosexuality becomes a genetic disease (perhaps a basis for a decision to abort a foetus bearing this gene) and the complex socio-political reasons why people identify themselves as gay or lesbian are obscured under biological determinism. The technology of genetic screening, therefore, acts as a highly individualized strategy of normalization, in which previously invisible aspects of people's genetic makeup are singled out and constructed as problems and certain groups are identified as deviating from the norm and rendered subject to intervention on the part of the medical and allied health professions.

Concluding comments

As this chapter has shown, risk and diagnostic testing are highly inter-related and central normalizing strategies in public health and health promotion. Even as they gain increased credibility and popular support, there are ethical and political aspects in the use of risk and testing discourses in public health which hitherto have been little questioned from within or even outside public health. While, as Beck (1992: 155) points out, there is a contradictory logic in the role of science in risk society – science is simultaneously the cause, the medium of definition, and the source of solutions to risks – there is less overt contradiction in medicine or public health's role. While medicine and public health may serve to define and deal with health risks, they are rarely positioned as their cause. Hence, although it may often seem necessary to limit the expansion of science as it relates to industry, it is far more difficult to question the expansion of medicine and public health, which promise only to improve people's states of health and quality of life in better, more effective (if often more expensive) ways. Individuals and political movements rarely call for *less* medical care or public health intervention, but rather, for *more*, citing neglect if it is not available. While the side-effects of medical treatment and public health interventions occasionally create public disquiet and critique, these institutions are subjected to far less criticism than is science in general. When medicine *is* subjected to criticism, it is often the areas where medicine and scientific development blur that creates disquiet; for example, assisted conception technologies and genetic manipulation. Furthermore, medicine rarely speaks publicly about the risks it has generated. It is not usually the iatrogenic outcomes of medical treatments or surgery to which medical risk discourse is directed, but causes of ill-health from other agents. Medical and public health risk discourses could therefore be seen as in some ways far less reflexive than scientific risk discourse.

The role and symbolic status of modern medicine and public health, compared with modern science, also effects distinctions between the fields in risk society. The fields of medicine and public health are commonly viewed as more politically neutral and beneficent than science, and those working in medical and public health fields are considered more altruistic and mindful of health, for after all, that is the focus of their work. The endeavour of health risk communication sponsored by the state as part of its public health activities is therefore rarely questioned as a political practice which can serve to maintain the interests of the powerful. The judgements of medical and public health workers on health risks seem far more value-free than those articulated by professionals in science and industry, who have an obvious career or pecuniary stake in the assessment of risk and the public's acceptance of it. The latter are seen as trying to underplay risk in the face of increasing public concern, whereas the former are regarded as beneficently raising concern about risk among the public.

Yet, as this chapter has demonstrated, as with other major public health strategies and discourses, the rationalized logic of risk discourse is by no means neutral or disinterested. The discourses of risk and testing serve to cast certain individuals and groups as dangerous, either to themselves or others, based on apparently objective medical and epidemiological classifications derived from statistical principles. The categorization of which risks are deemed to be external and which internal influences the moral judgements made about blame and responsibility for placing health in jeopardy. Because of the seemingly rational and scientific nature of medical advice on self-imposed risk – that it is the individual's choice whether to eat too much or not, for example – there is no external vested interest to blame or to question their assessment of risk. To locate ill-health as a social rather than an individual responsibility does not remove blame or moral judgement, it simply shifts blame from stigmatized individuals to the marginalized groups of which they are a member, while at the same time serving to obscure the suffering of individuals, who become anonymous 'risks' or 'threats' to the commonweal. Risk, as the concept is used in public health, therefore may be regarded as having less to do with the nature of 'danger' than the ideological purposes to which concerns about risk may be put.

4

Communicating Health: the Mass Media and Advertising in Health Promotion

A key strategy of health promotion remains the mass media advertising campaign directed towards large groups. Such campaigns use the tenets of commercial advertising to promote awareness of health risks and encourage subsequent behavioural change. The underlying premise of these campaigns is the notion that health promoters are 'communicating health'; that is, conveying the 'facts' about health risks to a complacent population, and strongly advising that individuals deemed 'at risk' of a disease change their behaviour in ways prescribed by authoritative professionals. The mass media health communication campaign is thus conceptualized as a health education session writ large.

This chapter critically analyses the conceptualization and use of the mass media in health promotion, with a particular focus on the favoured strategies of advertising and social marketing. It contrasts the understanding of mass communication prevailing in health promotion with the more sophisticated insights offered by cultural theory. Several health promotional campaigns are analysed for the primary discourses they draw upon and strategies they use to 'market' good health. The chapter ends with a discussion of the political function of mass media campaigns.

Models of communication in health promotion

The original adoption of commercial advertising techniques by health promoters largely rested on the belief that advertising in the mass media is an effective means of propaganda, able to persuade audiences to take up a desired behaviour, whether it be the purchasing of a commodity or the abandonment of a practice believed to undermine the achievement and maintenance of good health. Media campaigns are directed at creating docile citizens, who accept the truths of public health authorities without question. Evident in much health promotional literature on the use of the mass media are frank statements on how best to command audience members' attention, how to frighten them into acceptance of the message or persuade them to give up behaviours they currently enjoy. The primary goal is that of manipulation, often based on emotional appeals. Health promotion texts are replete with assertions concerning the importance of adopting appropriate language and discourse strategies to achieve this goal, outlining ways to achieve more 'effective' health communication campaigns by carefully 'targeting' or 'segmenting' the audience, emphasizing 'positive' behaviour change and 'current rewards' and using commercial marketing strategies to attract audiences' attention (for example, Backer et al., 1992: 30–2).

Consonant with the broader psychological approach to communication most evident in American communication theory, this approach to the mass media is primarily influenced by the stimulus–response model of communication. Fiske (1990: 2) calls this model of communication the 'process' school, for it is interested in questions of efficiency and accuracy, and with determining the linear mechanistic processes by which meaning is purposively generated by the producer of a discrete message with the intention of affecting the minds of the receivers. Media are viewed as the 'senders' of messages and audience members their 'receivers'. As one health promotion researcher explains it: 'The communicator uses a series of signs or symbols which he or she encodes in a message. The recipient, once his or her attention is aroused, decodes the message and, if motivated, acts on the information received' (Macdonald, 1992: 182). This model tends to use such mechanistic terms as 'noise', 'channel', 'signal', 'exposure' and 'feedback' to describe the communication process. The use of the term 'health communication', which has been adopted in the United States to describe a field of endeavour directed towards disseminating information about health and illness to members of the public, also conveys this meaning of 'health' as a phenomenon that may be 'transmitted' through communicative processes as if it were a message. The assumption is that as long as the 'message' is sent and successfully 'received' often enough, then the state of 'health' will be accomplished.

The process school became dominant in communication studies following the Second World War, when concerns were raised about the role of propaganda and the impact of the mass media in shaping people's beliefs and behaviours. The 'pessimistic mass society' thesis developed by members of the European Frankfurt School argued that individuals were vulnerable to manipulation by mass media propaganda which served to suppress political dissent. Some American writers adopted this perspective well into the 1960s, representing advertising as a means of 'brain-washing' populations into 'false needs' using subliminal as well as overt persuasive strategies (see, for example, Packard's *The Hidden Persuaders*, published in 1957). Individuals were viewed as gullible 'cultural dupes', with children, women and the less educated believed to be even more susceptible than other groups to the seductive influence of the mass media (Nava, 1992: 190). This approach is still evident in the health promotion literature, particularly in discussions of the effects of tobacco or alcohol advertising on children (for example, Ritchie, 1988). Other communication researchers took up this interest in the potential of the media for mass persuasion, but with a greater focus on the 'uses' made by audience members of media messages and their degree of 'openness' to the message they received (Jankowski and Wester, 1991: 49–50; Morley, 1992: 45–7).

Research became focused on controlled, laboratory-type experiments, directed towards measuring mental states, the gratification of needs and the phenomena of persuasion, attitude change, behaviour modification and conditioning. Jensen (1991: 137) has referred to such research as being 'functionalist in theory, quantitativist in methodology, and consensualist in politics'. It is this approach, emerging in the 1960s, which has dominated health education and promotion concepts of communication and which remains predominant today, with little modification.

While contemporary health promotional literature discussing the use of the mass media is frequently careful to emphasize that the media should not be considered as 'brainwashers', able to effect immediate change in their audiences, there remains a great deal of emphasis placed on the importance of using the media to further the goals of health promotion:

> Communication through the mass media is a fundamental component of many health promotion strategies designed to change health risk behaviours . . . The mass media can influence both personal behaviour and the community values that provide the environmental and individual supports so necessary to maintain difficult changes in behaviour. (Arkin, 1990: 219; see also, Atkin and Arkin, 1990; Flora and Wallack, 1990)

In much of the literature it is considered the role of the mass media campaign to 'establish a health problem as a priority concern' in the minds of members of the general public, to 'increase knowledge and change beliefs that impede the adoption of health-promoting attitudes and behaviour', 'motivate change by demonstrating the personal and social benefits of the desired behaviour', 'teach new behavioural skills', 'demonstrate how various barriers to behaviour change can be overcome', 'teach self-management techniques for sustaining change' and 'provide supports for maintaining change by stimulating interpersonal communication' leading ultimately to 'broad changes in perceived social norms' (DeJong and Winsten, 1990: 32). In their book *Designing Health Communication Campaigns: What Works?*, Backer et al. (1992: 3–4) define a mass media campaign as having four 'essential ingredients': it is 'purposive, and seeks to influence individuals . . . aimed at a large audience . . . has a more or less specifically defined time limit . . . [and] involves an organized set of communication activities'.

Despite evidence of a growing awareness in some of the health promotional literature of the complexity of the interaction between media products and their audiences, in many contemporary reports and articles media messages are typically portrayed as having a linear and measurable effect on audiences. Backer et al. (1992: 5), for example, describe a hierarchy of effect, ranging from audience exposure to a message as the lowest effect, moving to audience awareness of the message, the audience being informed by the message, being persuaded by the message, the audience expressing an intent to change behaviour, an actual change in behaviour in the audience, and lastly, maintenance of audience behaviour change. Studies into the effectiveness of health promotion campaigns commonly adopt the model of the clinical trials experiment of a new drug therapy, using a 'before and after' format. The campaign is viewed as the 'intervention' which may be 'evaluated' by measuring changes in beliefs, attitudes and behaviours occurring before the audience is 'exposed' to the intervention and afterwards. 'Exposure' is calculated by recording the number of people in the target audience who saw an advertisement, or who could remember the main message, or who liked the campaign, or requested more information or more ambitiously, who said they had changed their attitudes or behaviour because of the campaign. It is argued that 'it is possible for a campaign planner to know the exact number of people in each audience category that was exposed to a message on a particular day and time' (Solomon and Cardillo, 1985: 66).

An article published in an American communication research journal in 1994 on ways to prevent smoking in adolescents is telling in its use of language. The article reports the attempts of the authors to measure the influence of videos on more than 1,000 young adolescents in a mid-western American city, testing the videos' long-term 'effects' in terms of promoting 'resistance' to smoking (Pfau and van Bockern, 1994). Some students were shown the videos – referred to as 'an inoculation pre-treatment' – while the others, the 'control' group, received no such 'pre-treatment'. The goal of the researchers was to 'arrest attitude slippage'; that is, to preserve young adolescents' initial negative attitudes towards smoking so that they are not rendered 'vulnerable' to 'smoking onset' by virtue of a growing tolerance towards smoking (1994: 414). Such language conveys the image of adolescents as initially holding the 'correct' attitudes but liable, in spite of themselves and their 'true' attitudes, to cave in under pressure, easily weakened by others and therefore needing help to hold onto their 'true' attitudes: 'students were cautioned that, in spite of attitudes opposing smoking, as the result of peer pressure in the seventh grade, many of them would grow less certain about smoking, and some of them would change their minds and try smoking' (1994: 417). For these researchers, the solution to this is to 'inoculate' the adolescents with information, using threats and warnings to motivate the audience and strengthen their 'resistance' to taking up smoking (1994: 414). The resonance of such terms as 'inoculation', 'control group' and 'pre-treatment' with the language of medical trials to test the efficacy of drugs is evident in this article, as is the paternalistic approach taken. The researchers are positioning themselves as quasi-medical practitioners, working to save adolescents from themselves by 'injecting' them with the 'right' message so that they might develop an immunity to the temptation of smoking.

In such research, communication is thus represented as 'therapeutic', with better communication the basic 'prescription' to treat the pathogen of misunderstanding (Lievrouw, 1994: 96). This approach reduces health education via the mass media to a quasi-scientific formula, implying laboratory conditions in which as long as the formula is accurate and the intervention carefully carried out, then the desired outcome will eventuate.

For example, one article on the use of advertising for an anti-smoking campaign advocates the quantification of objectives so as best to plan the potential success of a campaign and redefine strategies: 'if the probability of reaching an individual is 50 per cent, and the probability of change is 50 per cent and the probability of maintaining the change is 50 per cent then one can readily see that out of 100 people, chances are that 12.5 per cent (.5x .5x .5) will change' (Solomon and Cardillo, 1985: 64). Any changes measured as statistically significant are then concluded to be due to the effectiveness of the media campaign in shaping attitudes and behaviour, while lack of demonstrated effectiveness is often attributed to such factors as not 'targeting' the audience well enough, not repeating the message often enough, wrong timing of the campaign, failure to involve influential people or 'gate-keepers', the goals set were not modest enough, the campaign entertaining enough, or it did not communicate enough incentives or motives for adopting the desired behaviour (see, for example, McGinnis, 1990; Backer et al., 1992: 30–2). Alternatively, the failure of a mass media health education campaign is often attributed not to the inappropriateness of the method of persuasion, but to insufficient expenditure upon the campaign materials. The solution often posited to deal with the failure of media campaigns is to design more sophisticated campaigns, taking more care in their planning and targeting and perhaps spending more resources.

There is therefore a slippage between education and indoctrination in the rhetoric of much health promotion and health communication; communication is far from being a two-way process. Once health communicators and promoters have discharged their responsibility in disseminating information and promoting awareness, the emphasis is upon the individual to act upon this knowledge to prevent illness. According to mainstream health promotion models of behaviour, if members of the target audience do not respond in the appropriate manner, they have adopted defence mechanisms or maladaptive coping responses, or they lack the required level of personal control and feelings of self efficacy, or they possess an 'addiction' to unhealthy behaviour (as outlined by Peterson and Stunkard, 1989, and Donovan, 1991). Members of the general public are often referred to as apathetic and ignorant in the literature, and as have-nots, illiterate, information poor, malfunctional, needful of persuasion to change their behaviour, resistant to change, obstinate, recalcitrant, chronically uninformed and 'hard to reach' (Freimuth and Mettger, 1990: 232). The very label 'hard to reach' implies the adoption of a one-way model of communication, implying that once the barriers to communication are broken down and 'noise' dispensed with, audiences will receive the message and subsequently change their ways.

Examples of this perspective abound in the health promotion and health communication literature. One Australian academic wrote in an article giving 'execution guidelines' for public health advertising that:

many [people] may actively avoid information that creates anxiety about their unhealthy behaviours. Hence it is often necessary, especially for some hard-to-reach target groups, to use an intrusive medium like television . . . One aim of these guidelines is to pre-empt the use of various defence mechanisms or maladaptive coping responses by individuals when they are confronted with evidence of ill-health or the negative consequences of a behaviour they enjoy or to which they are 'addicted'. (Donovan, 1991: 40)

In their discussion of mass communication and public health, American researchers Atkin and Arkin asserted that '[a] final barrier to be surmounted is *the ignorance and apathy of the general public*' (1990: 26, emphasis added). Although the authors give high priority to the application of 'theory' to the researching audience effects of media products, they see such theory as being social learning theory, the cognitive response model and the agenda-setting perspective (1990: 34), all of which are firmly rooted in the process model of communication. Likewise, when discussing the need for audience response research, Atkin and Arkin limit their suggestions to measuring 'effects' and 'outcome variables' such as the learning of 'useful' information and the formation of mental images of health-related concepts, objects and roles (1990: 37). Although most contemporary health communication and promotion literature is careful to emphasize the importance of taking into account the social and environmental factors influencing people's health-related attitudes and behaviour (such as ethnicity, gender, education level and socio-economic status), these are commonly represented as impediments or 'barriers' to successful transmission of the message, rendering certain social groups 'harder to reach' than others. The solution to these problems of communication is to uncover the beliefs and attitudes of such groups so as better to target them for more effective campaigns and to enhance 'receptivity' to the messages of campaigns (see, for example, Flay, 1987, and McGinnis, 1990). The focus thus stays firmly trained on using media campaigns to promote good health (albeit in conjunction with other strategies).

Social marketing has recently been adopted by some health promotion agencies as a somewhat more nuanced strategy for the mass dissemination of information about good health maintenance, and in some cases, changing attitudes. As the name suggests, the idea of social marketing centres around applying commercial marketing principles to social problems. The first assumption, then, is that marketing, as a persuasive strategy, 'works' in changing people's behaviour, and the second is that such a strategy is appropriate to apply to non-commercial social phenomena. In the discourse of social marketing, the language and orientation of the commercial economic world predominate. Based on the assumptions of marketing, which centre around the 'marketing mix' and the 'four Ps' (product, place, price and promotion), social marketing views information or 'correct' attitudes as a product to be marketed. Audiences are 'segmented' into discrete target groups for more effective persuasion

(Hastings and Haywood, 1991; Ling et al., 1992; Lefebvre, 1992). Under this model health becomes a commodity and members of the public 'consumers' who must be persuaded to acquire it at some cost to themselves, whether it be the giving up of smoking or salt or the loss of leisure time which is newly devoted to exercise. The advertising approach, as a central feature of commercial marketing, is privileged as a persuasive strategy for social marketing.

The 'consumer' is glossed in the discourse of social marketing as the individual who demands products or services. Social marketing exponents argue for a full understanding of the 'consumer', seeking knowledge of their 'needs, issues and unique situations' and keeping them in 'the centre of the programme' (Lefebvre, 1992: 62). It is asserted that 'the health promoter must understand and empathize with the perceptions, motivations, behaviour and above all, needs of the consumer in order to produce effective health communication' (Hastings and Haywood, 1991: 137). Social marketing, then, has been portrayed as a 'bottom up' rather than a 'top down' strategy in its interest in the consumer (Lefebvre, 1992: 62). It is also claimed that social marketing, like other forms of marketing, involves 'voluntary and mutually beneficial exchange' or a 'win-win situation'. The idea is to avoid 'coercion' for 'persuasion', by making the product appear desirable to the consumer (Hastings and Haywood, 1991; Lefebvre, 1992). However, while the emphasis of social marketing is overtly on understanding the consumer and fulfilling the consumer's needs, in reality it is directed towards attempting to create needs (or more commonly, anxieties) where they previously did not exist; the very antithesis of meeting consumer needs.

The 'consumer', as represented in the discourse of social marketing, is therefore a paradoxical figure. The discourse of meeting the consumer's needs constructs this individual as an actively choosing subject, employing the rational purchasing behaviour of *homo economicus* and highly aware of the 'buyer beware' approach to consumption. The rhetoric of marketing argues that 'the customer is always right'. Yet the approach of social marketing also constructs the consumer as malleable and amenable to persuasion, requiring the health-preserving advice of health promotion professionals: for example, the statement made in one health communication article: 'The notion, if it is good for you, you must want it, still lingers in the health field, but social marketers do not make such an assumption. In fact, marketers ask, "How can we *make* people want it?" ' (Ling et al., 1992: 355, emphasis added; see also, Lefebvre, 1992: 62). The customer, then, is not always right, but in fact is ignorant. As with other strategies of health promotion, the assumptions of the social marketers remain unchallenged; they seek knowledge of consumers better to influence or motivate them, not to ensure that the objectives of social marketing are considered by consumers as appropriate. Social marketing, therefore, is simply the old simplistic health promotion approach to persuasion dressed up in marketing jargon about products and consumers.

An alternative perspective to the mass media articulated in health promotion and health communication literature is that which sees the media not as the instruments of planned health promotion efforts, but as their enemy. The media are viewed as undermining attempts to disseminate 'healthy messages' by way of the entertainment and news media, who are seen as promoting the commercial interests of unhealthy products and broadcasting confusing stories on health and medical issues (Atkin and Arkin, 1990; Montgomery, 1990; Arkin, 1990). The media are criticized, for example, for allowing tobacco advertising, or depicting alcohol consumption as an accepted norm on television dramas. The news media are also often accused of inaccurately reporting health issues, of inciting unfounded panic and fear by making sensational statements, of distorting the 'facts' and of ignoring important details. One commentator has gone so far as to call the mass media 'agents of contagion' because of their allegedly influential role in presenting positive portrayals of unhealthy lifestyles and therefore 'transmitting' disease (Ling, 1989: 255). Here again, audiences are frequently represented as vulnerable to media manipulation (this time represented as non-beneficial), passively absorbing the 'viral' messages disseminated by the media, both intentional and unintentional, and thus becoming educated in the wrong way. To deal with this, the purposive use of television and other forms of popular mass media by health advocates and lobby groups, for example, by lobbying television soap opera producers to include storylines that promote healthy lifestyles and attitudes, has begun to be explored as a means for disseminating the 'correct' information.

Health promotional literature thus has a 'love/hate' relationship with the mass media. The mass media are viewed as highly influential, capable of subtly manipulating audiences into taking up or continuing unhealthy behaviours. Yet the manipulative use of the media to do so for the sake of promoting the public's health is championed. Advertising is represented both as a social good (if it supports the current claims of health promotion) in encouraging socially positive behaviour, but also as a potential source of harmful manipulation, creating false needs (if it undermines health promotion efforts). The media are both denounced as channels for propaganda, and praised for their potential to persuade people on a mass scale. It is argued on the one hand that 'people need to be informed consumers of health claims, conflicting news reports, and entertainment' so that they may be critical of media representations; on the other, health promoters are urged to 'seek media co-operation at all levels' so as to persuade the producers of media products to incorporate a health message into their products in the interests of better influencing audiences (Arkin, 1990: 222). Such health promotional activities are politically neutralized, narrowly confined to ensuring that the preferred message appears in the mass media in competition with commercially oriented marketing strategies, patronizing audiences and doing little actually to challenge public policy or the vested interests that shape media products.

These approaches to using the mass media for health promotion concerns are particularly evident in the American and Australian health promotion and health communication literature. Some British practitioners and researchers have been somewhat more open to the adoption of socio-cultural theory and qualitative research and more critical of models of communication drawn from social psychology, largely owing to the influence of the British school of cultural studies, which has only recently been taken up as a viable perspective in American communication studies. However, the traditional process models of communication continue to dominate much of British health promotion activity (see, for example, Macdonald's chapter on communication theory in health promotion, 1992).

The subject in health promotion campaigns

In the quest for publicizing the ill-effects of some behaviours on individuals' health, certain groups have been singled out for stigmatization in health promotion campaigns. For example, Wang (1992) points out that media campaigns directed at preventing disability (including campaigns focusing on gun control and motor cycle helmet or seat-belt wearing) simultaneously stigmatize disability by presenting it as a fate worse than death. She gives as an example an American television advertisement which showed a young woman sitting in a wheelchair with the accompanying words, 'The drunk driver got one year. She was sentenced to life', which inadvertently links criminality with disablement (1992: 1099). Hevey (1992) also criticizes the ways in which visual representations of disabled individuals are used to arouse concern and pity while underlining their position as members of a deviant outgroup. He argues that in advertising images, disabled people are represented as 'inhabit[ing] a living social death in a bone-cage bodily oblivion which is not of their own making. Inside the advertising image they are cripples, they are handicapped, they cannot function or work' (Hevey, 1992: 22). The viewpoints of these 'deviant' Others who are used as tragic exemplars are rarely canvassed when health promotion campaigns are designed.

AIDS education campaigns have provided copious examples of the propensity of state-sponsored health promotion to stigmatize certain social groups and bolster conservative moralistic positions towards sexual and illicit drug-using activities. One example is the notorious multi-million dollar Australian 'Grim Reaper' mass media campaign, run in 1987, which used the spectral icon of death and horror-movie effects to denote the seriousness of AIDS. The campaign was subject to much publicity and media attention because of its 'shock tactics' (Lupton, 1994c: 53–5). The advertisement followed the attempt to frighten people into awareness of AIDS used by the British 'Don't Die of Ignorance' mass media campaign run in 1986, which adopted the imagery of massive tombstones carved with the word 'AIDS', erupting volcanoes and looming icebergs to emphasize to the public that AIDS threatens everyone. The 'Grim Reaper' campaign was deliberately constructed to provoke shock: it was stated by a member of the government agency responsible for AIDS education that the advertisement was planned to 'stop people in their tracks and make them think seriously about AIDS . . . to make it explicitly clear that AIDS has the potential to kill more Australians than World War 2' (reported in *The Age* newspaper [Melbourne], 7 April 1987).

The discourse of punishment for sexual sins is overt in these appeals to people's anxiety and fear, as is the construction of 'deviant' sexualities as threats to the body public. In the United States health promotion advertising has overtly valorized marital fidelity over multiple partners (heterosexual or homosexual) in such advertisements as:

> The faithful have nothing to fear. Not everyone has to worry about AIDS. You're safe if you're in a long-term sexual relationship with someone who's just as faithful as you. And if neither of you is using needles and drugs. AIDS – It's Up to You [with accompanying photograph of two wedding rings]. (reproduced in Bolton, 1992: 175)

Similarly, part of the national 'America Responds to AIDS' television campaign run in 1988 featured characters such as the unfaithful husband warning the public of the dangers of such behaviour: 'I was cheating [on my wife] . . . it's not worth it' (Bush and Boller, 1991: 32). A British series of television advertisements depicted the scenarios of the pick-up at the disco and the enticing woman asking her dinner partner to 'stay the night', to both arouse and incite fear in the audience around the dangers of 'promiscuous' sexuality (Rhodes and Shaughnessy, 1989). One Australian media campaign, run in 1988 and 1989, featured television advertisements showing a heterosexual couple embracing in a double bed. The camera then panned out to show many other similar couples in beds. The wording of the campaign was as follows:

> Next time you go to bed with someone, how many people will you be sleeping with? It's quite possible your partner has had several previous partners. And it's just as likely that these partners have had several partners too, and they've had partners, and so on, and so on, and so on. And any one of them could have been infected by the AIDS virus and passed it on. But you don't know. That's why you should always use a condom. Because you can never be sure just how many people you're really going to bed with.

Such fear-invoking strategies represent members of the public as apathetic, requiring stern warnings to jolt them into action. Education via campaigns is portrayed as a 'weapon' in the war against disease and a 'punishment' for complacency (Lupton, 1994c: 59–60). For example, the 'Don't Die of Ignorance' campaign suggested that lack of knowledge was the only barrier to full protection against HIV infection. Posters used in Britain in 1987 proclaiming 'The longer you believe AIDS only infects others, the faster it'll spread' and 'AIDS: how big does it have to be before you take notice?' were direct attempts to create fear without providing accurate information or advice about how best to protect oneself (Watney, 1988: 180), as was the tag-line of an American campaign 'AIDS. If you think you can't get it, you're dead wrong' (van Dam, 1989: 145). Ironically, however, the campaigns served only to present paradoxical appeals to behaving 'rationally' on the part of the viewer by invoking highly irrational emotions of terror using horror-movie style imagery (Rhodes and Shaughnessy, 1990: 57).

Sexual behaviour characterized as 'immoral' has thus been represented in such campaigns as dangerous not on religious or ethical grounds, but on health grounds. The moralistic approach to 'deviant' or 'perverse' sexual behaviours is disguised by the appeal to the preservation of the public's health. The incursion into individuals' intimate sexual relationships on the part of such campaigns is legitimized by the apparent urgency of protecting the population from the AIDS epidemic. However, rather than publicizing alternative ways of engaging in sexual acts with as many partners as one likes (such as mutual masturbation instead of penetrative sex), health promotional material on HIV/AIDS has continued to privilege the strategies of monogamous relationships, 'knowing' one's partner and reducing multiple sexual contacts. In stark contrast, AIDS education materials developed by community and activist groups in Britain, the United States and Australia have largely rejected fear appeals and hints of punishment for positive and erotic representations of safer sex which demonstrate how individuals may continue to indulge and take pleasure in their sexual fantasies and desires while avoiding infection.

Like commercial advertising, many contemporary health promotion campaigns directly attempt to interpellate their target audience through the use of carefully chosen discursive strategies that seek to incite concern about body image and the gaze of others. One example, aimed at middle-aged men, was an advertisement for 'Gutbusters', a state-sponsored campaign appearing in Sydney newspapers during the 1994 summer months. The advertisement was in monochrome, comprised of text only. It was intriguingly headed '(For men only)', seeking to inspire an air of titillation, mystery and exclusion from the world of women. The advertisement went on to describe a crisis of conscience in the life of an ordinary 'bloke' (all emphases are in the original): 'There's a point in most of our lives when what we're used to seeing as we're, well, *peeing*, suddenly (or it seems like suddenly) isn't there any more. Or if it is, it's hidden by a rather disgusting growth. It's like you wake up one morning to a total eclipse of your manhood.' In these three sentences, the reader is interpellated as one of 'us/we' – an inhabitant of the world of men. The third sentence uses the pronoun 'you' to further invoke the genre of a confidential chat. The mystery is heightened by the coyness of the allusions to that part of a man's body he is used to seeing when 'well, *peeing*' (italicized in the advertisement's text to emphasize the rather naughty use of this colloquialism) and his 'manhood'. The advertisement goes on: 'Oh sure, we joke about it – "the patio over the playground". We even parade it (struth, you can hardly hide a pot belly). But the *truth is* we feel uncomfortable – and not just because of the extra weight we're carrying. What the hell's happening? It's not so much what we're gaining – it's what we're losing. Control. Youth. Dignity: "*Dad's got a beer gut*".'

By now it is evident that the 'disgusting growth' referred to in the second sentence is a pot or 'beer' belly. The problem is that of unwanted flesh, which the advertisement asserts makes its possessors 'uncomfortable', signifies loss of control, youth and dignity, and inspires the ridicule of others. The advertisement goes on to use the cartoon character Homer Simpson as a potent exemplar of the male pattern of middle-aged fat distribution as figure of fun. It is not the health effects of this extra flesh that is problematized, but its appearance, its grotesqueness and lack of aesthetics, its potential even to emasculate its possessor by obscuring the genitalia.

Another example of the type of subject constructed by health promotional discourses, this time sponsored by a drug company, is a one-page pamphlet distributed in Australian doctors' surgeries and pharmacies and supported by a billboard campaign in late 1993. One side of the pamphlet showed the photographic image of a middle-aged man, looking disconsolate, behind 'bars' of floating white smoke. The text above read, 'There is a way out for smokers who want to escape.' Turned over, the text read in large letters, 'If you have the will, we have the way', followed by:

> Congratulations! Your decision to quit smoking is the first step toward living a more healthy, smokefree life. Quitting is never easy. But now there is something which can help you achieve your goal. Simply see your doctor and ask how you can escape from your nicotine addiction and habit. Your doctor can give you the prescription to help you succeed.

The pamphlet asserts that 'You will begin to feel better very quickly', as breathing will be easier, the 'smoker's cough' will be lost, there will be more energy, breath will be fresher, teeth will look brighter and skin will improve and (lastly); 'You will be less likely to suffer from smoking related diseases (e.g. cancer and heart diseases).' In addition, ex-smokers will be able to save money, they will smell better (as will their house), they will not have to clear up any 'dirty' ashtrays and cigarette butts: 'You will soon begin to feel proud that you have the strength and willpower to kick the smoking habit . . . You will find your new, clean, healthy image makes you more appealing to others . . . You will no longer feel like a social outcast.' Finally, the pamphlet asserts: 'You will not be affecting the health of others.' This pamphlet represents smokers as lacking discipline and will power, needful of medical help and even a prescribed drug (nicotine patches) to beat their habit. The use of the graphics (suggesting a prisoner held against his will) and the word 'escape' several times, the representation of smokers as unhealthy, dirty, lacking pride in themselves, physically unappealing, outcasts and harming others' health, all work to stigmatize smokers, representing them not only as a threat to themselves but as endangering public health. It argues for the view of the subject as having a genuine, real persona, the authentic self – the non-smoker – versus the false self of the 'smoker' who is controlled by the drug. There is a non-smoker behind the bars of tobacco waiting to be freed.

Recent health education campaigns have encouraged people to carry out surveillance not only on themselves, but on others. For example, in a mass media campaign against passive smoking run by the New South Wales Department of Health in late 1993, people were warned that they should police the activities of others to protect their own health. In one newspaper advertisement, an accompanying computer-enhanced photograph, cropped just above the upper lip, showed a woman's lower lip being grotesquely drawn out by a 'fishing hook' made of smoke emitting from a lit cigarette, labelled not with a known brand-name but with the words 'Other People's Smoke'. The heading extended the 'hook' metaphor: 'Just because you don't smoke, it doesn't mean you're off the hook.' The text went on to claim:

> Think you're a Non-Smoker? Think again. If you live, work or play where other people smoke, you're inhaling – like it or not. 'Other People's Smoke'. Drifting from the burning end of other people's cigarettes, it accounts for 85% of the smoke in smoke-filled rooms. And being unfiltered, it also contains far higher concentrations of poisonous chemicals . . . Non-Smokers? There'll be no such thing until we clear the air.

The advertisement thus positions all individuals as smokers, the majority albeit involuntary smokers. In one suburban Sydney newspaper this advertisement was accompanied by a full-page of 'advertorial' advising people to plaster 'smoke-free' stickers on their front door and on their cars, remove all ashtrays and 'when smokers ask you if they can smoke in your home, say you'd prefer them to smoke outside'. They were encouraged to ensure that their workplace is smoke free by approaching management and to request smoke-free dining areas in restaurants that do not already have them. Readers were exhorted to remember that 'you are not alone. Three out of four people are non-smokers and everybody is affected by Other People's Smoke.'

While the intention to make people aware that side-stream cigarette smoke is potentially threatening to the health of both non-smokers and smokers seems an eminently reasonable goal, the manner in which the New South Wales Department of Health chose to publicize the risk is telling for its imagery and subtextual ideological stance. The rhetoric of this campaign positions the smoker as the stigmatized Other, both overtly in the slogan of 'Other People's Smoke', and less overtly, in the discursive strategies used throughout. The photograph, with its distorted image of the lip being pulled towards a cigarette's lighted end, the mouth grimacing in pain and fear, vividly denotes the threat posed by the unseen 'Other People'. Throughout the advertisement, it is assumed that the reader, the 'you' hailed by the text, is a non-smoker, one of a community of like-minded people reading the advertisement together. The language is didactic, using imperatives to exhort this non-smoking reader to take action against 'Other People'. The emphasis is on the non-smoker as an innocent bystander, forced to endure the health risks posed them by 'Other People' and urged to join with the community, hailed as 'we' and 'us' (as in the 'Let's'), to 'clear the air'. By this rhetoric, non-smokers are positioned as consorting with the Other in their own downfall by refusing to act to prevent others from smoking in their presence. The onus is placed on them to do something, to enforce their right to clean air and good health. The overall effect is to further stigmatize smokers as not only socially unacceptable, but as selfishly endangering the health of all others around them. Such individuals, the advertisement implies, must be policed by the majority of reasonable people around them, both in public and private places. Ironically, a month before the release of the campaign the *Sydney Morning Herald* newspaper published the results of a poll it had commissioned on whether Australians would allow people to smoke in their home. Of the sample surveyed, 73 per cent were non-smokers, of which almost half (46 per cent) agreed that they would let others smoke in their home (Carney, 1993).

Critics of health promotion campaigns have pointed out how they routinely reproduce gender stereotypes evident in commercial advertising: 'Women are to be seen as passive, vulnerable and sexually available, only distinguished by their youth and beauty, while men are seen as active, possessive, and masterful' (Rhodes and Shaughnessy, 1989: 27). As I noted in Chapter 1, since the nineteenth century public health strategies have traditionally represented women as mothers, the guardians of their families' health, and by extension, that of the nation, and have targeted them for intervention as agents of regulation. So too, contemporary health promotion campaigns tend to place the emphasis of responsibility for health promotion upon women, in their roles as wives and mothers, with little concern for women's own health status or the structural constraints under which they operate (H. Rose, 1990; Amos, 1993). Women are expected to regulate the diet of their partners and offspring according to the dictates of health guidelines, to monitor their partner's weight and exercise habits, to ensure the cleanliness of their children, to make sure that their children are vaccinated and to desist from smoking and alcohol consumption while pregnant and even afterwards. In 1993, an Australian woman was forced to give the Family Court an undertaking that she would not smoke in the presence of her two young children following an application made to the court by the woman's former husband. The woman also had to undertake to prevent her children's exposure to any cigarette smoke. The court supported her ex-husband's actions on the ground that the children were both asthmatic (Stenberg, 1993).

Media campaigns have vacillated between representing women as carers and women as the source of contagion. For example, in HIV/AIDS media campaigns women have either been represented as *femmes fatales*, seeking to tempt men into their web of infection (as in the British advertisement described earlier), or conversely as the 'responsible' partner in a hetero-

sexual relationship who is exhorted to negotiate condom use or other safe
sex techniques with her partner. As one pamphlet designed for Australian
women by the New South Wales Department of Health advised them:
'Women can reduce their risk of HIV infection by: insisting that their male
partner always uses a condom for sex . . . Finding a way to talk about HIV
and STD prevention with your partner is very important.'

Health promotional campaigns have often explicitly directed their
emotional appeals to incite women's anxiety around the attractiveness and
youthfulness of their bodies. Several anti-smoking advertisements, for
example, in Australia and Britain have attempted to manipulate young
women's concern about their physical appearance or general attractiveness
to frighten them into avoiding or giving up smoking. A television
advertisement run by the Western Australian Department of Health in the
late 1980s showed a young woman smoking, her face slowly ageing into
that of an old crone. The voice-over asserted: 'What good's a pretty face
when you've got ugly breath?' Health advertisements advocating breast
self-examination have routinely adopted the genre of soft porn to represent
the breast. Rarely is the woman depicted as ageing in such portrayals, even
though the older woman is most at risk from breast cancer. Instead, the
image of the breast is youthful, firm and shapely. Young, attractive women
are shown caressing their breasts like *Penthouse* Pets (Wilkinson and
Kitzinger, 1993). Alternatively women's bodily parts have been objecti-
fied, rendered as separate, for the purposes of health promotion. Wilkinson and Kitzinger (1993: 230) describe a British breast self-examination
advertisement which showed a photographed breast with dotted circles
superimposed around the nipple, with the instruction 'press', implying a
mechanistic metaphor which ill-fits with the dominant sexualized portrayal
of the female breast.

As these examples demonstrate, a dualism is routinely constructed in
health promotional campaigns between the civilized and the grotesque
body. The grotesque body is commonly vividly represented, often visually,
as a horror of flesh-out-of-control: the beer belly, the ugly, wrinkled face,
the distorted lip, the helpless, disabled body in the wheelchair, the
entrapped addict. These images provide visual evidence to support a moral
tale: this is what will happen to *your* body if you are not careful. In
contrast, the civilized body is that which will be achieved and preserved
through the regimens of health promotion, with due application of
personal control and continuous attention and awareness of the potential
of the body to revolt.

Throughout the health promotional literature (both commercial and
government-sponsored), the implicit assumption is that the information
disseminated to patients or the general public on the part of those in
authority is privileged over the lay health beliefs of those not in authority.
The subjects of health promotion are constructed in a similar manner to
the subject of the child in the school; needing the opportunity for self-
realization but also needful of training to become a citizen; capable of self-

control and self-discipline but only able to fulfil their 'health potential' via governmental regulation; encouraged to aquire the ability to recognize their own best interests and to be responsible for themselves (Tyler, 1993: 35). Under this notion, individuals who seemingly care little for their health status because of the desire to fulfil 'short-term desires' are viewed as needful of more education. More often than not, this individual is categorized as working class, or, more euphemistically, as a member of one of the 'lower socio-economic groups' or 'with lower educational attainment' (Better Health Commission, 1986: 39). Such understandings of health-related behaviour view it as 'a "problem" that will respond to help organized in such a way as to "correct" an incorrect perception of interpersonal relations, or to reconstruct the world view of particular subjects and their own calculation of personal capacities' (May, 1993: 60).

Commodity culture, advertising and cultural theory

The adoption of commercial advertising and marketing strategies to achieve health promotional goals is largely doomed to failure, both because they have wildly ambitious aims (to persuade large numbers of people to abandon pastimes they find pleasurable or to take up activities they have hitherto avoided) and because their conceptualization of audience response is naive. As noted above, the dominant approach to advertising adopted in health promotion has relied on understandings of communication and the effects of the mass media drawn largely from the process school of communication. Socio-cultural theory offers a different, more complex perspective on advertising and marketing activities which explores their symbolic role. As scholars from this perspective argue, advertising was originally used to give the public details about a commodity or service. This function of advertising has now receded, and few advertisements for commercial products use information alone as a selling point, apart from inexpensive advertisements for local services in community newspapers. The primary function of glossy advertising is to create an image around a product which entices consumers to purchase the product and incorporate it into their everyday lives. Advertising serves to bring the product and a representation of the culturally constituted world together within the frame of a particular advertisement; it is up to members of the audience to make that link, which they may or may not do. Therefore, 'advertising serves us as a lexicon of current cultural meanings' (McCracken, 1988: 79).

In order to attract purchases, in the marketing of consumer goods the aesthetics of commodities are emphasized over their actual use-value. The use-value of the product is only a small part of its image: the remainder, the exchange value, or 'floating signifier', is constituted by references to other products, certain archetypal lifestyles and abstract values. Advertising appropriates desired abstract values such as sensuality, glamour, exuberance, vitality and sophistication as floating signifiers which are used to give meaning to meaningless products. A soft-drink, for example, has the use-value of quenching thirst, and this value is overtly why consumers purchase it. However there are a large number of beverages available for purchase to quench thirst, and there even exists a liquid (water) which performs the same purpose but comes free from the tap. The advertising and marketing strategies around the product exist to persuade consumers that this particular soft drink is a more desirable thirst-quencher than any other beverage available. In doing so, the original use-value of the product is often subsumed under values unrelated to the product.

The concept of desire is central to understanding the symbolic nature of advertising and the meaning of commodities. Advertising appeals to both conscious and unconscious desires generated in the individual since infancy. Advertising addresses a lack, an absence felt by the individual that is never fully filled by consumption because it relates not to a physical need (such as hunger or thirst), but to symbolic meanings. Similarly, consumption itself promises the satisfaction of desire, but never delivers it (Bocock, 1993: 68). Advertising appeals to unfulfilled desire by inviting individuals to recognize themselves as the subject of the advertisement. By this process, the subject of the advertisement is voluntarily constituted as an 'active receiver'. Audiences create the meaning of the advertisement, but in doing so, create meanings of themselves through the advertisement. They must already recognize something of themselves in the advertisement to be attracted to its overt and subconscious appeals (Williamson, 1990: ch. 2).

Symbols and cultural metaphors are employed in advertising to make links between the initially meaningless product and desirable values. Thus, an advertisement for a soft drink may use scenes of young, athletic, attractive people cavorting on a golden beach in the attempt to transfer the values of youth, freedom, sexual attractiveness and joie de vivre to the product. The pre-existing desires to be youthful and sexually attractive are not the creations of the advertising industry alone, although that industry is part of the wider cultural milieux in which such values arise and are perpetuated. Rather, these abstract values are used and recirculated by the advertisement. It is therefore misleading to believe that commercial advertising creates a 'false' need by persuading consumers to desire commodities, and that health promotion activities should attempt to counter this 'false' need and create other, more beneficial needs. The intention is merely to attract the consumer who *already* wants to enter that lifestyle, be that type of person: 'Clearly, the more an advertisement is able to exploit images and beliefs that the viewer recognizes as familiar and reassuring and "knows" to be "true", then the more potentially effective it will be' (Rhodes and Shaughnessy, 1990: 56).

It is salutary to note that contemporary cultural advertising theory now recognizes that audiences are highly aware of the use of advertising to persuade them to adopt a behaviour; 'advertising is propaganda, and everyone knows it' (Schudson, 1984: 4). The idea of individuals as passive and absorptive, subject to manipulation by the mass media and seduced by the promises of commodities, has given way to a view of active, plural audiences and consumers, differentiated by membership of sub-cultural groups and by the interpretive repertoires with which they respond to and make use of commodities and media products. Consumers purchase and use products critically and selectively, and are highly media literate and cynical in their reception of advertising and publicity campaigns around consumer goods (Schudson, 1984; McCracken, 1988; Nava, 1992: ch. 9; Shields, 1992). The recognition that cultural products are polysemous, or have many meanings, is important to this argument. It is now commonly argued that while advertisements and other cultural artefacts are produced in such a way as to draw upon shared and accepted cultural meanings, and structured so that particular meanings are favoured over others, members of the audience may well resist the intended meaning to produce their own use of the product. A strong barrier of audience cynicism must be overcome for a commodity to be successful. Active and sceptical audiences may well enjoy clever and glossy advertisements but do not necessarily buy the products they advertise. As a result, proportionately less money is now spent on commercial advertising than on developing products with strong images, highly differentiated from other inherently similar products, based on intensive qualitative research with consumers (Mellencamp, 1992: 21; Nava, 1992: ch. 9).

Ironically, the vast weight of the economic power controlled by multinational companies and the intensive product research which taps into pre-existing symbolic images and meanings subsequently used in their promotions sometimes coincidentally serve to further the goals of health promoters. Among these commercial promotional activities are products which valorize the glamour and eroticism of the physically active body, or link sexual attractiveness with the consumption of health food products, such as Reebok and Nike advertisements, while fast-food outlets and the snack food industry have developed 'low-fat' products to meet consumer demand. For example, an advertisement for 'Lean Cuisine' (frozen, low calorie meals) that appeared in an Australian women's magazine in 1993 posed the question, 'Why should you make a habit of positive eating?' The advertisement went on to provide figures of how many Australians are overweight and reproduced a table showing the nutritious constituents of a typical Lean Cuisine meal. The advertisement asserted that 'you' should:

> think positively about what and when you eat. For example, do you really need a huge meal for dinner, every night? . . . LEAN CUISINE is an excellent example of a lighter, leaner meal because it has low, controlled levels of fat and cholesterol . . . Not only will you be tempting your tastebuds, you'll be taking positive steps towards a leaner, healthier you.

The discourses of control and positive thinking, the appeals to consumers to avoid fat and cholesterol for the sake of both their health and their figures, echo the dominant discursive strategies of health promotional advertising. It is clear that the boundaries between commercial advertising, directed towards selling a product for profit, and health promotional messages have therefore blurred: each genre now borrows freely from the other. There is a symbiotic relationship between the promotion of health and fitness and that of the body as commodity. As Featherstone argues:

> Consumer culture latches onto the prevalent self-preservationist conception of the body, which encourages the individual to adopt instrumental strategies to combat deterioration and decay (applauded too by state bureaucracies who seek to reduce health costs by educating the public against bodily neglect) and combines it with the notion that the body is a vehicle of pleasure and self-expression. (1991a: 170)

In commodity culture the ideal body is lean, fit, controlled, toned and youthful – such a body is also healthy. Just as health education discourses seek to use the desire for sexual attractiveness as a motivational point for people to regulate their diet, give up smoking or exercise regularly, commercial advertising uses the incentives of improved health and vitality to sell commodities.

In addition to the cynicism engendered in audiences by the genre of advertising as a whole, health promotional advertising has the major problem that it can be easily identified as a government sponsored message by its use of logos which accompany all promotional material, from the television advertisement to the pamphlet. These logos inform audiences that the advertisement has been produced by a health promotion body, and that by corollary, the message will most likely attempt to persuade them to give up a pleasurable activity or take up an unpleasant activity; whether it is wearing condoms during sex, giving up smoking or taking up jogging. People are rarely responsive to overt attempts to coerce them into changing their behaviour, unless they have already decided that they wish to do so, and resentment about the state's role in 'preaching' to its citizens may be generated by such campaigns. Commercial promotional activities are directed towards a view of the client/consumer as having the power to choose, positioning the consumer in the authoritative role (Fairclough, 1993: 157). By contrast, health promotion activities do not represent the consumer as authoritative; rather, as I have noted earlier, they routinely position members of the public as ignorant, apathetic and passive, needing guidance from state agencies to conduct their lives wisely. This is a fundamental philosophical difference which may go some way towards understanding the reasons why health promotion activities emulating commercial promotions often fail.

In the light of these observations on advertising and marketing activities, mass media health communication campaigns need to be examined for the role they serve in the context of commodity culture as a whole, especially if they attempt to borrow commercial advertising techniques and try to compete with commercial products. Public service advertising alone cannot create symbolic meanings around health-protective lifestyle choices which do not already exist. Messages and images must resonate with members of target audiences, striking a chord in their collective consciousness, making them want to position themselves within that world. This process is by no means linear, exact or predictable. As Wernick (1991: 37–8) comments:

> It would be impossible to valorize products symbolically if the symbolism employed to that end were itself unintelligible or without ideological appeal. Symbolic ads must therefore not only find effective pictorial and verbal devices by which to link the commodity with a significance. They must also build up significance from elements of an understood cultural code; and in such a way that the values in terms of which the product is endorsed are themselves endorsed by those to whom they make appeal.

Herein lies the dilemma and 'Catch 22' for health promoters. Advertising and other promotional activities are most effective if they tap into a corpus of existing meanings, rather than attempting to create new ones. Some health promotion advertising campaigns seek to reinterpret pleasurable activities as related to health risk. Yet it is only in the realm of medicine that sexual encounters, for example, are considered a 'health issue'; for most people, sex is about pleasure, danger, risk, romance, attraction, bonding and excitement, *not* health (Thorogood, 1992: 61). Any attempt to 'force' a cultural value upon such behaviours is doomed to failure.

The political function of media campaigns

Given the clear difficulties around the use of mass media campaigns for the purposes of health promotion, the question is begged why do they continue to be extensively used and funded as a major strategy? The simple answer is that mass media campaigns, quite apart from their actual content or 'effect' on mass audiences, provide a cost-effective means of demonstrating that the state considers the issue to be a 'problem' and is working to do something about it. Health promotion campaigns are nearly all funded by state agencies and are planned and carried out within bureaucratic departments of the state. When health promotional bodies depend on state funding, their activities effectively are tied to the objectives of the state; that is, to maintain the status quo. Hence the continued focus on individual behaviour in media campaigns to the exclusion of creating publicity around the social structural dimension of ill-health.

The continued use of fear appeals and the construction of subjects as apathetic, ignorant and uncontrolled serve to represent health promotion agencies, and through them, the state which funds them, as authoritative and active. Ill-health states and individual lifestyle choices are constructed as problems through media campaigns, and the health promotional agency is represented as the paternalistic educator providing the solution, identified by the logo accompanying the advertisement. The rhetorical strategies of risk, of impending doom, of the importance of physical attractiveness, are used to justify the incursion of the state into individuals' private lives. The underlying premise is that these warnings are for the good of the individual's health: follow this advice and all will be well. In producing the campaign the state is therefore able to discharge its responsibilities in preserving and improving the public's health by locating the causes of ill-health at the level of individual responsibility. The campaign serves to warn members of the public of these causes, leaving it in their hands to then take up the message for their own sake. It is worthy of note the attention given to proscribing 'deviant' or illegal personal behaviours, such as drug use (for example, the vastly expensive Australian National Campaign Against Drug Abuse, which cost approximately $100 million) or sexual activity (AIDS campaigns) to the exclusion of other health issues in mass media campaigns. State-sponsored media campaigns do not call attention to the deficiencies of the state-sponsored health promotional activities.

Fairclough (1993) has commented on the pervasiveness in contemporary western societies of 'promotional discourse', relating to the marketing and commodifying of most areas of social life, including people, ideas and organizations as well as objects (see also Wernick, 1991). Promotional discourse has incorporated the genre of advertising on a massive scale, 'generating many new hybrid partly promotional genres' (Fairclough, 1993: 141) to market a range of diverse activities. It is clear that most mass media health promotion campaigns adopt a dualistic promotional discursive strategy. They serve both to self-promote, to provide tangible evidence that the state is 'doing something' about that particular health problem (or is at least spending time and money on producing advertising materials and paying for air-time or column space), and to promote, or publicize, the health problem itself. One overt example of this strategy is a newspaper advertising campaign run by the New South Wales Department of Health during 'Health Week' at the end of October 1993. The advertisement was headed 'It's Health Week – Well?', followed by the questions:

> Can you honestly say you're as healthy as you could be? Do you know what the average life expectancy is? Do you take enough of the right kind of exercise? Is what you're eating good for you – and are there 'right' foods? If you do get sick, do you know where to go to get the right treatment? . . . There's a lot you don't know about looking after Number One. And that's what Health Week is all about . . . It's a major Health awareness initiative aimed at one person – You. The aim? Simply to get better health to be your goal as well as ours.

The advertisement went on to provide a glowing promotional description of how the New South Wales Department of Health is doing its job, describing 'improvements' in health status. It then provided details of drops in lengths of hospital stay, use of new surgical techniques and increases in life expectancy for men and women. It finished by asserting: 'They say that what you don't know can't hurt you. But when it comes to Health, that couldn't be further from the truth.' The internal logic of the advertisement is that readers should make themselves familiar with the achievements of the Department for the sake of their own health; that somehow, knowing what the average life expectancy is or being familiar with 'today's Health Services' will have a beneficial effect on an individual's health status. Paradoxically, combined with the advertisement's attempts to promote the imputed achievements of the Health Department in curing and treating illness is a discourse emphasizing personal responsibility for individual health status. This discourse is especially dominant in the first few sentences which call readers to task, attempting to shake their complacency and accusing them of almost wilful negligence and self-delusion in a style reminiscent of maternal exhortations – 'Can you honestly say you're as healthy as you could be? . . . Do you take enough of the right kind of exercise?' Indeed the very headline implies that because that week has been declared 'Health Week' by the Department of Health, it is up to readers to respond in some way – 'It's Health Week – Well?' Readers are both represented as clients of the Department (as taxpayers who fund its activities), requiring evidence of its achievements, but also as passive, dependent and ignorant, requiring the motivation offered by the Department to become actively involved in their own health. The advertisement exemplifies the hybrid promotional genre in its use of promotional discourse both to self-promote the Health Department and to promote (in this sense meaning 'improve') the health status or health-related knowledge or awareness of individuals.

As well as performing the role of publicizing the dynamic and philanthropic nature of state-sponsored health promotional activities, the discursive strategies of mass media health campaigns routinely serve the political purpose of obscuring the relationship between the state and vested interests by focusing on individual behaviour. State-sponsored messages warning of the danger of smoking or alcohol use may be viewed as covertly supporting this other intention; to continue to allow their sale and to reap the benefits of the taxes levied on these commodities, but doing so in a way that proclaims an overt interest in the health of the people. One example is the efforts to reduce the incidence of drink-driving in Australia, in which the emphasis is upon removing the drinking driver from the road through a combination of legislation and guilt-invoking or fear appeals. To that end, advertising campaigns are commonly employing menacing images of the police force using its power to incarcerate drivers who are found to have a blood alcohol level above the legal limit – 'Be under 0.5 or be under arrest' – or distressing images of young adults or children killed in horrific car accidents, their parents distraught, the drink-driver consumed with guilt. This emphasis on individuals and their alcohol consumption habits, the representation of alcohol as 'evil', ignores the wider socio-political and economic context in which car accidents occur, such as the availability of public transport, the production, distribution and marketing of alcohol and motor vehicles, the condition and planning of the road system, driving safety standards and density and location of housing in relation to places of employment and leisure activities (Petersen, 1989, 1991).

So too, the state's hypocritical stance on cigarette smoking is demonstrated by the proliferation of quit smoking programmes and media campaigns sponsored by the state and the prohibitions placed on cigarette advertising and smoking in public places in the name of providing clean, non-carcinogenic air, but the continuing lack of enthusiasm governments have demonstrated towards controlling the emissions of large industry and cars, the industrial use of massive amounts of pesticides and the hazardous wastes of petrochemical industries (Epstein, 1990). Klein (1993: 15) notes that a former American secretary of health 'castigated cigarette marketing during the very week that the White House chief of staff weakened the clean air bill'. Multinational tobacco companies continue to enjoy government support in both western and developing countries, and governments continue to reap the benefits of the taxes they place upon tobacco products at point-of-sale and to subsidize tobacco growers (Goodman, 1993: 243). Governments were slow to react to the discovery that tobacco use was strongly associated with the development of fatal diseases such as lung cancer, supported through the findings of epidemiological studies published in the 1950s and 1960s, and the eventual response was characterized by division: some state agencies were devoted towards protecting the tobacco industry, while others acted to disseminate the message that smoking damages health status and to take steps to inhibit tobacco use (1993: 126). Yet, like alcohol consumption, smoking has been individualized as a personal vice in health promotion campaigns. Rather than directing regulatory policies towards producing 'safer' cigarettes; for example by enforcing the use of filters, the state has focused its attentions on individual smokers' behaviours (Viscusi, 1992: 3). In tobacco control campaigns, smokers have become represented as the equivalent of addicted hard drug users, and tobacco use has become described as a disease itself, with terms such as 'nicotinism' and 'tobacconism' used to describe people's dependence on cigarettes (Goodman, 1993: 243).

Within the tightly controlled sphere of health promotion, it is very difficult for those working in health promotion to challenge orthodox strategies and attempt to engage in activities that divert resources away from funding mass media campaigns. Pattison and Player (1990) and Beattie (1991) contend, for example, that reports and research that have been critical of British health promotional policies and practices, or which have provided statistics demonstrating the continuing effect of material deprivation upon the health status of a large proportion of Britons, have frequently been suppressed or ignored by the very government ministers who commissioned them. Beattie (1991: 170) further suggests that the evidence that mass communication campaigns are largely ineffective in having an impact on people's health-related behaviours has been well known to British health promotion bodies (the Health Education Council and its successor, the Health Education Authority) since the early 1970s. However, reports outlining such a stance have been routinely suppressed and ignored for political purposes, including the avoidance of confrontations with vested interests. Beattie contends that the conservative British state health promotion agencies have been reluctant to eschew the process model of communication and have insisted on continuing to fund highly expensive mass media health education campaigns with the support of powerful bodies such as the medical establishment and commercial lobby groups: 'The dubious and discredited strategy of health persuasion regularly finds enthusiastic champions in Parliament. Numerous politicians, in both Houses, have made it their personal mission to resurrect the most blatant tactics of medico-moral persuasion around such issues as food and health, and sexuality and health' (Beattie, 1991: 170; see also Davison et al., 1991; Frankenberg, 1994).

Concluding comments

The use of the mass media for health promotional purposes is essentially a pedagogical activity, but it is a politically conservative pedagogy which generally uncritically accepts its objectives and is directed towards infusing audiences, seen as empty vessels, with knowledge, rather than a pedagogy which is oriented towards encouraging critical thinking and challenging of the status quo. The strategy has been adopted and continues to be used because the mass media are viewed as having a large, potentially malleable audience. Communication is largely regarded as a 'top-down' and somewhat paternalistic exercise, in which it is believed to be the role of those with the appropriate medical or epidemiological knowledge, whether they be physicians, other health care professionals or health educators, to disseminate the 'right' message to the masses for their own good. This taken-for-granted understanding obscures the self-promotional facet of the campaigns, their function in providing state agencies with the opportunity to publicize their concern, their dynamism and their disapproval of those behaviours deemed harmful to citizens' health to the exclusion of challenging the state's own role in supporting the health-damaging practices of certain industries. Mass media campaigns are little more than public relations exercises which simultaneously serve to censure behaviours deemed deviant and respond to pragmatic concern about the economic implications of health care provision, cloaked in the rhetoric of ameliorating the public's health.

While health promotional literature typically represents commercial advertising as antipathetical to the imperatives of public health, a symbiotic relationship exists between them. Both the genres of health promotional and commercially oriented advertising are explicitly directed towards the narcissistic management of the self relating to the body's appearance and deportment. They each contribute to the enterprise of health; they encourage readers to choose, to think positively, to *do* something for themselves: to make themselves healthy, attractive, and therefore socially acceptable and contented. Both health promotion discourse and commercial marketing directed at body care rely on appeals to anxieties around death and decay to motivate self-maintenance and promote the consumption of commodities marketed to fend off ageing and ill-health. Each seeks to construct the ideal-type of the controlled body which moves between the indulging of desire and the constraints of asceticism. In the next chapter I analyse this tension in more detail, discussing the ways in which individuals take up, negotiate, resist or simply ignore the imperatives of health promotional discourses in the context of the emotions, desires and pleasures invested in the practices of the self.

5

Bodies, Pleasures and the Practices of the Self

In previous chapters I have considered the ways in which public health and health promotion discourses are directed, both overtly and covertly, towards the construction of certain types of subjects. Like many other contemporary institutions and agencies, public health and health promotional discourses and practices privilege a certain type of subject, a subject who is self-regulated, 'health'-conscious, middle-class, rational, civilized. They also privilege a body that is contained, under the control of the will. Governmental strategies emerging from public health and health promotion, sponsored by the state and other agencies, are directed at fostering such subjects and bodies. These strategies *do* succeed, as is apparent in the ways people articulate their concerns about their health and the types of health-enhancing activities in which they engage, but not for all individuals, and not all of the time.

While the governmental tactics of health promotion and public health may have much to offer those who possess the appropriate economic, cultural or symbolic capital, for others their inducements will go unheeded or will be transformed or actively contested. If people do not find themselves interpellated by governmental discourses, if they do not recognize themselves therein or have no investment in these discourses, they will not respond accordingly. The practices of everyday life in particular are sites at which cultural norms are 'transgressed and reworked', taken up and used by individuals for purposes that may or may not coincide with the governmental goals of the state (Donald, 1992: 2–3). This chapter goes beyond describing the network of strategies devoted towards regulating the population's health, by examining the responses of individuals to such attempts in the context of everyday life. It is acknowledged that the constraints of socio-economic aspects such as gender, ethnicity, income, stage in the life course and social class categories also need to be considered in an analysis of the nexus between governmentality and subjectivity.

Resistance and desire

There is a central paradox in Foucauldian theory which is difficult to resolve for those interested in power relations, subjectivity and resistance. One confusing and ambiguous aspect of Foucault's writing about power is the dialectic between power as simultaneously productive and as repressive. Foucault insists that power is productive, for it brings institutions, objects and subjects into being, but at the same time, much of his writing, especially that focused on the development of the prison and the clinic and the regimes of governmentality, seem to represent power and discourse as pervasively and insidiously oppressive of the free will of humans, bent at creating 'docile bodies'. If power does not emanate from a central autocrat or institution, but is spread amongst all relationships in society, then power may be regarded as even more amenable to the abuse of the unsuspecting citizen. This implies that to use the term 'productive' in relation to the workings of power does not necessarily denote a positive production. Bringing something into open discourse serves to render it more amenable to control and surveillance. Coercive and confining relations of power may be produced and reproduced as part of the constitution of subjectivities and embodiment.

To what extent do discourses construct subjectivities and embodiment, and what is the role of the non-discursive? Is the challenging of or the non-conformity to the imperatives of governmentality possible within Foucault's schema? Foucault certainly appeared to believe so, at least in his later writings; for example, he argued that:

> Mastery and awareness of one's own body can be acquired only through the effect of an investment of power in the body: gymnastics, exercises, muscle-building, nudism, glorification of the body beautiful. All of this belongs to the pathway leading to the desire of one's own body, by way of the insistent, persistent, meticulous work of power on the bodies of children or soldiers, the healthy bodies. *But once power produces this effect, there inevitably emerge the responding claims and affirmations*, those of one's own body against power, of health against the economic system, of pleasure against the moral norms of sexuality, marriage, decency. Suddenly, what had made power strong becomes used to attack it. *Power, after investing itself in the body, finds itself exposed to a counter-attack in the same body.* (1980a: 56; emphases added)

This excerpt suggests that there are alternative, extra-discursive or non-discursive sources of resistance to external governmentality strategies, that there are imperatives and pleasures that challenge the dictates or conventions of 'moral norms'. Similarly, while Foucault comments elsewhere that the body is 'moulded by a great many distinct regimes; it is broken down by the rhythms of work, rest, and holidays, it is poisoned by food or values, through eating habits or moral laws', he adds that 'it constructs resistances' (1984b: 87). He discussed the sporadic 'transversal' struggles experienced by individuals in resisting forms directed at the constitution of the inner-self, and called for promoting new forms of subjectivity (Cotton, 1993: 99–100). However, Foucault did not adequately explain the ways in which this may occur, how individuals manage to dwell 'outside the field of possibilities made available by the dominant schema of subjection' (1993: 100) and why they choose to take up subject positions in some discourses rather than others; nor did he devote much time to discussing the structural constraints to free actions.

The term 'resistance' as it is used here does not refer solely to purposive, collective action directed towards political ends and the overt challenging of power. That is not to say that such acts of resistance do not happen: there *are* occasions where the more coercive elements of public health and health promotion are actively resisted through organized attempts. For example, AIDS activist groups in countries such as the United States, Australia and Britain have, for some years, directed collective action towards changing the state's policy and practices around AIDS education and health care provision. These groups have sought to expose the ways in which public health strategies frequently discriminate against individuals such as gay men and have challenged the construction of people living with HIV/AIDS in health promotional discourses as passive, helpless and deviant 'victims'. However, given the understanding of subjectivity as multiple and fragmented, the traditional, 'modern', notion of resistance cannot easily be adopted when discussing power relations, for it both assumes a model of power as always repressive, invested in institutions intent on domination, and the concept of the unified self, a self that has an exclusive allegiance to a certain social group or subculture. As I have discussed in previous chapters, these assumptions are no longer uncritically accepted in contemporary socio-cultural theory. A person may have an allegiance to one particular sub-culture in a certain context, and harbour conflicting loyalties in another, depending on the subject positions he or she takes up. It is therefore difficult to call for a unified movement that appeals to defined groups to act collectively in the struggle against oppression, for individuals are neither totally powerless nor powerful, but continually positioned and repositioned in relation to power (Henriques et al., 1984: 225).

Given these changes in understanding subjectivity and power relations, many discussions of resistance in response to Foucauldian theory tend to conceptualize struggle at the micro-level, related to the ways in which individuals fail to acquiesce in, conform or consent to the imperatives of governmentality. Resistance thus includes ways of contesting or non-conforming to a set of established dictums at the site of everyday life. At this micro-level, people may not conform to public health or health promotional advice because of a conscious sense of frustration, resentment or anger, or because they derive greater pleasure and satisfaction from other practices of the self, or because they experience an unconscious imperative that directs them to take up alternative subject positions and bodily practices. Indeed, these rationales for non-conformance to health imperatives may operate simultaneously or variously within the context of an individual's life course. Several theorists using the concept of govern-mentality to explain the moral regulation of individuals have emphasized the ways in which governmental attempts fail, or are resisted, related to the need for the governed to consent to an activity or way of governing: people must be willing to exist as subjects (Gordon, 1991: 48; Burchell, 1991:

145). In response to normalization, which attempts to render individuals more similar, practices of the self may promote idiosyncratic individuality. The concept of the care of the self therefore implies a degree of agency, suggesting that the techniques of governmentality are not simply imposed upon individuals, and that therefore, resistance and change may be generated and sustained (McNay, 1992: 84). As this implies, the governed subject has a highly ambivalent relationship with the apparatuses of governmentality. In relation to public health and health promotion for example, citizens continually move between resentment at the authoritative nature of the state and its incursion into their private lives, and the expectation that the state will take responsibility for ensuring and protecting their health.

But given the influence of dominant discourses in constituting subjectivity, from where does the potential to resist, to produce alternative forms of subjectivity using alternative discourses, emerge? Why do individuals choose to take up some subject positions over others? How is change both generated and resisted? People are never completely socialized into shared meanings, due partly to the continuing consciousness of their own bodily processes (Shilling, 1993: 178). One space for resistance may thus be created by the dissonance between the felt experiences of individuals and the 'official' version of those experiences, or 'the interstices of experience and representation' (McNay, 1992: 153). When external governmentality strategies conflict with the image of themselves that individuals hold, a certain dissonance, a sense of uneasiness, may be created that may lead to resistance at the personal level and possibly at the organized level (Burchell, 1991: 119). Another space for the constitution of alternative subjectivities is produced by the struggle between different rationales and competing ways of constructing subjectivity issuing from disparate governmental sites. As I explained in the Introduction, it is not solely the state's activities that contribute to the regulation of bodies via governmentality, but a myriad of other institutions and social settings: the media and commodity culture, the family, the school, the legal system. These are all to some extent part of the governmentality efforts of the state, but also have rationales beyond those of the state and on occasion contradict or even directly attempt to counter state imperatives. Thus, the competing discourses around the construction of the subject are too diverse and contradictory to ensure full alignment to the imperatives of public health. The sheer multiplicity of sites, techniques and forms of governmental power, the paradoxes that it encompasses, renders it vulnerable, not to a single form of oppositional politics but to resistance from a diversified array of sites (Hunter, 1993: 132). External governmentality attempts cannot simply impose themselves on the subject, nor are they able to constitute subjectivity seamlessly. There will always be the potential for governmentality to break down by virtue of its diversity. As Rose and Miller (1992: 190) argue, '[e]ach actor, each locale, is the point of intersection between forces, and hence a point of potential resistance of any one way of thinking and acting, or a point of organization and promulgation of a different or oppositional programme'.

Non-conformance to health imperatives thus may emerge from a conscious choice of alternative practices of the self, but also may be generated at the unconscious or non-discursive level. To address this level of self-formation, psychoanalytic theory is gradually being taken up by sociologists and cultural studies scholars theorizing the interplay of repression, incitement and desire. This use of psychoanalytic theory goes beyond the somewhat essentialist, structuralist concepts of the self offered by Freudian psychoanalysis to attempt to describe the intersection between the individual's psyche and the ways in which subjectivity is constructed via discursive formations and social relations. Donald (1991: 4) has character-ized the approach as 'after the feminist re-reading of Lacan's re-reading of Freud'. Critics from this perspective argue that Foucault's work largely ignored discussion of the 'positive, libidinal driving force'; or desire – that which is pre- or non-discursive (Lash, 1991: 277). They challenge the understanding of subjectivity as rationally constructed and fully conscious. Rather, they attempt to explain the nexus between agency and desire by examining the psychological processes through which cultural meanings are discovered, created and transformed. The psychoanalytic perspective views subjects as actively participating in the construction of meaning through the relations of power rather than simply being a passive object of language and discourse. It seeks to explain how subjects participate in their own domination as well as resisting it, why they have an emotional commitment to take up positions in some discourses rather than others, how both resistance to change and the desire to effect change are produced (Henriques et al., 1984: 205–7; Mahoney and Yngvesson, 1992: 46).

This brand of psychoanalytic theory posits that early libidinal drives and desires and their repression due to cultural norms construct the uncon-scious, which character is expressed through thoughts and behaviours individuals have the least conscious and rational control over such as dreams, memories, fantasies, slips of the tongue, neuroses and anxieties, erotic excitement and other sensual embodied experiences. Some scholars refer to the role of the repressed, desire, pleasure and the unconscious in constituting spaces for resistance in ways of which the subject has little awareness. Desire here does not refer merely to sexual desire, or a lack, but a positive force, the investment of libido in a person or thing, a will-to-power (Fox, 1993: 37). For theorists such as Deleuze, the body is 'the surface of intersection between libidinal forces, on the one hand, and "external", social forces on the other. It is the interplay of these forces which gives the body its shape and its specific qualities' (Lash, 1991: 277). Agency and resistance emerge from the libido as resisting discipline, meaning that the inscription of bodies by discourses is always in a state of flux (Fox, 1993: 37).

For psychoanalytic theory, the development of subjectivity and a sense of individuation in infancy and childhood is important to understanding agency. It is argued that the child's struggles in its relationship with its parents, the tension and ambiguity it experiences between dependence and resistance, is the space in which a sense of empowerment may be generated (Mahoney and Yngvesson, 1992). Resistance at the level of the unconscious does not emerge from self-reflection, but from the contradiction between desire and prohibition, meaning that 'the return of the repressed is always on the cards' (Game, 1991: 48). The resentment felt by individuals at being forced through social context and a knowledge of what is 'appropriate' or expected by social convention to engage in a behaviour which conflicts with their emotional state, or feels 'unnatural', is the point at which resistance to the expected norm emerges. It is through the tension between prohibition and realization of desire, the split between the conscious, logical self and the ungratified and guilty urges of the unconscious, that agency is created:

> This creation of the unconscious through repression is thus also the moment of individuation that allows conscious, intentional, autonomous agency within the terms of identification established through the authority of the social machinery. In this revised model, the *repression* of desires is as important to the formation of subjectivity as their incitement: it is a mechanism determining the form of expression of the repressed material and prompting its repetition. (Donald, 1993: 50, emphasis in the original)

Thus, even though the rational, logical self may consciously conform to social norms and external imperatives, the unconscious wills the self to explore new ways of being, to disrupt convention and coherence. This individual level of resistance may be translated to collective and organized acts of resistance if these desires and frustrations are recognized as shared rather than being confined to the individual's personal experience or psychic makeup.

Sexual desire provides one example. The sexual body is constructed in certain ways by dominant discourses that seek to constrain some forms of erotic expression deemed 'perverse' and to promote and legitimate others as 'normal'. However, the multiplication of discourses on the sexual body have also established sources of articulating sexual identities and have facilitated the formation of social groups amongst those who have been categorized as 'deviant' and resent this categorization, demanding certain rights and social change. Thus 'the sexed body is to be understood not only as the primary target of the techniques of disciplinary power, but also as the point where these techniques are resisted and thwarted' (McNay, 1992: 39). At the conscious level, individuals frequently engage in thoughts or activities they know to be strongly socially censured (such as sexual contact with a member of the same sex), deliberately flouting accepted norms. At either the conscious or unconscious levels, people may derive pleasure from 'deviant' sexual activities and fantasies because of their very status as perverse. As I shall argue in greater detail later in this chapter, the use of commodities is another area in which the interplay of repression, pleasure and desire plays a vital role in inspiring or motivating individuals both to take up and to challenge attempts at governmentality related to health promotion.

Further to this argument, certain practices of the self may be considered neither conscious nor unconscious, but simply non-subjective ways of behaving that are acculturated in individuals as part of their mode of life, such as styles of walking and sleeping (Hunter, 1993: 128). For example, most individuals brush their teeth every day, with generally little reflection on the reasons why they do so. The practice has become a habit, a practice of the self perpetuated not by the dictates of external imperatives or conscious motivation but by the individual's unthinking routines and rituals of everyday life. The notion of the 'habitus', as developed by the French sociologist Pierre Bourdieu (1984), is useful to conceptualize the ways in which individuals' choices and bodily presentations are both shaped and constrained by their social position. Bourdieu (1990: 9–10) developed the concept of the habitus to deal with the paradox that people may act in certain ways, directed towards certain ends, without being conscious of these ends, but also without being determined by them. For Bourdieu, the habitus describes the world in which individuals live, including their everyday habits, their working environment, their appearance and their sense of style. The habitus is formed within the structural conditions in which people are located, particularly their gender and class position. It is reproduced within the spheres of both the private and the public: the education system, the family, the workplace, the mass media and commodity culture. It is expressed in the ways in which people conduct themselves, dress, consume commodities, gesture, talk, their taste and preferences, the ways that they perceive and construct reality. Hence, social groups are distinguished from each other not only by their possession of wealth, but by their consumption patterns and their body shape, deportment, stance and expression.

These perspectives on power, subjectivity and bodily practices recognize that there is a tension between the notion of the body and subjectivity as constituted by discursive processes, and that of subjectivity and the project of the self as agential, the point of resistance. It is accepted that this dialectic can never be fully resolved; subjects are neither wholly governed by discourse nor fully capable of stepping out of discourse. Rather, there is a continuing struggle over meaning; governmentality both enables the construction of subjectivity and embodiment and constrains it in certain ways. This approach conceptualizes the human body as 'a series of processes of becoming, rather than a fixed state of being' (Grosz, 1994: 12) and as a site of contestation. Therefore, while the importance of conscious self-control needs to be recognized to understand the ways in which people conduct and regulate their bodies, and construct forms of subjectivity, the unconscious and non-conscious dimensions of behaviour also require consideration. There might be said to be a continuum along which resistance, or the construction of alternatives, is conscious, ranging from highly conscious radical oppositional struggles, at both the group and individual levels, to the unconscious, at which resistance takes place through emotional impulses and desire and may not necessarily be recognized or articulated by the subject as resistance. The non-conscious dimension of practices of the self, where behaviours are acculturated through the habitus and are performed 'automatically', also requires recognition.

Health promotional discourses in everyday life

As earlier chapters have shown, the logic of health promotion is directed at allowing individuals to uncover their true state of health, to reveal their moral standing and indeed shape their true selves by strategies of bodily management. To what extent are 'official' discourses on health mainten-ance and personal responsibility accepted and taken up by individuals in their construction of subjectivity and in the practices of everyday life? There is evidence from indepth interviews with people about their concepts and practices of health that the official governmental discourses of health promotion are often articulated in people's discourses at the conscious level. For example, Saltonstall (1993) interviewed middle-class American men and women between the ages of 35 and 55. She found that health was conceptualized as an accomplishment of the individualized self, a conscious creation, the result of deliberate action involving the body. Both men and women referred to such body maintenance routines as avoiding smoking, eating the right diet and abstaining from drinking as being essential to the accomplishment of good health. Health was routinely glossed as 'fitness', as being toned and in 'good shape'. As one of her male respondents commented; 'Health to me is the food you eat, how you carry yourself, from the clothes you wear, to the size you are, body fat, skin tone, and whether you're sick. I feel if you take care of yourself by working out and eating right, . . . you will be stronger and healthier' (1993: 8).

Such understandings of health appear widespread. Crawford's (1984) earlier study of people living in the Chicago area and more recent studies of people living in an area of Scotland (MacInnes and Milburn, 1994) and in Sydney (Lupton, 1994d), elicited similar responses about concepts of health that revolved around the notion of health as self-control, encom-passing concepts of self-discipline, self-denial and will power. Health was thus represented as a goal, to be achieved by intentional actions, involving restraint, perseverance and the commitment of time and energy. Health is what one does, as well as the condition one is in: as stated by one of Crawford's interviewees: 'I get exercise. I don't smoke. I don't eat a lot of red meat. I don't have a lot of cholesterol. I take vitamins. I get a physical every year. I think I'm healthy . . . I try to do all of those things, so I think I'm healthy' (1984: 66–7). Judgement of others and self-blame were themes that recurred throughout the interviews in these studies, reflecting a general moralization of health achievement similar to that of the work ethic. Fatness thus stood as a tangible sign of lack of control, impulsive-ness, self-indulgence, while the thin body was a testament to the power of self-discipline, 'an exemplar of mastery of mind over body and virtuous self-denial' (1984: 70).

When people fall ill they often explain their misfortune using the dominant discourses of health promotion. Johnson (1991) interviewed Americans who had experienced one or more heart attacks. She found that the respondents' attempts to 'make sense' of the experience were strongly related to the notion that one is responsible for heart disease. Respondents scrutinized their lifestyles for reasons why they had fallen ill. Some looked at their 'unhealthy' lifestyles, characterized by high stress or overweight, and decided that they were to blame, that they 'got what [they] deserved' or 'I guess one could almost say I had it coming to me', in the words of two such respondents (1991: 32). Such respondents felt remorse for their 'mistakes' and were ashamed of their illness, the nature of which so loudly proclaimed the fault of the individual. Others found it difficult to rationalize their heart problems, given that they had lived 'model' lives according to health education rationale, and some felt 'cheated' because they had followed the rules but had still been vulnerable to heart disease, in contravention of health promotion wisdom. As one individual said, 'I felt mad because I did all the right things. I thought, "I walk up and down eight flights. I swam every day. I walk wherever I can." *I'd been doing all the right things.* I'd also been watching my diet like mad.' Another observed, 'I felt that I shouldn't have had the heart attack, and yet I know it's heredity [sic] in our family. But I don't smoke . . . I've been eating pretty regular diets [sic], and I don't drink that much. I've been pretty active . . . *I shouldn't get a heart attack.* I'm too young. I don't smoke, and I'm pretty healthy' (Johnson, 1991: 31, emphases added).

Such comments demonstrate the extent to which people have used health promotion discourses to make sense of theirs or others' illnesses in ways that cast moral judgements upon the ill. They also demonstrate the disillusionment felt when people have accepted the healthism discourse of health promotion, and have done their best to conform to its warnings, yet have found themselves 'unprotected' by their cautious modification of behaviour. Even if people knew that the disease was strongly associated with genetic factors, as in the comment of the individual quoted above, they found it difficult to accept such an explanation as valid because of the dominance of the 'healthism' discourse.

In Britain, North America and Australia, health promotion is a middle-class movement dominated by women from English-speaking back-grounds. While their appeals to rationality and self-control may strike a chord with others of a similar socio-economic and cultural background, different social groups receive and interpret health promotional discourses in different ways. Members of less economically privileged groups, or in different stages of the lifecycle, do not necessarily share these meanings and often actively seek to challenge them. People may also articulate

conflicting discourses and strategies that both support the imperatives of
public health and challenge them. In-depth research has thrown light upon
the interaction of health-related knowledges and behaviours in the context
of people's everyday lives. The findings from these studies suggest that
people are highly aware of the political role of institutional discourses on
health maintenance, and are well able to distinguish between the demands
of institutional imperatives and how these should be applied to their
private lives. This is particularly the case when interviewers have been able
to go beyond people's 'public' accounts of health, which tend to conform to
official orthodoxies on the individual's responsibility for her or his health,
to their 'private' accounts. As one working-class man interviewed by
Crawford (1984: 84) maintained: 'I don't want to be forced by any kind of
worry about health that is really not based in reality of fact . . . Now they
start coming out with everything under the sun is going to cause cancer.
What does that do to people? I just say to hell with it. If I've been eating it,
I'm going to keep eating it.' Another study of ten English households of
differing socio-economic status (Calnan and Williams, 1991) found that
while most people articulated a belief in the link between smoking and ill-
health, the working-class respondents were both more likely to smoke and
to deny that the habit affected their health, and while acknowledging that
exercise is good for one's health, tended to see deliberate efforts to take
exercise as an irrelevance to their lives.

Many people appear to oscillate between accepting the orthodoxies of
health promotion as an explanation for ill health – the 'public account' –
and rejecting the victim-blaming implications of these discourses, particularly in relation to their own state of health – the 'private account'.
Backett's (1992) research into the lay health moralities of middle-class
families resident in Edinburgh was aimed at understanding the ways in
which lay health beliefs are constructed and enacted in the everyday,
domestic context. She found that her respondents viewed being obsessive
about one's health as just as much a taboo as being overly cavalier. While
the respondents at first interview tended to give socially acceptable views
on achieving good health according to prevailing official medical and public
health discourses, by the later interviews they were more likely to be
forthcoming about the practical difficulties of putting such ideologies into
practice in the everyday context. Backett concludes, therefore, that
'health-relevant behaviours are simply one aspect of prioritizing and
decision making about time allocation in daily life' (1992: 267). Other
studies have revealed the paradoxical approach people hold towards health
promotional strategies, both accepting the orthodoxies and rejecting them
as too difficult to apply to their own lives (MacInnes and Milburn, 1994;
Lupton, 1994d).

The fatalistic notion that health status is largely a 'matter of luck' tends
to be more often articulated by members of the working class than the
middle class, and by older rather than younger age groups (Pill and Stott,
1982; Lewis et al., 1989; Calnan and Williams, 1991). This assessment is

based largely on personal experience rather than ignorance of dominant health promotional messages, incorporating a recognition that a person's family background, individual constitution and life circumstances are important factors in influencing health status and the length of one's lifespan. For example, research investigating the beliefs on coronary heart disease evinced by people living in Wales (Davison et al., 1992) found that the respondents had a detailed and accurate knowledge of the risk factors for coronary heart disease as disseminated by health promotion agencies and the mass media but did not necessarily follow the guidelines in their own lives. Davison et al. argue that people develop a response to such information they term 'lay epidemiology', which includes 'the routine observation of cases of illness and death in personal networks and the public arena' (1992: 678). Their respondents had come to the recognition that there are barriers to the universal achievement of good health that were beyond individual control, including heredity, inherent traits, relative wealth and access to resources, one's occupation, social networks and support, the climate, natural dangers, environmental contamination and the sheer random nature of luck, or personal destiny (1992: 679).

In addition to the social class differences in the ways in which people respond to health promotional discourses, there has also emerged a gender difference. While women tend to express more concern about their health and body shape and size, men seem to have more of an instrumental view of their bodies and their health, perceiving health-enhancing behaviour as allowing them to participate actively in work or active leisure rather than enhancing their appearance (Morgan, 1993; Saltonstall, 1993). The male body is far less visible in cultural representations, greater attention is devoted to women's health issues than men's health, and in the sociological literature there is more writing and critique on female embodiment than that of men. In many respects, men tend to deny embodiment, except in relation to sporting or other physical prowess or action. The passive, sickly, problematized male body is culturally under-represented (Morgan, 1993). Indeed, in Anglo-Celtic cultures, to express concern about one's health is often considered 'unmasculine'. In interviews with predominantly middle-class Scottish men, Watson (1993) found that although they drew on moralistic discourses concerning 'slobs' and 'couch potatoes', the respondents were quite contemptuous of other men who displayed an interest in dieting or too much concern with the appearance of their bodies. Rather than put into action the imperatives of health promotion them-selves, they were more likely to take the view that if there was nothing 'wrong' (as in obvious symptoms of illness or disease), there was no need to worry about body maintenance. For young men, deliberate health risk taking may be valued as a means of expressing rebellion against parental and other authority, of demonstrating one's independence and transition from child to adult, and of articulating masculinity (Willis, 1990: 100–2).

Such studies have shown that the discourses of health as control and health as release, existing in tension with each other, are both evident in people's explanations of health maintenance. Health is conceptualized as being both an individual accomplishment and a matter of fate. It is wise to be cautious about one's living habits for the sake of one's health, but to be overly obsessive and deny oneself life's pleasures is to be unhealthy. Crawford (1984) found that the privileging of release was particularly evident in the discourses of the working-class people he interviewed, who expressed less control over their life situation. For these individuals, health is to be achieved by relaxing control, escaping from the discipline of work and the worries of everyday life (see also, Herzlich and Pierret, 1987: 232–3). The discourse of release draws on the logic of freedom and the satisfaction of desire. This discourse resists those imperatives of health promotion that valorize discipline, conceptualizing health as an outcome of enjoyment, the relief of stress and emotional tension. The grotesque body – plump, drunk, belching, stuffed to the gills with rich food, sucking on a cigarette, fornicating – becomes a site of pleasure and self-indulgence, and through the pleasures of consumption, resistance, in its rejection of dominant social norms (Morgan, 1993: 82–3).

Yet there is a paradox implicit in the dualism of control and release: discipline intensifies desire in denying it, the intensification of which may in turn lead to further restraint (Crawford, 1984: 101). This paradox emerges from the dialectic of capitalism, in which self-discipline is required to produce commodities, but the consumption of these commodities depends on the gratification of desire, albeit in carefully managed ways. As an advertisement for a Chicago health club worded it, 'We'll work you out and then we'll pamper you' (quoted in Crawford, 1984: 93). Health promotion co-exists with commodity culture in a symbiotic, mutually supportive relationship. Desire and self-indulgence are incited in one forum and restraint urged in the next, leading back to a compensatory search for self-indulgence, followed by a need to exert control. Thus individuals are placed in a 'double-bind', in which they move between consumption and asceticism, between the 'performance principle' and 'letting go' (Bordo, 1990: 97). In this context, health imperatives are taken up at some times and dropped at others in a continuing cycle of control and release.

Fitness, sport and exercise

With its emphasis on lifestyle, many of the tenets of health promotion are directed towards the regulation of consumption activities. In health promotional discourse, lifestyle is pathologized as a source of ill-health, the constellation of a diverse range of specific and discrete behaviours identified as risky, including tobacco and alcohol use, weight, diet, exercise patterns, stress management, driving behaviour, sexual activity, sleep patterns and medication use (Coreil et al., 1985: 428). Questions that remain largely unanswered include: Why do people choose certain behaviours and activities over others? What do these choices mean for individuals, in terms of the construction of subjectivity? Where do health-maintaining practices fit in the context of everyday life? Within commodity culture, lifestyle has yet another, albeit more positive meaning, connoting 'individuality, self-expression, and a stylistic self-consciousness' (Featherstone, 1991b: 83). Lifestyle is thus conceived of as an aesthetic project of the self, a central means of constructing subjectivity (Wearing and Wearing, 1992; Veal, 1993).

From this perspective, engaging in sporting activities or exercise is strongly associated with the construction of subjectivity. The terms 'fitness' and 'health' have generally become synonymous in everyday discourse, especially for members of the middle class. Fitness activities represent the attempt of individuals to find their 'true selves', to uncover the 'fit' and lean individual hiding beneath the layers of flesh, to bring together the mind and the body, to cope with the seemingly chaotic nature of life in the late twentieth century by mastering the body: 'By means of vital, rationalized, and self-directed action, the practitioner of fitness strives to construct an integral biography during a time when roles and collective morality are inconsistent and rapidly changing' (Glassner, 1989: 183). Thus, for some individuals, the imperatives of public health and health promotion around body management and exercise provide them with guidelines for self-transformation, ways of dealing with external and internal pressures, a conduit of agency and self-expression.

To exercise regularly, especially if it involves physical activities which are not 'game-like' and associated with enjoyment (such as racquet sports or team sports) but are solely devoted to body maintenance (for instance, jogging and working-out in gymnasia), acts as a marker of an individual's capacity for self-regulation. This concept of exercise is strongly linked with the concept of health as a 'creation' or an accomplishment of the self. It is also related to broader contemporary notions of the 'ideal' body as one that is tightly controlled, contained in space, devoid of excess fat or flabby muscle. In both health promotional discourses and commodity culture, bodies are routinely segmented in 'problem' areas that require extra attention either because they are too large and fleshy or because they are not well enough defined and toned; the thighs, the buttocks, the pectorals, the biceps. This segmentation reaches its apotheosis in body building, where special machines and exercises are designed to 'work' discrete areas of the body. As one female bodybuilder commented: 'I think that calves are an outrageously sexy body part. I have been able to put a lot more size on them in the past year. I love to train them and I love to watch them grow' (quoted in Mansfield and McGinn, 1993: 54).

These notions of sport as another kind of work, a means of displaying the strength of one's personal character, self-restraint and dedication to a common cause, the body as outward sign of inward moral standing, have been evident in both the medical literature and popular culture since the late nineteenth century (Armstrong, 1983; Mrozek, 1989: 19). As described in Chapter 1, over the past century and a half there has emerged a strong governmental class and gender-based structuring of the type of sporting activities deemed appropriate for different social groups. Yet the imperatives of the ideal-type sporting man have largely been resisted by members of the working class. Hargreaves (1987: 147) contends that even though the nineteenth-century British middle classes attempted to instill self-discipline and asceticism among working-class men through encouraging them to engage in organized sports, the latter much preferred recreational past-times that were more entertainment oriented, such as drinking and gambling. For the working classes, the 'sporting man' was an individual who was 'down-to-earth, sociable, enjoys a drink and a smoke and a good time'. Sports that require good timing and hand–eye coordination, and which take place in environments where individuals can smoke, drink and socialize, such as snooker, pool and darts, remain more popular amongst the working class than the middle class (1987: 153). In his account of the habitus, Bourdieu categorizes the contemporary working-class concept of the body as being instrumental, demonstrated by members of that group's choice of sports that often involve pain, suffering and a sense of gambling with the body, such as boxing, motor cycling, parachuting and rugby. He argues that by contrast the privileged classes treat the body as an 'end in itself', focusing on its state of health, its aesthetics, and engaging in rites of 'an ascetic exaltation of sobriety and dietetic rigour' (Bourdieu, 1993: 354). Bodies within this habitus are constantly self-surveilling themselves and each other, checking for bulges, flab, lack of tone. They look in the mirror, they cast covert glances in public spaces, partners remind each other that they are 'getting too fat' and urge restraint.

The binary oppositions healthy/sickly, masculine/feminine, real/artificial, moral/venal, active/passive, to name but a few, are highly evident in exercise and fitness discourses. Although Glassner (1989) argues that both men and women are exhorted to exercise qualitatively in the same ways, Mansfield and McGinn (1993) have shown, for example, that large muscles on women's bodies are not considered attractive nor feminine, even in the world of body-building, and that women are actively dissuaded against becoming bulky in the same way that men are encouraged to build up muscle tissue. For Bordo (1990), the anxiety around the uncontrolled body is symbolically expressed in such media products as the horror films 'The Fly' and 'Alien', both of which involved nightmarish figures that are combinations of monster and human. This concept of the monstrous, uncontained body is also expressed in women's descriptions of their own bodies, in which they express emotions of disgust at their inability to contain their flesh: for example, one woman commented 'my breasts, my stomach – they're just awful lumps, bumps, bulges. My body can turn on me at any moment; it is an out-of-control mass of flesh' (1990: 89). Bordo argues that 'the construction of the body as an alien attacker, threatening to erupt in an unsightly display of bulging flesh, is a ubiquitous cultural image', at least for women (1990: 89–90).

Is the women's fitness movement merely another example of the way that women's bodies are subjected to dominant discourses, pandering to the narcissistic 'tyranny of slenderness', or is it expressing women's need to resist the stereotypical discourse that represents their bodies as weak and submissive (Crawford, 1984: 95–6)? Choosing to take up the discourse of slenderness and tautness may signify for some women their participation in the valued qualities of western societies – detachment, self-containment, self-mastery, mind-over-matter – that have been traditionally considered the preserve of masculinity rather than femininity (Bordo, 1990: 105; Willis, 1991). Redican and Hadley (1988) found in their interviews with women in paid employment who were regular attenders of a gym in a large English city that the motivation to take up and continue such exercise was more strongly related to positive feelings of self-control and the outer maintenance of the body than to the achievement of good health. The women had invested in a collection of fashionable exercise outfits to train in and were concerned about their body shape and physical deterioration. They viewed the gym as a place to publicly demonstrate their fitness, to relieve the stresses of the working day and to experience a glow of achievement. However, they also expressed guilt about their laziness if they did not engage in regular exercise. The respondents viewed their level of fitness and participation in the exercise activities as symbolizing the achievement of a goal, and saw themselves in a hierarchy of fitness which they aspired to climb. Their participation in exercise thus was both a release from work but also took on the structure of work. Attendance at the gym for the women was also a source of social support, as they became friends with other attenders and staff.

The constellation of meanings surrounding such activities suggest that people exercise because it is fashionable, because it is virtuous and ascetic, representing self-control and self-discipline, but also because it is glamorous and sexy, involving form-fitting Lycra body-wear and expensive, hi-tech shoes (Bordo, 1990; Featherstone, 1991a). As Hargreaves (1987: 151) has commented: 'What links consumer culture with sports culture so economically . . . is their common concern with, and capacity to accommodate the body meaningfully in the constitution of the normal individual.' For some women, engaging in exercise may represent their desire to escape the bounds of the feminine role, to subvert the notion of the female body as weak and dependent, while for other women, and most men, the primary motivation is to acquire the lean, hard, firm athletic body so prized as sexually attractive by consumer culture (Hargreaves, 1987; Bordo, 1990; Willis, 1991; Saltonstall, 1993). For those people of both sexes approaching middle-age, exercise may signify an attempt to secure youth and attractiveness in a culture which views the ageing or overweight body as physically repulsive (Featherstone and Hepworth, 1991; Mellencamp, 1992). In all these cases, exercise offers an opportunity to reshape one's flesh, to either pare it down and rid it of unwanted fat, or to build it up with muscle. When these cultural meanings are examined, the desire for 'good health' becomes a very minor component of people's reasons for engaging in exercise regimens, superseded by concerns engendered by the powerful ideologies of morality, asceticism, self-discipline and control which underlie consumption patterns in a culture which is intent upon self-promotion and achieving 'the look' (Wernick, 1991; Featherstone, 1991a). Notions of 'health' are reinterpreted, particularly in middle-class commodity culture, as concerning attractiveness and body maintenance; as one respondent interviewed by Saltonstall commented, 'Well, it's pretty easy. I just look at them, if they're not in shape, I say, "Those people are not healthy" ' (1993: 11).

While these concepts of the idealized body are clearly strongly linked to consumer culture, in representing bodies as commodities, and health promotional discourses, in valorizing the controlled body, other institutions, such as the military and the education system, have been integral to the construction of the 'healthy' and 'fit' body. As discussed in Chapter 1, since the nineteenth century the education system has been a primary site at which dominant discourses around sport and physical exercise have been produced and reproduced. At the end of the twentieth century, health education and physical development programmes in schools continue as forums for the reproduction of dominant ideologies and discourses around appropriate bodily deportment. There are a number of dominant ideologies circulating in contemporary school physical education: individualism, or the emphasis on values that support the individual's achievement in competition; healthism, the valorization of fitness as leading to good health and the notion of good health as emerging from careful control; technocratic rationality, emphasizing efficiency, value-free facts, the control of time and the notion of the human body as a machine and physical education as a 'science' devised by 'experts' and merely implemented by teachers; and mesomorphism, or a privileging of the fit, slim, muscular body over the thin and rounded body (Kirk and Colquhoun, 1989; Tinning, 1990).

Hargreaves (1986: 162) sees physical education as quite overtly directed towards cooperation, self-control and body management, symbolizing individual responsibility for the maintenance of harmonious social order. He further points out (1986: 164) that such terms as 'preparation for society', 'knowledge of right and wrong' and 'integrating the odd man [sic] out' are frequently used in the discourse of physical education, as is the potential for exercise to maximize such qualities as 'initiative', 'creativity', 'competence', 'discipline', 'loyalty' and 'cooperation'. Social processes and structures are obscured by such a discourse with its emphasis on individual achievement and social integration: 'Where the discourse does touch on social structure it is in terms of a pervasive "communitarianism", whereby the school and its pupils are depicted as forming part of a vague, undefined entity – "the community" ' (1986: 165). In the context of schooling, teachers view themselves as doing the right thing by their pupils in encouraging them to achieve their goal of the healthy body, in turn allowing pupils to succeed physically but also socially. As this suggests, the notion of the ideal body does not simply conform to state imperatives relating to producing a fit labour force. Its rationale is far more individualized in that it valorizes the importance of being 'fit' and 'healthy' as a project for oneself, to fulfil the individual's objectives, rather than those of the state.

Quite apart from the moral meanings of sporting activities, the emotions they induce also need consideration. Sports and games are exciting: they engage the emotions and the passions, they incite feelings of nationalism and community (Mennell, 1992: 141). The combination of uncertainty and the dramatic, ritualistic and theatrical quality of sporting activities results in a rich investment of meaning which uniquely endows them with the capacity to deploy the body so as to reproduce hegemonic ideologies and discourses (Hargreaves, 1987: 142). Since the turn of the century, participation in sporting activities has been viewed as an intense experience, uniting sensual pleasure, self-discipline, self-discovery, self-expression and fulfilment: 'Sport was a joy, but it was also a duty – a peculiar but essential paradox not unlike that arising in religious conversion' (Mrozek, 1989: 42-3). In highly regulated western societies, where the public containment of emotions such as hatred, aggression and wild joy is expected, participation in sporting activities as either a competitor or a spectator allows the spontaneous release of feeling. Hence the representation in popular culture of professional sporting bouts as the discursive equivalent of wars; the common use of aggressive military terms such as 'battle', 'fight', 'vanquish' and 'warrior' in coverage of sporting activities. In such activities, argues Elias (quoted in Mennell, 1992: 142); 'Imaginary danger, mimetic fear and pleasure, sadness and joy are produced and perhaps resolved by the setting of past-times. Different moods are evoked and perhaps contrasted, such as sorrow and elation, agitation and peace of mind.' The stimulation and then the resolving of these emotions in the controlled setting of the sporting arena serve, for a short time at least, to take participants out of the everyday world of 'real life' with its risks and perils. Moreover sporting activities allow participants to display their feelings in the company of others (sometimes thousands of others) in ways which are prohibited in other social arenas, allowing the collective manifestation of emotion (Mennell, 1992: 142–3).

A study which elicited memories of sport from individuals demonstrated the link between sporting activities, social relationships and emotion. Healey (1991) asked 132 Americans for their single clearest memory connected with sport. He found that most of the events recalled occurred during childhood and adolescence and most concerned high or moderate emotional intensity, relating to such feelings as joy, pride, excitement, embarrassment, frustration and humiliation. The most common theme of the memories related around positive self-discovery, where individuals remembered an incident in which they 'proved' themselves and gained self-confidence or a renewed appreciation of their own talents. Other common themes included the experience of strengthening social bonds through sport (such as neighbourhood games in childhood or school team sports), images of personal heroism, where the protagonists 'saved the day' for their team, stories about overcoming obstacles due to determination and fighting spirit, or conversely about failure, and stories about pain. Healey concludes that 'people freely and commonly associate sport with their closest relationships and the most meaningful moments in their lives' (1991: 226–7). Participation in sporting activities, then, is motivated by a complex admixture of discourses, in which the imperative of health is but one consideration.

. As this research suggests, the practices of the self privileged by public health and health promotional discourses should not necessarily be viewed as constraining and oppressive. Consider the example of a young middle-class male, working in a highly paid professional occupation, who responds to dominant discourses on fitness, health and the commodified body by attending a gym regularly. He can well afford the expensive Nike shoes and Lycra outfits he wears to the gym as well as the monthly gym membership. He enjoys many aspects of his gym experience: the break from sitting at a desk, the opportunity to engage in physical exercise to release the tensions of his demanding job, the physical pleasures of sweating, moving muscles, working out to the throbbing beat of dance music, an increased heart-rate and oxygen intake and release of endomorphins, making him feel vital and full of energy, the hot shower afterwards, the notion of being part of a community of athletes, the feeling of well-deserved physical tiredness that facilitates a deep sleep when he goes to bed. While he generally eats a low fat diet, because of his regular attendance at the gym he permits himself little indulgences – a beer or two, the occasional chocolate bar – that he knows will not make him overweight as long as he keeps up the exercise. He can say airily to friends or work colleagues, 'I'm off to the gym', thus reinforcing his self-identity as that of the healthy, active, fit young man. He feels no embarrassment when lounging at the beach dressed only in a skimpy swimming costume, or removing his clothes in front of sexual partners. Indeed he enjoys showing off his well-defined abdominals, biceps and quadriceps to others, and even permits himself the occasional parade in front of the mirror at home. This young man is no victim, he is not oppressed by dominant discourses; indeed, he is highly aware of, and revels in, the discourses of self-control, asceticism and aestheticism that construct the meaning of his exercising.

Consider this same man a decade later. He shares his house with his partner and perhaps young children. He has achieved a high position in his workplace, but with this comes more responsibility, lunch-times which must be worked through or devoted to eating rich food and drinking with clients and long hours spent working at his desk in the evenings and at the weekend. He no longer goes to the gym simply because he lacks the time. What little spare time he has is mostly spent relaxing in front of the television with his partner and a few calming drinks. From time to time he feels guilty and anxious about his lack of physical exercise. He knows he should engage in regular aerobic exercise to maximize his cardiovascular fitness, but most importantly from his perspective, he has lost his muscle tone and bulk and his once trim stomach, of which he was so proud, has become flabby and there is the beginning of a middle-aged spread. All his trousers have become tight, and his partner has started to make carping comments about his 'love-handles' and to nickname him 'tubby'. He secretly worries that his partner might no longer find him attractive, and may even leave him for another, trimmer, man. He avoids looking at his naked body in the mirror, and no longer parades at the beach. He is still the same 'person', albeit with a somewhat physically different body, but his subjectivity has changed. The discourses of fitness, healthism, self-discipline and asceticism that once made him feel attractive and vital, in control, now constitute him as lazy, unattractive, a loser, out of control.

As this example demonstrates, the interaction of discourse, practices of the self and subjectivity in the context of health promotional and other governmental imperatives is not stable. The ways in which discourses are taken up and integrated into self-identity are at least partially contingent on the flux of individuals' positions in the workforce, in the lifecycle and the interaction of institutions such as the economy, the family, the school.

Alcohol and tobacco use: a symbolic perspective

Health promotional discourses represent both cigarette smoking and alcohol use as 'problems' and 'risky activities' that must be fought against in the interests of the public's health. Those individuals or social groups who are deemed to have a 'problem' with alcohol or smoking tend to be represented in health promotional discourses as weak and easily susceptible to external pressures. They are portrayed as uncontrolled, needful of a higher level of rationality: indeed, as 'uncivilized'. In the case of groups who continue to smoke or drink alcohol, such reasons as 'peer group' pressure are often put forward. The concept of 'peer group pressure', notes May (1993: 161) in the context of youths and alcohol consumption, adopts 'the notion of an underdeveloped or distorted rationality, embodied in the apparent failure of individuals to make socially competent decisions about their drinking behaviours'. 'Peer group pressure' is viewed as negative, 'forcing' people to do things that are not good for them, whereas it may equally act as a restraint on behaviours. Indeed, such factors as membership of an occupational group have been shown to be more relevant to behaviours such as smoking and alcohol use than peer group (Daykin, 1993: 96). In health promotional discourses, alcohol use and smoking tend therefore to be removed from both their social meaning and their social context. The problem is viewed as that of the individual rather than the product they consume.

Most health promotional literature tends to emphasize the negative health effects of alcohol, concentrating on excessive use, without acknowledging the research indicating that moderate alcohol consumption appears beneficial for health status, for example protecting against heart disease (McCormick, 1994: 390). Similarly there are a number of epidemiological studies which have suggested that the nicotine in cigarettes can protect against such diseases as Parkinson's disease, Alzheimer's disease, ulcerative colitis, rheumatoid arthritis and some cancers. Such studies have tended to be downplayed in the medical and public health literature, and funding is generally not forthcoming from national funding bodies to follow-up their findings because of the stigmatization around cigarettes and the current obsession with their health side-effects (Mundell, 1993).

The decline in cigarette smoking amongst some social groups (mostly older middle-class men and women) in western countries has led some health promoters to claim that their strategies directed at tobacco control have been successful. Yet just as the growing consumption of cigarettes following the Second World War was intimately linked to popular culture (not only advertising, but cinematic and televisual representations and popular novels), the decline of smoking (amongst the middle class at least) cannot be simply explained by the health promotional efforts, but also by concurrent movements within popular culture and everyday life. Central to understanding why it is that people either desist from smoking or excess drinking, or continue to participate in these activities, is the symbolic nature of alcohol and tobacco as commodities and conduits of pleasure and desire. The emotions – pleasures, fears, anxieties and desires – around the use of commodities such as alcohol and cigarettes in the face of health promotional discourses warning against them have been little explored in public health research. So, too, the use of these commodities in the construction of subjectivity is rarely acknowledged.

Commodities have properties which link them to a certain way of life, a certain personality, a certain social class (Bourdieu, 1984). Ritual is used to transfer meaning from goods to individuals by way of exchange, possession, grooming and divestment rituals: each represents a different stage in a more general process in which meaning is moved from consumer good to individual consumer (Douglas and Isherwood, 1978; McCracken, 1988: 84). Just as commodities have their obvious use-value, they also have the qualities of a more symbolic value, expressing the owner's taste and sense of style. Goods thus act as a message system, indicating to oneself and others the type of image one would like to fit. As I noted in Chapter 4, advertising is an important part of adding meaning to consumer products.

Scanning of sociological and anthropological research reveals some important dimensions of the pleasures and needs fulfilled by alcohol and cigarette use. Unlike the majority of health promoters, anthropologists do not necessarily view alcohol use as a problem. Rather, from the anthropological perspective alcohol use has been viewed as part of celebration, a social act performed in a recognized social context, and a problem only for a small minority of people (Douglas, 1987: 3-4). Anthropological and interpretive sociological research has revealed that alcoholic drinks function symbolically to mark shifts from worktime to leisure; serve as markers of personal identity and of boundaries of exclusion and inclusion; as a means of making the world intelligible and bearable, as well as having a political economy of production and distribution that affects their use and meaning (Douglas, 1987; Mars, 1987; Thornton, 1987).

Moore (1992), for example, has argued that academic writing on the alcohol 'problem' in Aborigines often tends not to take into account the socio-cultural and political meanings of drinking for Aborigines. Much psychological and psychiatric literature on Aboriginal drinking tends to represent Aborigines as suffering from 'cultural disintegration' and 'maladjustment' compared with an idealized notion of past 'noble' Aboriginal societies. Moore asserts that rather than viewing drinking as the pathological product of anomie, it should be regarded as an activity laden with social meaning. Drinking on the part of Aborigines may be viewed as an act of rebellion against increased white interference and decreased autonomy, a mark of personal productivity, social status and independence and a means of reciprocity and engaging in communal life. Hence, rather than there being no rules around drinking in Aboriginal groups, there is a network of mores which shape Aboriginal consumption of alcohol within specific social contexts. Drinking for Aborigines is not simply destructive and pathological, but also has beneficial aspects, just as it does for other groups. Indeed, Aboriginal acts of drinking may be viewed as 'an essentially political act' (Moore, 1992: 187), a concept which challenges individualistic attempts at prevention. Ironically, the attempts of non-Aboriginal authorities to change drinking habits are thus often interpreted by Aborigines as yet more interventions and impositions on their lives, impositions to which they have responded by continuing to drink alcohol.

Gusfield (1987: 79), in a discussion of alcohol as a marker of time, notes that 'alcohol appears in American society deeply connected with mood-setting. It is a mood which contrasts with the serious and the work-a-day world.' Alcohol acts as a 'cover' for embarrassing moments, lapses of responsibility, gaucheries and improper actions. It signifies festiveness and gaiety, and acts to dissolve social hierarchies, allowing alternative subjectivities to be expressed. It is a ritual to celebrate the end of the working day or week, and involves relationships of moral economies in terms of buying rounds (1987: 79–81). Dorn (1983) undertook a detailed study into drinking behaviour amongst youths in Britain, focusing on sub-cultures. He found that forms of drinking practice in 'pub culture', including 'round buying', were important parts of working-class male youth culture. Round buying symbolically demonstrated the economic independence and equality of individuals, and enabled reciprocal public exchange, serving to contribute to the cohesiveness of the group. In such a sub-culture, health promotion activities directed at fear warnings or 'rational' behaviour has little effect, simply because the social practices of pub culture are so important to such youths' sense of group and personal identity, and serve to insulate these underprivileged individuals from outside cultural imposition, of which health promotion activities are a part.

Similarly, Willis' (1990: 100–1) study of young British men and women found that drinking in pubs was a central leisure activity, especially for the white youths. They went to the pub to escape boredom, the restrictions of the family home, to be with others in a convivial and social environment dedicated to leisure and informality. Willis notes that the imbibing of alcohol serves to relax the self, to distance oneself from the real world within a warm, friendly environment. For many young men, entry into the pub represents the promise of adventure in suspending the mundane and the everyday. Round buying and drunkenness becomes a competitive activity, a way of reinforcing solidarity and of demonstrating 'manliness'. Drunkenness, and being in the pub itself, offer the opportunity of uncertainty and of the pleasurable frisson of danger, an atmosphere in which anything might happen: 'The physiological effects of alcohol are interpreted to mean loss of control – an existential freeing of the self to an uncertainty which seems to be "new" or "different" every time. It opens the way to adventure' (Willis, 1990: 102). For young women, the meanings of alcohol consumption are somewhat different. Drinking is not competitive, and excess drinking has negative connotations with the danger of potential attack and the risk of appearing to be too sexually available. Alcohol means uncertainty for women too, but this uncertainty is feared rather than welcomed (1990: 102).

Research routinely finds that people are highly aware of the health promotional and news media messages about the health-effects of such behaviours as excess alcohol consumption and smoking. For instance, middle-aged Scottish men interviewed about their smoking articulated feelings of embarrassment, shame, of being social outcasts, of demonstrating lack of self-discipline. As one man commented, 'nowadays to smoke is a sign of weakness, a sign of ill-health' (Mullen, 1987: 240; see also Crawford, 1984: 69). But yet they also argued that smoking offers them much pleasure, giving them 'something to do with their hands', relieving boredom, helping them to relax. Smoking is a way of managing negative emotion, but also is a potential incitement of such emotion in the context of the growing social condemnation of smoking and the smoker. Smoking is a way of dealing with a stressful work environment, or unemployment, a means of giving oneself a 'reward': 'It's like a pat on the back to myself' (Mullen, 1992: 83).

For many working-class or impoverished women, it appears that the combination of material deprivation and acting as primary carer for young children encourages the need to smoke. In three separate studies with underprivileged British women caring for children with little social support (Graham, 1987; Oakley, 1989; Calnan and Williams, 1991), women spoke of the pleasure they derived from sitting down with a cigarette, and perhaps a cup of coffee or tea, to take 'time-out' from the rigours of their day; for example one woman commented, 'If I was economizing, I'd cut down on cigarettes, but I wouldn't give up. I'd stop eating. That sounds terrible, doesn't it? Food just isn't that important to me but having a cigarette is the only thing I do just for myself' (Graham, 1987: 55). In situations where the women have had to deal with misbehaving children or marital conflict, sitting down and having a cigarette is a strategy of coping, of dealing with feelings of anger towards children or partner. Daykin (1993) conducted a study of young women smokers living in England, and discovered that they used cigarettes in similar ways. Her interviews found that the young women experienced disputes around the degree of autonomy allowed them within the family. More of those who had not managed to find a job since leaving school had increased their consumption of cigarettes, as did those who reported a greater degree of domestic tension, suggesting the role of smoking as a relief of feelings of boredom, insecurity, lack of autonomy and conflict. Smoking provided them with symbolic adult status, and helped the women to manage their tension and suppress their anxiety and anger.

Klein's paean to cigarette smoking, entitled *Cigarettes are Sublime* (1993), is one of the few theoretical examinations of the ways in which the cigarette acts as fetish, prop, object and conduit of beauty and an expression and extension of the innermost self. For Klein, cigarettes are 'sublime' because they combine aesthetic satisfaction with intimations of mortality. Cigarettes are a 'negative pleasure'; they risk death even as they fulfil desire (1993: 2). Smoking becomes an expression of one's emotional state, and also a means of releasing negative feelings, diffusing them from the body through the cigarette and into the air via the smoke. It combines a physiological 'rush', a heightening of the pulse, with a psychological need, but each cannot be removed from the other as they are symbiotically intertwined. Klein discusses vividly the sensual, almost erotic pleasure of drawing in smoke, releasing it in a cloud hovering around one's head, watching it dissipate:

> Take a long, deep puff on a cigarette; fill yourself up with its venomous smoke; let it touch the innermost convolutions of your lungs; then exhale it, slowly, past nose and lips in a swirling, expanding stream about your head. *Tout est la*. The smoke penetrates sharply, then exudes, softly envelops you in the experience of extending your body's limits, no longer fixed by the margin of your skin. The tobacco's vapour is atomized into atmosphere that halos your exterior form, after having been condensed within the cavities that harbour your most intimate interior. Joining inside and out, each puff is like a total immersion: it baptizes the celebrant with the little flash of a renewed sensation, an instantaneous, fleeting body image of the unified *Moi*. An inhaling moment of concentration, centralizing the self to make it more dense, more opaquely present to itself, is trailed by a moment of evaporation, as the self exhales itself, ecstatically, in a smoky jag – as it grows increasingly tenuous, progressively less differentiated from the exterior world it becomes. (1993: 105)

Cigarettes work to defeat anxiety by displacing the internal state of tension onto the cigarette. The physiological effects of the nicotine rush mimic and intensify the heightened feelings of anxiety, but bind these feelings and responses to the cigarette rather than the internal state, assisting their mastery. When the cigarette is smoked, consumed and then stubbed out, so too is some of the anxiety dispersed, released and extinguished. The rise and then sudden drop in blood pressure that accompanies the smoking act gives a precise, contained resolution of the anxious state, allowing relaxation to overcome anxiety. Discomfort is first elevated and then alleviated. On the more unconscious level, smoking becomes a definite route to death, a death of one's own choosing, over which one has control, representing a kind of freedom over death (Klein, 1993: 142–3).

Cigarettes therefore provide for smokers one of the few moments of 'dark beauty' and expression of defiance that are available to them: 'At a time when war seems to have been banished from the West, cigarettes are one of the last adventures left' (Klein, 1993: 141). There may be very few alternative strategies available for people suffering material and social disadvantage. While middle-class people may find solace and the reinforcement of self-image in the gym, or by engaging in leisure activities such as going out for a meal or to the cinema, lack of opportunity confines the disadvantaged to activities such as smoking. Alcohol and cigarettes are therefore a means of maintaining emotional equilibrium in the face of great social pressure. It is not the cigarette itself that is necessarily important to smokers, even though physical addiction may well be involved, but what it symbolizes. The cigarette is an object with which individuals living highly stressful lives may attempt to exert emotional control. Smoking is pleasurable and relaxing not merely because tobacco is a drug, but because it represents, albeit briefly, a space to sit down, gather one's thoughts, take stock, indulge oneself, engage in hedonism and experience the thrill of danger. Participation in smoking or alcohol use enables the self to escape from the constraints of civility and the management of the body, into release, bodily pleasure, self-indulgence.

When people are living in a world in which everything else seems out of their control, when anger and frustration seem almost overwhelming, the act of smoking is a way of regaining composure, a means of release, but paradoxically, through release it is also a means of control. As symbolic markers of relaxation, both alcohol and cigarettes prepare the body for enjoyment, for the evocation of pleasure, even before their biophysiological effects take place. It may therefore be argued that cigarettes and alcohol evoke emotion because of what they *are*, and not merely because of what they *do* (bearing in mind that there is an inextricable link between the two). The need, or desire for a cigarette or alcoholic drink may thus be viewed as an emotion – like other emotions, a complex intertwining of physical and socio-cultural phenomena.

For Klein, the pleasures and consolations of smoking constitute a redefinition of health, one that challenges the dominant meaning represented in health promotional discourse. He argues that smokers live through their cigarettes, making systematic use of cigarettes as a resource to achieve ends they consider important. Without cigarettes, Klein asserts, smokers would not *have* a life, for life would lose the meaning and sense of self that have been constructed with the aid of cigarettes: 'The notion that by giving up smoking we will attain health is the illusion that feeds the impulse to stop smoking that smoking itself creates . . . Ultimately, health is the realization that there is no health, only disease and parasites. But that's life' (1993: 103). Ironically, the health promotional discourses around the prohibition of alcohol or smoking may thus serve to underline these meanings, promoting these actions rather than discouraging them. Knowing that cigarettes are bad for the health may, indeed, be considered a precondition for taking up and maintaining the habit; for 'if cigarettes were good for you, they would not be sublime' (Klein, 1993: 1–2). Klein points to the contradiction of repression as incitement; the more a behaviour is discussed, overtly prohibited, denounced as evil, sinful or health-damaging, the more pleasurable it becomes. Censorship thus fosters its use (1993: 182). These insights recall the control/release cycle mentioned earlier in this chapter, the dialectic between repression and the incitement of desire, between rationality and irrationality, between the consumption of commodities and the asceticism of health-maintenance regimens. Health promotional imperatives, thus, may be conceptualized as an integral dimension of the 'dark pleasures' of the behaviours they prohibit, serving to intensify their enjoyment by rendering them sins.

Concluding comments

The insights described in this chapter into the social uses, pleasures, fears and desires, both conscious and unconscious, around 'lifestyle' activities such as sports and exercise, cigarette smoking and alcohol consumption, construct an alternative perspective on 'health' from that evident in health promotional discourses. They recognize that health-maintaining practices do not stand alone and above other practices of everyday life, but are incorporated seamlessly into the life-world of the individual, often in ways that submerge any overt 'health' associations under other meanings and pleasures experienced as more important. They also go some way to elucidating the nexus between governmentality and the construction of subjectivity and bodily practices in the context of contemporary public health and health promotion.

Public health and health promotion have provided a set of central interpretive repertoires for individuals to draw upon in their ceaseless working to construct subjectivity. The dominant discourses of public health and health promotion, with links to other social institutions and vested interests, may produce anxiety, concern about one's body or relationships, even a hatred of the self. Yet they also serve to help us know ourselves and our worlds, and produce forms of subjectivity that allow some individuals to feel in control of their lives and bodies, at least on some occasions. The vast majority of people are well aware of the health promotional orthodoxies concerning lifestyle modification. In the context of a constellation of opposing as well as supportive discourses and tactics of other governmental enterprises, the imperatives of health are taken up but are just as often resisted, ignored or negotiated. Many individuals adopt or at least attempt to take up the imperatives of health promotion for the sake of their health status. Yet others steadfastly resist adopting the advised strategies of health preservation, and many give up their attempts quite quickly. Some people at times find pleasure and a sense of certainty in the adoption of health promotional practices and beliefs into their everyday lives, while others find the imperatives simply too limiting, or enjoy the guilty pleasure of flouting their dictums. Resistance to and negotiation of public health imperatives may originate from the conscious will, from a recognition that they do not fit the self or because they chafe upon cherished notions of autonomy. They may also originate at the emotional level or the unconscious, places where desire, fear and pleasure are repressed, emerge and are constantly in tension with external governmental imperatives, or at the level of the non-conscious, where bodily practices are adopted and reproduced as part of the habits of everyday life.

It therefore cannot be argued that public health and health promotional discourses are uniformly coercive, repressive or confining, for they provide ways of shaping embodiment and a range of subject positions. However, these bodily practices and sources of subjectivity are not available to all individuals equally, and do frequently serve to perpetuate relations of social inequality, often organized around the drawing of distinctions between gender, categories of sexual preference, ethnicity and social class. Where the imperatives of health are constraining is in their inward focus, their linking to the narcissistic care of the self, body management and control. The promotion of such self-obsession serves to obscure social differences, to cover over the traces of structural social inequity and often to reproduce it. While 'resistance' to health promotional discourses may occur at the individual level, in the flouting of health imperatives and the enjoyment of the pleasures of commodities such as cigarettes and alcohol, at this micro-level of non-conformance dimensions of the relationship between the state, commodity culture and public health at the macro-level tend to be obscured. The contingent and political nature of public health knowledges and 'truths' are little challenged at the micro-level of resistance. Whether individuals take pride in their body management, their achievement of fitness and 'health', whether they wallow in guilt over their body-out-of-control, or whether they revel in the self-indulgence of the grotesque body, their concerns, pleasures and anxieties are limited to the self. Not only, then, do the constructions of the ideal subject in public health and health promotional discourses require problematizing for their limitations, moral judgements and tendency to support and reproduce social inequality, but so too does the often myopic focus of the philosophy of the care of the self into which they fit.

Conclusion

Throughout this book I have sought to problematize the taken-for-granted nature of health promotion discourses. I have attempted to demonstrate that public health and health promotion act as apparatuses of moral regulation, serving to draw distinctions between 'civilized' and 'uncivilized' behaviour, to privilege a version of subjectivity that incorporates rationality, to promote notions of the human body as separate from the mind/will, needful of careful management and control and to represent certain social groups as uncontrolled, and therefore, the threatening Other. However I have also argued that these governmental texts, discourses and practices should not simply be regarded as means of brainwashing, oppression or indoctrination, but as the sites of struggle and the constant renegotiation of meaning, subjectivity and bodily practices. Indeed, as I have shown, the imperatives of public health and health promotion may also be considered both sources of pleasure in themselves and incitements of the 'sins' they seek to control. As I have observed in earlier chapters, in health promotional discourses the privileging of rationality may be viewed as an attempt to suppress the disorderly aspects of human nature, as well as those threatened by disease and illness states and death, to deny the body, to project anxieties about contamination and dirt onto marginalized groups. Yet the continued attempts to suppress the body only serve to reincite desire and highlight embodiment. As the psychoanalytic perspective argues, rationality and irrationality are in a dialectical relationship; each could not exist without the other. Indeed, the quest for rationality itself emerging from the Enlightenment could be described as an irrational fantasy of mastery and domination, an expression of the desire for a perfectly ordered universe (Sofia, 1993: 26). Hence the ultimate irrationality and perverse nature of rationality as it is expressed in public health and other governmental sites.

I began this book by discussing the importance of reflexivity on the part of researchers and practitioners in the fields of public health and health promotion. I argued that the adoption of socio-cultural theory and critique encourages workers and researchers to devote more attention to the epistemological and ontological aspects of their endeavours. Their ability to question the practices, knowledges and belief systems of public health and health promotion, including their own privileging of 'health', 'knowledge' and 'rationality', needs to be fostered. The critical analysis of discourse encourages practitioners and researchers constantly to be reflexive and to confront the political dimension of their own use of language and discourse, including their truth claims, as part of their professional activities. Such praxis should include not only analysing the discriminatory or stereotyping characteristics of discourses and practices and interrogating their normalizing assumptions, but also highlighting the multiple and alternative forms of subjectivity, rationality and bodily practices that are available in the dispersed and contested sites of governmentality. Questioning the dualisms, or binary oppositions, that dominate meaning is an important aspect of the critical awareness of language and discourse. For example, as shown throughout this book, the insistence on discriminating between men/women, the masculine/the feminine, moral/depraved, well/ ill, controlled/chaotic, active/passive, Self/Other and disciplined/unruly has been central to medical and public health discourses and remains so. Such essentialisms are too reductive, failing to recognize the plurality of difference that exists in the social world.

One approach to develop reflexivity is the use of writing tasks to encourage individuals to explore the conditions of their own lives in the context of broader power relations. Writing narratives or stories and reading them 'across and against each other' is a means of laying bare the socio-political nature of the construction of individual lives and allows for the possibility of 'rewriting' stories (Game, 1991: 47–8). There are strong possibilities here for the manner in which health promoters and educators and other public health workers might be trained themselves, and in turn learn to train others in different 'ways of seeing'. Fox (1993: 114-15) describes a postgraduate programme at a British university training individuals in the caring professions (including health workers) which uses ficto-critical writing as a means of encouraging reflexive thought on work practices. The participants write fictional accounts based on issues in their lives, past or present, on a topic decided by the group each week. They then read their writing aloud and discuss them in a small group setting. The use of fiction is to enable participants to write about potentially sensitive or embarrassing issues without feeling as if they are exposing themselves. Sociological writing and practices are themselves challenged by this approach, including questions concerning the nature of knowledge and theorizing, and the dialectic between subjectivity and the social collective.

Students and practitioners may also be encouraged to engage in media analysis, discourse analysis and other methods of revealing the ways in which knowledges and truths are created and power relations reproduced through language and discourse. For example, the AIDS cultural activist and academic Cindy Patton (1990: 158–9) has described her strategies for teaching about AIDS at the tertiary level, involving encouraging discussion on the political nature of 'facts' and how they make a difference to people's experiences and concerns, comparing different genres of writing about and visually portraying AIDS, from New Right pamphlets and government policy documents to novels and plays about living with AIDS, inviting outside speakers who can provide a number of different perspectives on the epidemic, from hospice workers to lawyers, and teaching 'practical deconstruction', or reading texts such as pamphlets, media reports, everyday conversations and medical literature for their discursive practices. She gives as an example the interrogation of the term 'emergency' to describe the AIDS epidemic. Patton looks at whose interests are served by describing the epidemic as an 'emergency', the ways in which this discursive choice implicates certain public health laws, invokes issues of blame, quarantine and the policing of marginalized groups. She and her students pursue discourses related to 'emergency', including gender, post-colonial social organization, definitions of 'public' and 'health' and who is empowered to make such definitions (1990: 107–8; see also Grover, 1992; Lupton, 1994c).

The process of interrogating a text, of laying bare its discursive and ideological dimensions, may create resistant readings which may 'disarticulate to one extent or another the intertextual articulation of a text' (Fairclough, 1992: 136). An example of a 'demystification' of a commodity through such a critical interrogation of discourse and representation is that conducted by Klein in his book *Cigarettes are Sublime* (discussed in Chapter 5). According to Klein (1993: ix), one of the purposes of writing his psychoanalytically informed work on the sublime nature of the cigarette and smoking (which process he dubs 'fumo-analysis') was to acquire another perspective on the satisfactions that smoking provides. He argues that attempts to elucidate the smoking experience will provide smokers with a new perspective on their habit, perhaps disenthralling cigarettes by removing the mystique around them, and thus stripping them of their very attractiveness (1993: 2–3). Klein himself had written his book as a (successful) strategy for giving up smoking, and therefore describes his work as 'both an ode and an elegy to cigarettes' (1993: 3).

It is important to bear in mind that such pedagogical processes have themselves the potential to be confining and authoritarian, perpetuating rather than challenging relations of power. Donald (1992: 142–3) points to the paradox in teaching people to be autonomous and 'think for themselves'; in doing so, one is directing them to behave in certain ways, thus restricting their autonomy (see also Lather, 1991: 101). This dilemma, I believe, does not negate attempts to demystify the taken-for-granted nature of public health and health promotion, to expose their epistemological bases, to construct alternative positions, viewpoints and knowledges with the awareness of their nature as cultural practices. To disrupt the confining nature of the types of subjects and bodies offered by public health and health promotion, it is necessary to realize their contingent, constantly moving and dispersed nature, to acknowledge that 'positions of resistance can never be established once and for all. They must, instead, be perpetually refashioned to address adequately the shifting conditions and circumstances that ground them' (Lather, 1991: 100). The point is not to seek a certain 'truth', but to uncover the varieties of truth that operate, to highlight the nature of truth as transitory and political and the position of subjects as inevitably fragmentary and contradictory. If it is acknowledged that discourse formations and subject positions are not bounded systems, but are open to dispersal, contradiction, contestation and opposition, then the opportunity to construct alternative discourses and subject positions is facilitated. Public health and health promotion become recognized as institutions that reproduce accepted understandings of truth and certain versions of the subject within specific historical and social conditions.

There may seem to be a certain lack of security and order in this approach to subjectivity and the social world, particularly in this post-Enlightenment age, when individuals are acculturated to accept the notion of the unified self as the ideal towards which they should strive. But ontological uncertainty, ambivalence and fragmentation need not be negative. As Smart (1993: 103) has asserted, '[t]he prospect of living without certainty or necessity may cause us to respond with fear, anxiety, and insecurity, but equally it allows us to live with imagination and responsibility . . . it constitutes a site, space, or clearing for political possibilities, rather than a distinctive political strategy'. He (1993: 103–6) argues that this perspective allows individuals to assume responsibility with others for their shaping of their destiny, rather than accepting fate, providing a space for the acknowledgment of differences and diversity, new ways of relating, new forms of experience and the social. As this suggests, the 'resistance' emerging from such processes of interrogation need not be confined to the micro-level. Individual recognition of the processes by which one's own subjectivity is shaped through the discursive practices and regulatory activities of institutions such as public health and health promotion in ways that are often confining and discriminatory, if articulated and shared by others may lead to collective action that seeks to contest taken-for-granted imperatives and strategies.

References

Abrams, M.H. (ed.) (1979) *The Norton Anthology of English Literature*, 4th edn. New York: W.W. Norton and Co.

Almond, B. and Ulanowsky C. (1990) HIV and pregnancy. *Hastings Center Report*, March/April, pp. 16–21.

Amos, A. (1993) In her own best interests? Women and health education: a review of the last fifty years. *Health Education Journal*, 52(3), 141–50.

Arkin, E.B. (1990) Opportunities for improving the nation's health through collaboration with the mass media. *Public Health Reports*, 105(3), 219–23.

Armstrong, D. (1983) *Political Anatomy of the Body: Medical Knowledge in Britain in the Twentieth Century*. Cambridge: Cambridge University Press.

Armstrong, D. (1993) Public health spaces and the fabrication of identity. *Sociology*, 27(3), 393–410.

Ashmore, M., Mulkay, M. and Pinch, T. (1989) *Health and Efficiency: A Sociology of Health Economics*. Milton Keynes: Open University Press.

Ashton, J. and Seymour, H. (1988) *The New Public Health*. Milton Keynes: Open University Press.

Atkin, C. and Arkin, E.B. (1990) Issues and initiatives in communicating health information to the public. In Atkin, C. and Wallack, L. (eds), *Mass Communication and Public Health: Complexities and Conflicts*. Newbury Park, CA: Sage, pp. 13–39.

Backer, T.E., Rogers, E.M. and Sopory, P. (1992) *Designing Health Communication Campaigns: What Works?* Newbury Park, CA: Sage.

Backett, K. (1992) Taboos and excesses: lay health moralities in middle class families. *Sociology of Health and Illness*, 14(2), 255–73.

Bauer, W.W. and Hull, T.G. (1942) *Health Education of the Public: A Practical Manual of Technic*, 2nd edn, rev. Philadelphia: W.B. Saunders.

Bauman, Z. (1992) Survival as a social construct. *Theory, Culture and Society*, 9, 1–36.

Beattie, A. (1991) Knowledge and control in health promotion: a test case for social policy and social theory. In Gabe, J., Calnan, M. and Bury, M. (eds), *The Sociology of the Health Service*. London: Routledge, pp. 162–202.

Beck, U. (1992) *Risk Society: Towards a New Modernity*. London: Sage.

Bennett, P. and Hodgson, R. (1992) Psychology and health promotion. In Bunton, R. and Macdonald, G. (eds), *Health Promotion: Disciplines and Diversity*. London: Routledge, pp. 23–41.

Better Health Commission (1986) *Looking Forward to Better Health: Volume One*. Canberra: Commonwealth of Australia.

Billings, P.R., Beckwith, J. and Alper, J.S. (1992) The genetic analysis of human behaviour: a new era? *Social Science and Medicine*, 35(3), 227–38.

Bilson, G. (1988) Public health and the medical profession in nineteenth-century Canada. In MacLeod, R. and Lewis, M. (eds), *Disease, Medicine, and Empire: Perspectives on Western Medicine and the Experience of European Expansion*. London: Routledge, pp. 156–75.

Bocock, R. (1993) *Consumption*. London: Routledge.

Bolton, R. (1992) AIDS and promiscuity: muddles in the models of HIV prevention. *Medical Anthropology*, 14, 145–223.

Bordo, S. (1990) Reading the slender body. In Jacobus, M., Keller, E.F. and Shuttleworth, S. (eds), *Body/Politics: Women and the Discourses of Science*. New York: Routledge, pp. 83–112.

Bourdieu, P. (1984) *Distinction: a Social Critique of the Judgement of Taste*. London: Routledge and Kegan Paul.

Bourdieu, P. (1990) *In Other Words: Essays Towards a Reflexive Sociology*. Cambridge: Polity Press.

Bourdieu, P. (1993) How can one be a sports fan? In During, S. (ed.), *The Cultural Studies Reader*. London: Routledge, pp. 339–57.

Brandt, A.M. (1985) *No Magic Bullet: A Social History of Venereal Disease in the United States since 1880*. New York: Oxford University Press.

Brown, E.R. and Margo, G.E. (1978) Health education: can the reformers be reformed? *International Journal of Health Services*, 8(1), 3–26.

Bunton, R. (1992) More than a woolly jumper: health promotion as social regulation. *Critical Public Health*, 3(2), 4–11.

Bunton, R. and Macdonald, G. (1992) Introduction. In Bunton, R. and Macdonald, G. (eds), *Health Promotion: Disciplines and Diversity*. London: Routledge, pp. 1–19.

Bunton, R., Murphy, S. and Bennett, P. (1991) Theories of behavioural change and their use in health promotion: some neglected areas. *Health Education Research*, 6(2), 153–62.

Burchell, G. (1991) Peculiar interests: civil society and governing 'the system of natural liberty'. In Burchell, G., Gordon, C. and Miller, P. (eds), *The Foucault Effect: Studies in Governmentality*. Hempel Hempstead: Harvester Wheatsheaf, pp. 119–50.

Bush, A.J. and Boller, G.W. (1991) Rethinking the role of television advertising during health crises: a rhetorical analysis of the federal AIDS campaigns. *Journal of Advertising*, 20(1), 28–37.

Calnan, M. and Williams, S. (1991) Style of life and the salience of health: an exploratory study of health related practices in households from differing socio-economic circumstances. *Sociology of Health and Illness*, 13(4), 516–29.

Caplan, R. (1993) The importance of social theory for health promotion: from description to reflexivity. *Health Promotion International*, 8(2), 147–57.

Carney, S. (1993) Most are tolerant of others smoking. *Sydney Morning Herald*, 9 October.

Catania, J.A., Kegeles, S.M. and Coates, T.J. (1990) Towards an understanding of risk behaviour: an AIDS risk reduction model (ARRM). *Health Education Quarterly*, 17(1), 53–72.

Christie, D., Gordon, I. and Heller, R. (1987) *Epidemiology: An Introductory Text for Medical and Other Health Science Students*. Sydney: New South Wales University Press.

Cipolla, C.M. (1992) *Miasmas and Disease: Public Health and the Environment in the Pre-Industrial Age*. New Haven, CT: Yale University Press.

Colquhoun, D. (1991) Health education in Australia. *Annual Review of Health Social Sciences*, 1, 7–29.

Conrad, P. and Walsh, D.C. (1992) The new corporate health ethic: lifestyle and the social control of work. *International Journal of Health Services*, 22(1), 89–111.

Corbin, A. (1986) *The Foul and the Fragrant: Odour and the French Social Imagination*. Cambridge, MA: Harvard University Press.

Coreil, J., Levin, J.S. and Jaco, E.G. (1985) Life style – an emergent concept in the sociomedical sciences. *Culture, Medicine and Psychiatry*, 9, 423–37.

Cotton, P. (1993) Foucault and psychoanalysis. *Arena*, 1, 63–105.

Coward, R. (1989) *The Whole Truth: the Myth of Alternative Health*. London: Faber and Faber.

Crawford, R. (1977) You are dangerous to your health: the ideology and politics of victim blaming. *International Journal of Health Services*, 7, 663–80.

Crawford, R. (1980) Healthism and the medicalization of everyday life. *International Journal of Health Services*, 19, 365–88.

Crawford, R. (1984) A cultural account of 'health': control, release, and the social body. In McKinlay, J.B. (ed.), *Issues in the Political Economy of Health Care*. New York: Tavistock, pp. 60–103.

Crawford, R. (1994) The boundaries of the self and the unhealthy other: reflections on health, culture and AIDS. *Social Science and Medicine*, 38(10), 1347–65.

Curson, P.H. (1985) *Times of Crisis: Epidemics in Sydney, 1788–1900*. Sydney: Sydney University Press.

Daly, J. (1989) Innocent murmurs: echocardiography and the diagnosis of cardiac normality. *Sociology of Health and Illness*, 11(2), 99–116.

Davenport-Hines, R. (1990) *Sex, Death and Punishment: Attitudes to Sex and Sexuality in Britain since the Renaissance*. London: Collins.

Davies, S. (1991) *The Historical Origins of Health Fascism*. London: Forest.

Davison, C., Davey Smith, G. and Frankel, S. (1991) Lay epidemiology and the prevention paradox: the implications of coronary candidacy for health education. *Sociology of Health and Illness*, 13(1), 1–19.

Davison, C., Frankel, S. and Davey Smith, G. (1992) The limits of lifestyle: re-assessing 'fatalism' in the popular culture of illness prevention. *Social Science and Medicine*, 34(6), 675–85.

Davison, C., Macintyre, S. and Davey Smith, G. (1994) The potential social impact of predictive genetic testing for susceptibility to common chronic diseases: a review and proposed research agenda. *Sociology of Health and Illness*, 16(3), 340–71.

Daykin, N. (1993) Young women and smoking: towards a sociological account. *Health Promotion International*, 8(2), 95–102.

Dean, M. (1991) *The Constitution of Poverty: Toward a Genealogy of Liberal Governance*. London: Routledge.

Dean, M. (1994) 'A social structure of many souls': moral regulation, government, and self-formation. *Canadian Journal of Sociology*, 19(2), 145–68.

DeFriese, G.H. and Fielding, J.E. (1990) Health risk appraisal in the 1990s: opportunities, challenges, and expectations. *Annual Review of Public Health*, 11, 401–18.

DeJong, W. and Winsten, J.A. (1990) The use of mass media in substance abuse prevention. *Health Affairs*, 9(2), 30–46.

Donald, J. (1991) On the threshold: psychoanalysis and cultural studies. In Donald, J. (ed.), *Psychoanalysis and Cultural Theory: Thresholds*. Houndsmills: Macmillan, pp. 1–10.

Donald, J. (1992) *Sentimental Education: Schooling, Popular Culture and the Regulation of Liberty*. London: Verso.

Donald, J. (1993) The natural man and the virtuous woman: reproducing citizens. In Jenks, C. (ed.), *Cultural Reproduction*. London: Routledge, pp. 36–54.

Donovan, R.J. (1991) Public health advertising: execution guidelines for health promotion professionals. *Health Promotion Journal of Australia*, 1(1), 40–5.

Donzelot, J. (1979) *The Policing of Families*. New York: Pantheon Books.

Dorn, N. (1983) *Alcohol, Youth and the State: Drinking Practices, Controls and Health Education*. London: Croom Helm.

Douglas, M. (1980) *Purity and Danger: An Analysis of Concepts of Pollution and Taboo*. London: Routledge and Kegan Paul.

Douglas, M. (1986) *Risk Acceptability According to the Social Sciences*. London: Routledge and Kegan Paul.

Douglas, M. (1987) A distinct anthropological perspective. In Douglas, M. (ed.), *Constructive Drinking: Perspectives on Drink from Anthropology*. Cambridge: Cambridge University Press, pp. 3–15.

Douglas, M. (1990) Risk as a forensic resource. *Daedalus*, Fall, 1–16.

Douglas, M. and Calvez, M. (1990) The self as risk-taker: a cultural theory of contagion in relation to AIDS. *Sociological Review*, 38(3), 445–64.

Douglas, M. and Isherwood, B. (1978) *The World of Goods*. Harmondsworth: Penguin.

Douglas, M. and Wildavsky, A. (1982) *Risk and Culture*. Oxford: Basil Blackwell.

Draper, E. (1992) Genetic secrets: social issues of medical screening in a genetic age. *Hastings Center Report*, July/August Supplement, pp. 15–18.

Duffy, J. (1990) *The Sanitarians: A History of American Public Health*. Urbana, IL: University of Illinois Press.

Edwards, P.J. and Hall, D.M.B. (1992) Screening, ethics, and the law. *British Medical Journal*, 305, 267–8.

Elias, N. (1978) *The Civilizing Process*. New York: Urizen.

Epstein, S.E. (1990) Losing the war against cancer: who's to blame and what to do about it. *International Journal of Health Services*, 20(1), 53–71.

Ewald, F. (1991) Insurance and risk. In Burchell, G., Gordon, C. and Miller, P. (eds), *The Foucault Effect: Studies in Governmentality*. Hempel Hempstead: Harvester Wheatsheaf, pp. 197–210.

Fairclough, N. (1992) *Discourse and Social Change*. Cambridge: Polity Press.

Fairclough, N. (1993) Critical discourse analysis and the marketization of public discourse. *Discourse and Society*, 14(2), 133–68.

Farrant, W. (1991) Addressing the contradictions: health promotion and community health action in the United Kingdom. *International Journal of Health Services*, 21(3), 423–39.

Featherstone, M. (1991a) The body in consumer culture. In Featherstone, M., Hepworth, M. and Turner, B.S. (eds), *The Body: Social Process and Cultural Theory*. London: Sage, pp. 170–96.

Featherstone, M. (1991b) *Consumer Culture and Postmodernism*. London: Sage.

Featherstone, M. and Hepworth, M. (1991) The mask of ageing and the postmodern life course. In Featherstone, M., Hepworth, M. and Turner, B.S. (eds), *The Body: Social Process and Cultural Theory*. London: Sage, pp. 371–89.

Fee, E. and Fox, D.M. (eds) (1988) *AIDS: The Burdens of History*. Berkeley, CA: University of California Press.

Fee. E. and Fox, D.M. (eds) (1992) *AIDS: The Making of a Chronic Disease*. Berkeley, CA: University of California Press.

Fee, E. and Porter, D. (1992) Public health, preventive medicine and professionalization: England and America in the nineteenth century. In Wear, A. (ed.), *Medicine in Society: Historical Essays*. Cambridge: Cambridge University Press, pp. 249–76.

Fentiman, S. (1988) Pensive women, painful vigils: consequences of delay in assessment of mammographic abnormalities. *Lancet*, i, 1041–2.

Fielding, J.E. (1982) Appraising the health of health risk appraisal. *American Journal of Public Health*, 72(4), 337-40.

Figlio, K. (1987) The lost subject of medical sociology. In Scambler, G. (ed.), *Sociological Theory and Medical Sociology*. London: Tavistock, pp. 77–109.

Figlio, K. (1989) Unconscious aspects of health and the public sphere. In Richards, B. (ed.), *Crises of the Self: Further Essays on Psychoanalysis and Politics*. London: Free Association Books.

Finch, L. (1993) *The Classing Gaze: Sexuality, Class and Surveillance*. Sydney: Allen and Unwin.

Fiske, J. (1990) *Introduction to Communication Studies*. London: Routledge.

Flay, B.R. (1987) Evaluation of the development, dissemination and effectiveness of mass media health programming. *Health Education Research: Theory and Practice*, 2(2), 123–9.

Flora, J.A. and Wallack, L. (1990) Health promotion and mass media use: translating research into practice. *Health Education Research: Theory and Practice*, 5(1), 73–80.

Foucault, M. (1975) *The Birth of the Clinic: An Archaeology of Medical Perception*. New York: Vintage Books.

Foucault, M. (1979) *The History of Sexuality: Volume 1, An Introduction*. London: Allen Lane.

Foucault, M. (1980a) Body/Power. In Gordon, C. (ed.), *Power/Knowledge: Selected Interviews and Other Writings, 1972–1977*. New York: Pantheon Books, pp. 55–62.

Foucault, M. (1980b) Two lectures. In Gordon, C. (ed.), *Power/Knowledge: Selected Interviews and Other Writings, 1972–1977*. New York: Pantheon Books, pp. 78–108.

Foucault, M. (1980c) The eye of power. In Gordon, C. (ed.), *Power/Knowledge: Selected Interviews and Other Writings, 1972–1977*. New York: Pantheon Books, pp. 146–65.

Foucault, M. (1984a) The politics of health in the eighteenth century. In Rabinow, P. (ed.), *The Foucault Reader*. New York: Pantheon Books, pp. 273–89.

Foucault, M. (1984b) Nietzche, genealogy, history. In Rabinow, P. (ed.), *The Foucault Reader*. New York: Pantheon Books, pp. 76–100.

Foucault, M. (1985) *The Use of Pleasure: Volume 2 of the History of Sexuality*. New York: Pantheon Books.

Foucault, M. (1986) *The Care of the Self: Volume 3 of the History of Sexuality*. New York: Pantheon Books.

Foucault, M. (1988a) Technologies of the self. In Martin, L.H., Gutman, H. and Hutton, P.H. (eds), *Technologies of the Self: A Seminar with Michel Foucault*. London: Tavistock, pp. 16–49.

Foucault, M. (1988b) The political technology of individuals. In Martin, L.H., Gutman, H. and Hutton, P.H. (eds), *Technologies of the Self: A Seminar with Michel Foucault*. London: Tavistock, pp. 145–62.

Foucault, M. (1991) Governmentality. In Burchell, G., Gordon, C. and Miller, P. (eds), *The Foucault Effect: Studies in Governmentality*. Hemel Hempstead: Harvester Wheatsheaf, pp. 87–104.

Fox, D.M. and Lawrence, C. (1988) *Photographing Medicine: Images and Power in Britain and America since 1840*. New York: Greenwood.

Fox, N.J. (1991) Postmodernism, rationality and the evaluation of health care. *Sociological Review*, 39(4), 709–44.

Fox, N.J. (1993) *Postmodernism, Sociology and Health*. Buckingham: Open University Press.

Frankenberg, R.J. (1992) The other who is also the same: the relevance of epidemics in space and time for prevention of HIV infection. *International Journal of Health Services*, 22(1), 73–88.

Frankenberg, R.J. (1994) The impact of HIV/AIDS on concepts relating to risk and culture within British community epidemiology: candidates or targets for prevention. *Social Science and Medicine*, 38(10), 1325–35.

Freimuth, V. and Mettger, W. (1990) Is there a hard-to-reach audience? *Public Health Reports*, 105(3), 232–8.

French, K., Porter, A.M.D., Robinson, S.E., McCallum, F.M., Hoie, J.G.R. and Roberts, M.M. (1982) Attendance at a breast screening clinic: a problem of administration or attitudes. *British Medical Journal*, 285, 617–20.

Fujimura, J. and Chou, D.Y. (1994) Dissent in science: styles of scientific practice and the controversy over the cause of AIDS. *Social Science and Medicine*, 38(8), 1017–36.

Game, A. (1991) *Undoing the Social: Towards a Deconstructive Sociology*. Buckingham: Open University Press.

Gamson, J. (1990) Rubber wars: struggles over the condom in the United States. *Journal of the History of Sexuality*, 1(2), 262–82.

Gane, M. and Johnson, T. (1993) Introduction: the project of Michel Foucault. In Gane, M. and Johnson, T. (eds), *Foucault's New Domains*. London: Routledge, pp. 1–9.

Gifford, S. (1986) The meaning of lumps: a case study of the ambiguities of risk. In Janes, C.R., Stall, R. and Gifford, S.M. (eds), *Anthropology and Epidemiology: Interdisciplinary Approaches to the Study of Health and Disease*. Dordrecht: Reidel, pp. 213–46.

Glassner, B. (1989) Fitness and the postmodern self. *Journal of Health and Social Behaviour*, 30, 180–91.

Goldstein, R. (1989) AIDS and the social contract. In Carter, E. and Watney, S. (eds), *Taking Liberties: AIDS and Cultural Politics*. London: Serpent's Tail, pp. 81–94.

Goodman, J. (1993) *Tobacco in History: The Cultures of Dependence*. London: Routledge.

Gordon, C. (1991) Government rationality: an introduction. In Burchell, G., Gordon, C. and Miller, P. (eds), *The Foucault Effect: Studies in Governmentality*. Hemel Hempstead: Harvester Wheatsheaf, pp. 1–52.

Grace, H. (1993) A practical man: portraiture between word and image. *Continuum*, 6(2), 156–77.

Grace, V.M. (1991) The marketing of empowerment and the construction of the health consumer: a critique of health promotion. *International Journal of Health Services*, 21(2), 329–43.

Graham. H. (1987) Women's smoking and family health. *Social Science and Medicine*, 25(1), 47–56.

Greco, M. (1993) Psychosomatic subjects and the 'duty to be well': personal agency within medical rationality. *Economy and Society*, 22(3), 357–72.

Grimshaw, J. (1987) Being HIV antibody positive. *British Medical Journal*, 295, 256–7.

Grosz, E. (1989) *Sexual Subversions: Three French Feminists*. Sydney: Allen and Unwin.

Grosz, E. (1994) *Volatile Bodies: Toward a Corporeal Feminism*. Sydney: Allen and Unwin.

Grover, J.Z. (1992) AIDS, keywords, and cultural work. In Grossberg, L., Nelson, C. and Treichler, P. (eds), *Cultural Studies*. New York: Routledge, pp. 227–39.

Gusfield, J. (1987) Passage to play: rituals of drinking time in American society. In Douglas, M. (ed.), *Constructive Drinking: Perspectives on Drink from Anthropology*. Cambridge: Cambridge University Press, pp. 73–90.

Hacking, I. (1990) *The Taming of Chance*. Cambridge: Cambridge University Press.

Handwerker, L. (1994) Medical risk: implicating poor pregnant women. *Social Science and Medicine*, 38(5), 665–75.

Haraway, D. (1989) The biopolitics of postmodern bodies: determinations of self in immune system discourse. *Differences*, 1(1), 3–44.

Hargreaves, J. (1986) *Sport, Power and Culture: A Social and Historical Analysis of Popular Sports in Britain*. Cambridge: Polity Press.

Hargreaves, J. (1987) The body, sport and power relations. In Horne, J., Jary, D. and Tomlinson, A. (eds), *Sport, Leisure and Social Relations*. London: Routledge and Kegan Paul, pp. 139–59.

Hart, G., Boulton, M., Fitzpatrick, R., McLean, J. and Dawson, J. (1992) 'Relapse' to unsafe sexual behaviour among gay men: a critique of recent behavioural HIV/AIDS research. *Sociology of Health and Illness*, 14(2), 216–32.

Hastings, G. and Haywood, A. (1991) Social marketing and communication in health promotion. *Health Promotion International*, 6(2), 135–45.

Hayes, M.V. (1992) On the epistemology of risk: language, logic and social science. *Social Science and Medicine*, 35 (4), 401–7.

Healey, J.F. (1991) An exploration of the relationships between memory and sport. *Sociology of Sport Journal*, 8, 213–27.

Henriques, J., Hollway, W., Urwin, C., Venn, C. and Walkerdine, V. (1984) Theorizing subjectivity. In Henriques, J., Hollway, W., Urwin, C., Venn, C. and Walkerdine, V. (eds), *Changing the Subject: Psychology, Social Regulation and Subjectivity*. London: Methuen, pp. 203–26.

Herzlich, C. and Pierret, J. (1987) *Illness and Self in Society*. Baltimore, MD: Johns Hopkins University Press.

Hevey, D. (1992) *The Creatures Time Forgot: Photography and Disability Imagery*. London: Routledge.

Hewitt, M. (1991) Bio-politics and social policy: Foucault's account of welfare. In Featherstone, M., Hepworth, M. and Turner, B.S. (eds), *The Body: Social Process and Cultural Theory*. London: Sage, pp. 225–55.

Hindess, B. (1989) Rationality and modern society. *Political Theory Newsletter*, 1, 111–25.

Hochbaum, G.M., Sorenson, J.R. and Lorig, K. (1992) Theory in health education practice. *Health Education Quarterly*, 19(3), 295–313.

Holman, C.D.J. (1992) Something old, something new: perspectives on five 'new' public health movements. *Health Promotion Journal of Australia*, 2(3), 4–11.

Hoy, D.C. (1986) Introduction. In Hoy, D.C. (ed.), *Foucault: A Critical Reader*. Oxford: Basil Blackwell, pp. 1–26.

Hubbard, R. (1984) Personal courage is not enough: some hazards of childbearing in the 1980s. In Arditti, R., Klein, R.D. and Minden, S. (eds), *Test-tube Women: What Future for Motherhood?* London: Pandora, pp. 331–55.

Hunter, I. (1993) Subjectivity and government. *Economy and Society*, 22(1), 123–34.

Illich, I. (1976) *Limits to Medicine: Medical Nemesis: the Expropriation of Health*. London: Marion Boyers.

Imhoff, A.E. (1992) The implications of increased life expectancy for family and social life. In Wear, A. (ed.), *Medicine in Society: Historical Essays*. Cambridge: Cambridge University Press, pp. 347–76.

Jameson, M. (1993) Why I don't treat cigarette smokers. *Tobacco Control*, 2, 236.

Jankowski, N.W. and Wester, F. (1991) The qualitative tradition in social science inquiry: contributions to mass communication research. In Jensen, K.B. and Jankowski, N.W. (eds), *A Handbook of Qualitative Methodologies for Mass Communication Research*. London: Routledge, pp. 44–74.

Jensen, K.B. (1991) Reception analysis: mass communication as the social production of meaning. In Jensen, K.B. and Jankowski, N.W. (eds), *A Handbook of Qualitative Methodologies for Mass Communication Research*. London: Routledge, pp. 135–48

Johnson, J.L. (1991) Learning to live again: the process of adjustment following a heart attack. In Morse, J.M. and Johnson, J.L. (eds), *The Illness Experience: Dimensions of Suffering*. Newbury Park, CA: Sage, pp. 13–88.

Johnson, R. (1993) Expertise and the state. In Gane, M. and Johnson, T. (eds), *Foucault's New Domains*. London: Routledge, pp. 139–52.

Jones, G. (1986) *Social Hygiene in Twentieth Century Britain*. Beckenham: Croom Helm.

Kagawa-Singer, M. (1993) Redefining health: living with cancer. *Social Science and Medicine*, 37(3), 295–314.

Kelman, S. (1975) The social nature of the definition problem in health. *International Journal of Health Services*, 5(4), 625–42.

Kemm, J. (1991) Health education and the problem of knowledge. *Health Promotion International*, 6(4), 291–6.

Kendall, G. and Wickham, G. (1992) Health and the social body. In Scott, S., Williams, G., Platt, S. and Thomas, H. (eds), *Private Risks and Public Dangers*. Aldershot: Avebury, pp. 8–18.

Kirk, D. and Colquhoun, D. (1989) Healthism and physical education. *British Journal of Sociology of Education*, 10(4), 417–34.

Kirk, D. and Spiller, B. (1993) Schooling for docility-utility: drill, gymnastics and the problem of the body in Victorian elementary schools. In Meredyth, D. and Tyler, D. (eds), *Child and Citizen: Genealogies of Schooling and Subjectivity*. Brisbane: Griffith University Institute for Cultural Policy Studies, pp. 103–27.

Kirmayer, L.J. (1988) Mind and body as metaphors: hidden values in biomedicine. In Lock, M. and Gordon, D.R. (eds), *Biomedicine Examined*. Dordrecht: Kluwer, pp. 57–93.

Klein, R. (1993) *Cigarettes are Sublime*. Durham, NC: Duke University Press.

Knowles, J.H. (1977) Responsibility for health. *Science*, 198(4322), 1103.

Kristeva, J. (1982) *Powers of Horror: An Essay on Abjection*. New York: Columbia University Press.

La Berge, A.F. (1992) *Mission and Method: The Early Nineteenth-Century French Public Health Movement*. Cambridge: Cambridge University Press.

Laqueur, T. (1987) Orgasm, generation, and the politics of reproductive biology. In Gallagher, C. and Laqueur, T. (eds), *The Making of the Modern Body: Sexuality and Society in the Nineteenth Century*. Berkeley, CA: University of California Press, pp. 1–41.

Larriera, A. (1994) Smoking said to increase birth risk. *Sydney Morning Herald*, 3 February.

Lash, S. (1991) Genealogy and the body: Foucault/Deleuze/Nietzche. In Featherstone, M., Hepworth, M. and Turner, B.S. (eds), *The Body: Social Process and Cultural Theory*. London: Sage, pp. 256–80.

Lather, P. (1991) Post-critical pedagogies: a feminist reading. *Education and Society*, 9(2), 100–111.

Latour, B. (1988) *The Pasteurization of France*. Cambridge, MA: Harvard University Press.

Lears, T.J.J. (1989) American advertising and the reconstruction of the body, 1880–1930. In Grover, K. (ed.), *Fitness in American Culture: Images of Health, Sport, and the Body, 1830–1940*. Amherst and New York: University of Massachusetts Press and the Margaret Woodbury Strong Museum, pp. 47–66.

Lefebvre, R.C. (1992) The social marketing imbroglio in health promotion. *Health Promotion International*, 7(1), 61–4.

Levenstein, H.A. (1988) *Revolution at the Table: The Transformation of the American Diet*. New York: Oxford University Press.

Levidow, L. (1987) Sex selection in India: girls as a bad investment. *Science as Culture*, 1(1), 141–52.

Lewis, J. (1986) *What Price Community Medicine? The Philosophy, Practice and Politics of Public Health Since 1919*. Brighton: Wheatsheaf Books.

Lewis, J. (1992) The medical journals and the politics of public health 1918–90. In Bynum, W.F., Lock, S. and Porter, R. (eds), *Medical Journals and Medical Knowledge: Historical Essays*. London: Routledge, pp. 207–27.

Lewis, M. (1988) The 'health of the race' and infant health in New South Wales: perspectives on medicine and empire. In MacLeod, R. and Lewis, M. (eds), *Disease, Medicine, and Empire: Perspectives on Western Medicine and the Experience of European Expansion*. London: Routledge, pp. 301–15.

Lewis, P.A., Charny, M., Lambert, D. and Coombes, J. (1989) A fatalistic attitude to health amongst smokers in Cardiff. *Health Education Research: Theory and Practice*, 4(3), 361–5.

Lievrouw, L.A. (1994) Health communication research reconsidered: reading the signs. *Journal of Communication*, 44(1), 90–9.

Ling, J.C. (1989) New communicable diseases: a communication challenge. *Health Communication*, 1(4), 253–60.

Ling, J.C., Franklin, B.A.K., Lindsteadt, J.F. and Gearon, S.A.N. (1992) Social marketing: its place in public health. *Annual Review of Public Health*, 13, 341–62.

Lippman, A. (1992) Led (astray) by genetic maps: the cartography of the human genome and health care. *Social Science and Medicine*, 35(12), 1469–76.

Lorig, K. and Laurin, J. (1985) Some notions about assumptions underlying health education. *Health Education Quarterly*, 12(3), 231–43.

Lupton, D. (1994a) *Medicine as Culture: Illness, Disease and the Body in Western Societies*. London: Sage.

Lupton, D. (1994b) The condom in the age of AIDS – newly respectable or still a dirty word? A discourse analysis. *Qualitative Health Research*, 4(3), 304–20.

Lupton, D. (1994c) *Moral Threats and Dangerous Desires: AIDS in the News Media*. London: Taylor and Francis.

Lupton, D. (1994d) 'Everything in moderation': responses to news media coverage of the cholesterol controversy. Presented at the British Sociology Association Medical Sociology Group 26th Annual Conference, York, England, September.

Lupton, D., McCarthy, S. and Chapman, S. (1995) 'Panic bodies': discourses on risk and HIV antibody testing. *Sociology of Health and Illness*, 17(1), 89–108.

Lupton, D., McCarthy, S. and Chapman, S. (in press) 'Doing the right thing': the symbolic meanings and experiences of having an HIV antibody test. *Social Science and Medicine*.

McCombie, S. (1986) The cultural impact of the 'AIDS' test: the American experience. *Social Science and Medicine*, 23(5), 455–9.

McCormick, J. (1994) Health promotion: the ethical dimension. *Lancet*, 344, 390–1.

McCracken, G. (1988) *Culture and Consumption: New Approaches to the Symbolic Character of Consumer Goods and Activities*. Bloomington, IN: Indiana University Press.

Macdonald, G. (1992) Communication theory and health promotion. In Bunton, R. and Macdonald, G. (eds), *Health Promotion: Disciplines and Diversity*. London: Routledge, pp. 182–201.

McGinnis, J.M. (1990) Communication for better health. *Public Health Reports*, 105(3), 217–18.

MacInness, A. and Milburn, K. (1994) Belief systems and social circumstances influencing the health choices of people in Lochaber. *Health Education Journal*, 53, 58–72.

McKeown, T. (1976) *The Role of Medicine: Dream, Mirage or Nemesis?* London: Nuffield Provincial Hospitals Trust.

Maclean, U., Sinfield, D., Klein, S. and Harnden, B. (1984) Women who decline breast screening. *Journal of Epidemiology and Community Health*, 38, 278–83.

McNay, L. (1992) *Foucault and Feminism: Power, Gender and the Self*. Cambridge: Polity Press.

Mahoney, M.A. and Yngvesson, B. (1992) The construction of subjectivity and the paradox of resistance: reintegrating feminist anthropology and psychology. *Signs: Journal of Women in Culture and Society*, 18(1), 44–73.

Mansfield, A. and McGinn, B. (1993) Pumping irony: the muscular and the feminine. In Scott, S. and Morgan, D. (eds), *Body Matters: Essays on the Sociology of the Body*. London: Falmer, pp. 49–68.

Mars, G. (1987) Longshore drinking, economic security and union politics in Newfoundland. In Douglas, M. (ed.), *Constructive Drinking: Perspectives on Drink from Anthropology*. Cambridge: Cambridge University Press, pp. 91–101.

Marshall, S. (1990) Picturing deviancy. In Boffin, T. and Gupta, S. (eds), *Ecstatic Antibodies: Resisting the AIDS Mythology*. London: Rivers Oram Press, pp. 19–36.

Marteau, T.M. (1990) Reducing the psychological costs. *British Medical Journal*, 310, 26-8.

May, C. (1993) Resistance to peer group pressure: an inadequate basis for alcohol education. *Health Education Research: Theory and Practice*, 8(2), 159–65.

Mayne, A. (1988) 'The dreadful scourge': responses to smallpox in Sydney and Melbourne, 1881-2. In MacLeod, R. and Lewis, M. (eds), *Disease, Medicine, and Empire: Perspectives on Western Medicine and the Experience of European Expansion*. London: Routledge, pp. 219–41.

Mellencamp, P. (1992) *High Anxiety: Catastrophe, Scandal, Age and Comedy*. Bloomington, IN: Indiana University Press.

Mellor, P.A. and Shilling, C. (1993) Modernity, self-identity and the sequestration of death. *Sociology*, 27(3), 411–31.

Mennell, S. (1992) *Norbet Elias: An Introduction*. Oxford: Basil Blackwell.

Miles, L. (1993) Women, AIDS, and power in heterosexual sex: a discourse analysis. *Women's Studies International Forum*, 16(5), 497–511.

Miller, P. and Rose, N. (1993) Governing economic life. In Gane, M. and Johnson, T. (eds), *Foucault's New Domains*. London: Routledge, pp. 75–105.

Minkler, M. (1989) Health education, health promotion and the open society: an historical perspective. *Health Education Quarterly*, 16(1), 17–30.

Montgomery, K. (1990) Promoting health through entertainment television. In Atkin, C. and Wallack, L. (eds), *Mass Communication and Public Health: Complexities and Conflicts*. Newbury Park, CA: Sage, pp. 114–28.

Moore, D. (1992) Beyond the bottle: introducing anthropological debate to research into Aboriginal alcohol use. *Australian Journal of Social Issues*, 27(3), 173–93.

Morgan, D. (1993) You too can have a body like mine: reflections on the male body and masculinities. In Scott, S. and Morgan, D. (eds), *Body Matters: Essays on the Sociology of the Body*. London: Falmer, pp. 69–88.

Morley, D. (1992) *Television, Audiences and Cultural Studies*. London: Routledge.

Mort, F. (1987) *Dangerous Sexualities: Medico-Moral Politics in England Since 1830*. London: Routledge and Kegan Paul.

Moscucci, O. (1990) *The Science of Woman: Gynaecology and Gender in England, 1800–1929*. Cambridge: Cambridge University Press.

Mrozek, D.J. (1989) Sport in American life: from national health to personal fulfilment, 1890–1940. In Grover, K. (ed.), *Fitness in American Culture: Images of Health, Sport, and the Body, 1830–1940*. Amherst and New York: University of Massachusetts Press and the Margaret Woodbury Strong Museum, pp. 18–46.

Mullen, K. (1987) The beliefs and attitudes of a group of men in mid-life towards tobacco use. *Drug and Alcohol Dependence*, 20 (3), 235–46.

Mullen, K. (1992) A question of balance: health behaviour and work context among male Glaswegians. *Sociology of Health and Illness*, 14(1), 73–97.

Mundell, I. (1993) Peering through the smoke screen. *New Scientist*, 9 October, 14–15.

Musto, D.F. (1988) Quarantine and the problem of AIDS. In Fee, E. and Fox, D.M. (eds), *AIDS: the Burdens of History*. Berkeley, CA: University of California Press, pp. 67–85.

Nava, M. (1992) *Changing Cultures: Feminism, Youth and Consumerism*. London: Sage.

Nelkin, D. (1989) Communicating technological risk: the social construction of risk perception. *Annual Review of Public Health*, 10, 95–113.

Nelkin, D. and Brown, M.J. (1984) *Workers At Risk: Voices from the Workplace*. Chicago: University of Chicago Press.

Nelkin, D. and Hilgartner, S. (1986) Disputed dimensions of risk: a public school controversy over AIDS. *Milbank Quarterly*, 64(Suppl. 1), 118–42.

Nelkin, D. and Tancredi, L. (1989) *Dangerous Diagnostics: the Social Power of Biological Information*. New York: Basic Books.

Nettleton, S. (1991) Wisdom, diligence and teeth: discursive practices and the creation of mothers. *Sociology of Health and Illness*, 13(1), 98–111.

New, S.J. and Senior, M.L. (1991) 'I don't believe in needles': qualitative aspects of a study into the uptake of infant immunisation in two English health authorities. *Social Science and Medicine*, 33(4), 509–18.

Nicoll, A. and Brown, P. (1994) HIV: beyond reasonable doubt. *New Scientist*, 15 January, 24–8.

Nutbeam, D., Wise, M., Bauman, A., Harris, E. and Leeder, S. (1993) *Goals and Targets for Australia's Health in the Year 2000 and Beyond*. Canberra: Australian Government Publishing Service.

Nutton, V. (1992) Healers in the medical market place: towards a social history of Graeco-Roman medicine. In Wear, A. (ed.), *Medicine in Society: Historical Essays*. Cambridge: Cambridge University Press, pp. 15–58.

Oakley, A. (1989) Smoking in pregnancy: smokescreen or risk factor? Towards a materialist analysis. *Sociology of Health and Illness*, 11(4), 311–35.

Oakley, A. (1992) *Social Support and Motherhood: the Natural History of a Research Culture*. Oxford: Basil Blackwell.

Oppenheimer, G.M. (1988) In the eye of the storm: the epidemiological construction of AIDS. In Fee, E. and Fox, D.M. (eds), *AIDS: the Burdens of History*. Berkeley, CA: University of California Press, pp. 267–300.

Osborne, T. (1993) On liberalism, neo-liberalism and the 'liberal profession' of medicine. *Economy and Society*, 22(3), 345–56.

Packard, V. (1957) *The Hidden Persuaders*. London: Penguin.

Palmer, R. (1993) In bad odour: smell and its significance in medicine from antiquity to the seventeenth century. In Bynum, W.F. and Porter, R. (eds), *Medicine and the Five Senses*. Cambridge: Cambridge University Press, pp. 61–8.

Park, K. (1992) Medicine and society in medieval Europe, 500–1500. In Wear, A. (ed.), *Medicine in Society: Historical Essays*. Cambridge: Cambridge University Press, pp. 59–90.

Parsons, E. and Atkinson, P. (1992) Lay constructions of genetic risk. *Sociology of Health and Illness*, 14(4), 437–55.

Pattison, S. and Player, D. (1990) Health education: the political tensions. In Doxiadis, S. (ed.), *Ethics in Health Education*. Chichester: John Wiley and Sons, pp. 63–79.

Patton, C. (1990) *Inventing AIDS*. New York: Routledge.

Petchesky, R.P. (1987) Foetal images: the power of visual culture in the politics of reproduction. In Stanworth, M. (ed.), *Reproductive Technologies: Gender, Motherhood and Medicine*. Cambridge: Polity Press, pp. 57–80.

Peters, M. and Marshall, J.D. (1991) Education and empowerment: postmodernism and the critique of humanism. *Education and Society*, 9(2), 123–34.

Petersen, A.R. (1989) Alcohol control in the age of advertising. *Drug Education Journal of Australia*, 3(1), 1–8.

Petersen, A.R. (1991) Alcohol, the medical model and the politics of defining problems. *Drug Education Journal of Australia*, 5(2), 89–95.

Petersen, A.R. (1994) *In a Critical Condition: Health and Power Relations in Australia*. Sydney: Allen and Unwin.

Peterson, C. and Stunkard, A.J. (1989) Personal control and health promotion. *Social Science and Medicine*, 28(8), 819–28.

Pfau, M. and van Bockern, S. (1994) The persistence of inoculation in conferring resistance to smoking initiation among adolescents: the second year. *Human Communication Research*, 20(3), 413–30.

Pill, R. and Stott, N.C.H. (1982) Concepts of illness causation and responsibility: some preliminary data from a sample of working class mothers. *Social Science and Medicine*, 16, 43–52.

Pirrie, D. and Dalzell-Ward, A.J. (1962) *A Textbook of Health Education*. London: Tavistock.

Porter, D. and Porter, R. (1988) The enforcement of health: the British debate. In Fee, E. and Fox, D.M. (eds), *AIDS: The Burdens of History*. Berkeley, CA: University of California Press, pp. 97–120.

Porter, R. (1992) The patient in England, c.1660–c.1800. In Wear, A. (ed.), *Medicine in Society: Historical Essays*. Cambridge: Cambridge University Press, pp. 91–118.

Posner, T. (1991) What's in a smear? Cervical screening, medical signs and metaphors. *Science as Culture*, 2(2), 167–87.

Posner, T. and Vessey, M. (1988) *Prevention of Cervical Cancer: the Patient's View*. London: King Edward's Hospital Fund for London.

Prior, L. (1989) *The Social Organization of Death: Medical Discourse and Social Practices in Belfast*. Basingstoke: Macmillan.

Prior, L. and Bloor, M. (1993) Why people die: social representations of death and its causes. *Science as Culture*, 3(3), 346–75.

Quilliam, S. (1990) Positive smear: the emotional issues and what can be done. *Health Education Journal*, 49(1), 19–20.

Rapp, R. (1988) Chromosomes and communication: the discourse of genetic counselling. *Medical Anthropology Quarterly*, 2(2), 143–57.

Rawlings, B. (1989) Coming clean: the symbolic use of clinical hygiene in a hospital sterilising unit. *Sociology of Health and Illness*, 11(3), 279–93.

Rawson, D. (1992) The growth of health promotion theory and its rational reconstruction. In Bunton, R. and Macdonald, G. (eds), *Health Promotion: Disciplines and Diversity*. London: Routledge, pp. 202–24.

Redican, B. and Hadley, D.S. (1988) A field studies project in a city health and leisure club. *Sociology of Sport Journal*, 5, 50–62.

Rhodes, T. and Shaughnessy, R. (1989) Selling safer sex: AIDS education and advertising. *Health Promotion*, 4(1), 27–30.

Rhodes, T. and Shaughnessy, R. (1990) Compulsory screening: advertising AIDS in Britain, 1986–89. *Policy and Politics*, 18(1), 55–61.

Richards, M.P.M. (1993) The new genetics: some issues for social scientists. *Sociology of Health and Illness*, 15(5), 567–86.

Richardson, J. (1992) Cost–utility analyses in health care: present status and future issues. In Daly, J., McDonald, I. and Willis, E. (eds), *Researching Health Care: Designs, Dilemmas, Disciplines*. London: Routledge, pp. 21–44.

Risse, G.B. (1988) Epidemics and history: ecological perspectives and social responses. In Fee, E. and Fox, D.M. (eds), *AIDS: the Burdens of History*. Berkeley, CA: University of California Press, pp. 33–66.

Risse, G.B. (1992) Medicine in the age of Enlightenment. In Wear, A. (ed.), *Medicine in Society: Historical Essays*. Cambridge: Cambridge University Press, pp. 149–96.

Ritchie, J. (1988) Commerce or con: young people and cigarette advertising. *Community Health Studies*, 12(1), 9–15.

Roberts, M.M. (1989) Breast screening: time for a rethink? *British Medical Journal*, 299, 1153–4.

Rodmell, S. and Watt, A. (eds) (1986) *The Politics of Health Education: Raising the Issues*. London: Routledge and Kegan Paul.

Rogers, N. (1992) *Dirt and Disease: Polio Before FDR*. New Brunswick, NJ: Rutgers University Press.

Rose, H. (1990) Activists, gender and the community health movement. *Health Promotional International*, 5(3), 209–18.

Rose, N. (1990) *Governing the Soul: the Shaping of the Private Self*. London: Routledge.

Rose, N. and Miller, P. (1992) Political power beyond the State: problematics of government. *British Journal of Sociology*, 43(2), 173–205.

Rosen, G. (1974) *From Medical Police to Social Medicine: Essays on the History of Health Care*. New York: Science History Publications.

Rowland, R. (1992) *Living Laboratories: Woman and Reproductive Technologies*. Sydney: Pan Macmillan.

Salt, H., Boyle, M. and Ives, J. (1990) HIV prevention: current health promoting behaviour models for understanding psycho-social determinants of condom use. *AIDS Care*, 2(1), 69–75.

Saltonstall, R. (1993) Healthy bodies, social bodies: men's and women's concepts and practices of health in everyday life. *Social Science and Medicine*, 36(1), 7–14.

Sapolsky, W.M. (1990) The politics of risk. *Daedalus*, Fall, 83–96.

Saul, H. (1994) Screening without meaning? *New Scientist*, 19 March, 14–15.

Schiller, N.G., Crystal, S. and Lewellen, D. (1994) Risky business: the cultural construction of AIDS risk groups. *Social Science and Medicine*, 38(10), 1337–46.

Schudson, M. (1984) *Advertising, the Uneasy Persuasion: Its Dubious Impact on American Society*. New York: Basic Books.

Sears, A. (1991) AIDS and the health of nations: the contradictions of public health. *Critical Sociology*, 18(2), 31–50.

Sears, A. (1992) 'To teach them how to live': the politics of public health from tuberculosis to AIDS. *Journal of Historical Sociology*, 5(1), 61–83.

Sedgwick, E.K. (1993) Axiomatic. In During, S. (ed.), *The Cultural Studies Reader*. London: Routledge, pp. 243–68.

Seidman, S. (1991) *Romantic Longings: Love in America, 1830–1980*. New York: Routledge.

Sennett, R. (1976) *The Fall of Public Man*. Cambridge: Cambridge University Press.

Shields, R. (1992) Spaces for the subject of consumption. In Shields, R. (ed.), *Lifestyle Shopping: the Subject of Consumption*. London: Routledge, pp. 1–20.

Shilling, C. (1991) Educating the body: physical capital and the production of social inequalities. *Sociology*, 25(4), 653–72.

Shilling, C. (1993) *The Body and Social Theory*. London: Sage.

Singer, L. (1993) *Erotic Welfare: Sexual Theory and Politics in the Age of Epidemic*. New York: Routledge.

Skrabanek, P. (1985) False premises and false promises of breast cancer screening. *Lancet*, ii, 316–20.

Skrabanek, P. (1989) Mass mammography: time for a reappraisal. *International Journal of Technology Assessment in Health Care*, 5, 423–30.

Slovic, P. (1987) Perception of risk. *Science*, 230, 280–5.

Smart, B. (1993) *Postmodernity*. London: Routledge.

Smith, D. (1990) *The Conceptual Practices of Power: A Feminist Sociology of Knowledge*. Boston, MA: Northeastern University Press.

Sofia, Z. (1993) *Whose Second Self? Gender and (Ir)rationality in Computer Culture*. Geelong, Victoria: Deakin University Press.

Solomon, D.S. and Cardillo, B.A. (1985) The elements and process of communication campaigns. In van Dijk, T.A. (ed.), *Discourse and Communication*. Berlin: Walter de Gruyter, pp. 60–8.

Stenberg, M. (1993) Mother's smoking outlawed by court. *Sydney Morning Herald*, 27 July.

Stenson, K. (1993) Social work discourse and the social work interview. *Economy and Society*, 22(1), 42–76.

Stevenson, H.M. and Burke, M. (1991) Bureaucratic logic in new social movement clothing: the limits of health promotion research. *Health Promotion International*, 6(4), 281–9.

Strong, P. (1990) Epidemic psychology: a model. *Sociology of Health and Illness*, 12(3), 249–59.

Taylor, I. and Knowelden, J. (1957) *Principles of Epidemiology*. London: J. and A. Churchill.

Tesh, S.N. (1988) *Hidden Arguments: Political Ideology and Disease Prevention Policy*. New Brunswick, NJ: Rutgers University Press.

Thornton, M.A. (1987) Sekt versus schnapps in an Austrian village. In Douglas, M. (ed.), *Constructive Drinking: Perspectives on Drink from Anthropology*. Cambridge: Cambridge University Press, pp. 102–112.

Thorogood, N. (1992) What is the relevance of sociology for health promotion? In Bunton, R. and Macdonald, G. (eds), *Health Promotion: Disciplines and Diversity*. London: Routledge, pp. 42–65.

Tinning, R. (1990) *Ideology and Physical Education: Opening Pandora's Box*. Geelong, Victoria: Deakin University Press.

Tones, B.K. (1986) Health education and the ideology of health promotion: a review of alternative approaches. *Health Education Research: Theory and Practice*, 1(1), 3–12.

Tones, B.K. (1992) Health promotion, self-empowerment and the concept of control. In Colquhoun, D. (ed.), *Health Education: Politics and Practice*. Geelong, Victoria: Deakin University Press, pp. 29–89.

Tones, K. (1993) Changing theory and practice: trends in methods, strategies and settings in health education. *Health Education Journal*, 52(3), 125–39.

Tsing, A.L. (1990) Monster stories: women charged with perinatal endangerment. In Ginsburg, F. and Tsing, A.L. (eds), *Uncertain Terms: Negotiating Gender in American Culture*. Boston, MA: Beacon Press, pp. 282–99.

Turner, B.S. (1984) *The Body and Society: Explorations in Social Theory*. Oxford: Basil Blackwell.

Turner, B.S. (1990) The interdisciplinary curriculum: from social medicine to postmodernism. *Sociology of Health and Illness*, 12(1), 1–23.

Turner, B.S. (1992) *Regulating Bodies: Essays in Medical Sociology*. London: Routledge.

Turner, B.S. (1994) Theoretical developments in the sociology of the body. *Australian Cultural History*, 13, 13–30.

Tyler, D. (1993) Making better children. In Meredyth, D. and Tyler, D. (eds), *Child and Citizen: Genealogies of Schooling and Subjectivity*. Brisbane: Griffith University Institute for Cultural Policy Studies, pp. 35–60.

van Dam, C.J. (1989) AIDS: is health education the answer? *Health Policy and Planning*, 4(2), 141–7.

Veal, A.J. (1993) The concept of lifestyle: a review. *Leisure Studies*, 12(4), 233–52.

Vigarello, G. (1988) *Concepts of Cleanliness: Changing Attitudes in France since the Middle Ages*. Cambridge: Cambridge University Press.

Viscusi, W.K. (1992) *Smoking: Making the Risky Decision*. Oxford: Oxford University Press.

Waldby, C., Herdman, E., Kippax, S. and Crawford, J. (1994) Discriminatory language in medical teaching texts. Presented at the Second International Conference on Biopsychosocial Aspects of AIDS, Brighton, UK, July.

Wang, C. (1992) Culture, meaning and disability: injury prevention campaigns and the production of stigma. *Social Science and Medicine*, 35(9), 1093–102.

Watney, S. (1988) Visual AIDS – advertising ignorance. In Aggleton, P. and Homans, H. (eds), *Social Aspects of AIDS*. London: Falmer, pp. 177–82.

Watney, S. (1991) AIDS: the second decade: 'risk', research and modernity. In Aggleton, P., Hart, G. and Davies, P. (eds), *AIDS: Responses, Interventions and Care*. London: Falmer, pp. 1–17.

Watson, J.M. (1993) Male body image and health beliefs: a qualitative study and implications for health promotion practice. *Health Education Journal*, 52(4), 246–52.

Wear, A. (1992) Making sense of health and the environment in early modern England. In Wear, A. (ed.), *Medicine in Society: Historical Essays*. Cambridge: Cambridge University Press, pp. 119–48.

Wearing, B. and Wearing, S. (1992) Identity and the commodification of leisure. *Leisure Studies*, 11(1), 3–18.

Webb, J. (1993) A fragile case for screening? *New Scientist*, 25 December, 10–11.

Weindling, P. (1992) From infectious to chronic diseases: changing patterns of sickness in the nineteenth and twentieth centuries. In Wear, A. (ed.), *Medicine in Society: Historical Essays*. Cambridge: Cambridge University Press, pp. 303–16.

Wernick, A. (1991) *Promotional Culture: Advertising, Ideology and Symbolic Expression*. London: Sage.

Whatley, M.H. and Worcester, N. (1989) The role of technology in the co-optation of the women's health movement: the cases of osteoporosis and breast cancer screening. In Ratcliff, K.S., Ferree, M.M., Mellow, G.O., Wright, B.D., Price, G.D., Yanoshik, K. and Freston, M.S. (eds), *Healing Technology: Feminist Perspectives*. Ann Arbor, MI: University of Michigan Press, pp. 199–220.

Whorton, J.C. (1989) Eating to win: popular conceptions of diet, strength, and energy in the early twentieth century. In Grover, K. (ed.), *Fitness in American Culture: Images of Health, Sport, and the Body, 1830–1940*. Amherst and New York: University of Massachusetts Press and the Margaret Woodbury Strong Museum, pp. 86–122.

Wikler, D.I. (1978) Persuasion and coercion for health: ethical issues in government efforts to change life-styles. *Milbank Memorial Fund Quarterly*, 56(3), 303–38.

Wilkinson, S. and Kitzinger, C. (1993) Whose breast is it anyway? A feminist consideration of advice and 'treatment' for breast cancer. *Women's Studies International Forum*, 16(3), 229–38.

Williamson, J. (1990) *Decoding Advertisements: Ideology and Meaning in Advertising*. London: Marion Boyers.

Willis, P. (1990) *Common Culture: Symbolic Work at Play in the Everyday Cultures of the Young*. Milton Keynes: Open University Press.

Willis, S. (1991) *A Primer for Daily Life*. London: Routledge.

Wilton, T. and Aggleton, P. (1991) Condoms, coercion and control: heterosexuality and the limits to HIV/AIDS education. In Aggleton, P., Hart, G. and Davies, P. (eds), *AIDS: Responses, Interventions and Care*. London: Falmer, pp. 149–56.

Wohl, A.S. (1983) *Endangered Lives: Public Health in Victorian Britain*. London: J.M. Dent and Sons.

Wright, P.W.G. (1988) Babyhood: the social construction of infant care as a medical problem in England in the years around 1900. In Lock, M. and Gordon, D. (eds), *Biomedicine Examined*. Dordrecht: Kluwer, pp. 299–330.

Wright, P. and Treacher, A. (1982) Introduction. In Wright, P. and Treacher, A. (eds), *The Problem of Medical Knowledge: Examining the Social Construction of Medicine*. Edinburgh: Edinburgh University Press, pp. 1–22.

Young, I. and Whitehead, M. (1993) Back to the future: our social history and its impact on health education. *Health Education Journal*, 52(3), 114–19.

Yoxen, E. (1982) Constructing genetic diseases. In Wright, P. and Treacher, A. (eds), *The Problem of Medical Knowledge: Examining the Social Construction of Medicine*. Edinburgh: University of Edinburgh Press, pp. 144–61.

Index